# CHARLES
## AT SEVENTY
### *Thoughts, Hopes and Dreams*

*About the author:*

**Robert Jobson** is a leading royal commentator and writer dubbed 'the Godfather of Royal Reporting' by the *Wall Street Journal*. He is Royal Editor of London's respected *Evening Standard* newspaper and Australia's top-rated Channel 7 breakfast show, *Sunrise*, as well as royal contributor to ABC's *Good Morning America* in the USA. In the UK he is a regular guest on BBC, ITV and Sky News. A bestselling author and award-winning correspondent, he has been at the forefront of royal reporting for more twenty-eight years.

# CHARLES
## AT SEVENTY
### *Thoughts, Hopes and Dreams*

~

## ROBERT JOBSON

JOHN BLAKE

Published by John Blake Publishing,
2.25 The Plaza,
535 Kings Road,
Chelsea Harbour,
London SW10 0SZ

www.johnblakebooks.com

www.facebook.com/johnblakebooks 🇫
twitter.com/jblakebooks 🇹

First published in hardback in 2018

ISBN: 978-1-78606-887-3

British Library Cataloguing-in-Publication Data:

A catalogue record for this book is available from the British Library.

Design by www.envydesign.co.uk

Printed and bound in Great Britain by Clays Ltd, Elcograf S.p.A

1 3 5 7 9 10 8 6 4 2

Text copyright © Robert Jobson 2018

Papers used by John Blake Publishing are natural, recyclable products made from
wood grown in sustainable forests. The manufacturing processes conform to the
environmental regulations of the country of origin.

Every attempt has been made to contact the relevant copyright-holders, but some
were unobtainable. We would be grateful if the appropriate people could contact us.

John Blake Publishing is an imprint of Bonnier Books UK
www.bonnierbooks.co.uk

Dedicated to Charles L. Jobson
(1933–2017)

A regent, from the Latin *regens*, '[one] ruling', is a person appointed to administer a state because the monarch is a minor, or is absent or incapacitated. The title 'Prince Regent' is given officially to a prince who acts as regent at the monarch's side.

# CONTENTS

'I have spent most of my life trying to propose and initiate things that very few people could see the point of or thought were plain bonkers at the time. Perhaps some of them are now beginning to recognise a spot of pioneering in all this apparent madness.'

HRH The Prince of Wales, 7 September 2016, in a speech on being named 'Londoner of the Decade' at the *Evening Standard*'s Progress 1000 party, held at the Science Museum to honour the UK capital's innovators

# INTRODUCTION

———— ∼ ————

'The afternoon of human life must also have a
significance of its own and cannot be merely a pitiful appendage
to life's morning.'

CARL JUNG, SWISS PSYCHIATRIST AND PSYCHOANALYST, 1875–1961

In his seventieth year, His Royal Highness Charles, Prince of
Wales, has travelled hundreds of thousands of miles around
the world on official business, from the tiny Lady Elliot Island,
the southernmost coral cay of the Great Barrier Reef, Australia,
to the former New Hebrides colony, now Vanuatu, in the South
Pacific, where the indigenous Melanesian people honoured him
with the title 'paramount chief'. In that time, too, he has carried
out hundreds of public duties representing the Queen in his role
as heir to the throne, meeting presidents and princes as well as
ordinary people going about their daily lives on visits to villages,
towns and cities across the UK and the Commonwealth.

On a visit to the Caribbean, he toured Antigua and Barbuda

and the British Virgin Islands, where the Queen is head of state, as well as the former crown colony Dominica, to see for himself the destruction caused by Caribbean hurricanes Irma and Maria, which he described as 'utterly devastating'. In Europe, too, he visited Ireland, France and Greece on overseas visits that further cemented Britain's ties with our closest neighbours in this uncertain post-Brexit Europe. A few months before the start of his seventieth year he conducted a major tour of the Commonwealth on behalf of the government to Singapore, Malaysia, Brunei and India, and, before that, to Romania, Italy, Austria, the Papal See and Malta. In that time, too, it was confirmed he would be the next head of the Commonwealth, and it is now assured that he will succeed his mother, the Queen, in that non-hereditary role when the time comes.

His increased workload sees the prince regularly working fourteen-hour days and he carries out more than six hundred engagements a year at home and abroad; and increased responsibility means he is much more than a deputy, stepping up to stand in for the Queen. As we approach the end of 2018, a more accurate description of Charles's role is 'Shadow King', as it is he, not Her Majesty, who is now doing most of the 'heavy lifting' for the monarchy at home and abroad while representing Elizabeth II, who turned ninety-two in April 2018.

The Queen has not travelled on long-haul flights since her visit to Australia in 2011. Her last state visit overseas was to Germany in June 2015. The previous year she paid a state visit to France and went by Eurostar. She now restricts her journeys to short flights, 'away-days' by royal train, commercial railway or car all within the United Kingdom.

# INTRODUCTION

Her once ever-present 'liege man', her loyal consort and husband of more than seventy years, His Royal Highness the Duke of Edinburgh (who turned ninety-seven in June 2018) has effectively retired from public life having, as he put it, 'done his bit'. With perfect timing, he walked off the royal stage in a summer downpour on 2 August 2017 at Buckingham Palace, doffing his bowler hat as he departed. He marched off the forecourt as the Plymouth Band of the Royal Marines played 'For He's a Jolly Good Fellow'. As he went back inside he made one of his trademark quips, joking with two Royal Marine corporals, who had run 1,664 miles over 100 days as part of the 1664 Global Challenge (which recognised the year the Royal Marines were founded in 1664), that they should be 'locked up' for the corps' fundraising efforts. It was certainly the end of an era. His departure from public life, however, marked a new beginning for his son the Prince of Wales. With his father no longer ever present at the Queen's side, Charles would now be the lead man in the unfolding royal story.

Throughout the prince's milestone seventieth year (and several months before that, in fact), I have accompanied him at home and abroad, as he crisscrossed the globe on official business, joining him aboard royal jets and following him in support helicopters as he ventured deep into rainforests and other remote regions. I was there, too, at his early seventieth Birthday Patronage Celebration in the immaculate gardens of Buckingham Palace, and also enjoyed conversations with him, aboard a royal jet and at royal receptions overseas, as well as being his dinner guest at Dumfries House, an eighteenth-century Palladian country house set on a 2,000-acre estate in Ayrshire, Scotland.

I have enjoyed tea and conversation with the prince, too, at his beloved country estate, Highgrove House, his private residence, also built in the late eighteenth century and situated southwest of Tetbury, Gloucestershire. I have been invited to a tour of the gardens, where in the Orchard Room he joked of his 'backyard', by which he meant the magnificently cultivated Royal Gardens at Highgrove (they are well worth seeing, and are now open to the public on select dates between April and October each year). It has been a life's work and clearly reflects the deeper side of the man. 'The garden at Highgrove really does spring from my heart and, strange as it may seem to some, creating it has been rather like a form of worship,' he wrote in an introduction to a book about the estate published in 1993.

I was the only British journalist present at the Cotroceni Palace on 29 May 2017, when Prince Charles was formally welcomed to Romania by President Klaus Iohannis, and he seemed baffled that there was no photographer present. The Romania head of state pointed out his official photographer, while Charles looked around for a UK photographer, but our pool man had failed to show, so he pointed at me saying, 'Well, he's been following me around the world for thirty years.' 'It's not quite that long,' I mumbled, not knowing if a response was invited or if it was best that I say nothing in response, although I suspect the latter. Later at a reception, after he had joined in with a troop of Romanian dancers earlier in the day of engagements, he joked that he would quite like Romanians dancing in all the costumes at his seventieth birthday party.

As a result of devoting so much time to following, observing and chronicling what the prince has done publicly over eighteen months or so, I have been able to watch our future king with a discerning eye as I have scrutinised him at close quarters. I note what the prince does on a daily basis when on overseas tours and how he meticulously prepares for and goes about his business. Despite the fact that I have reported on the British Royal Family as a Fleet Street correspondent for national newspapers for nearly three decades, even for me, refocusing the lens and not just looking for the daily story or news photo-opportunity, but trying to see the bigger picture, has been an illuminating experience. Only when you take time to do that do the dots in the bigger picture join and the integrity and passion of the man emerge.

The prince himself noted in his trailblazing thesis *Harmony*, 'Perhaps I should not have been surprised that so many people failed to fathom what I was doing. So many appeared to think – or were told – that I was merely leaping from one subject to another – from architecture one minute to agriculture the next – as if I spent a morning saving the rainforests, then in the afternoon jumping to help young people start new businesses.'

Understandably, there is a degree of exasperation in the tone of his writing. It is only when you examine all that he does in detail that the integrated and interrelated picture of his life's work becomes clearly visible, not diluted or reduced to a few half-baked soundbites for the evening television, or to silly picture captions of him pulling bizarre facial expressions or wearing daft costumes that some of the photographers who follow him encourage, forgetting who he is and what he represents. Even as a journalist who once took the Murdoch shilling when I worked for the tabloid *Sun* newspaper, I found myself cringing at the cheap caricature they painted of him in October 2017 after a passionate speech at the Our Ocean summit in Malta.

Charles told delegates it was now crucial to create a circular economy that allows plastics to be 'recovered, recycled and reused instead of created, used and then thrown away', and pointed out that plastic is now 'on the menu' in the fish we eat the next day. *The Sun*, however, decided to mock up a photo of him wearing a pirate's hat and stuck it on the front page. They had plucked out a quote (and said it had caused a 'storm', which of course it hadn't) in which he said gangs of pirates off Somalia had been 'fantastic' for fish stocks. It was, of course, taken out of context and once again the messenger had done the prince and readers a disservice, making the heir to the throne appear ridiculous.

It is risible, too, when every year the prince is criticised for what is reported as an excessive royal travel bill. At the time of writing in 2018 the figure was revealed to be £4.7 million, the most expensive trip being £362,149 for the Prince of Wales and Duchess of Cornwall to visit India, Malaysia, Brunei and Singapore. But it is a visit taken at the government's behest and, not least for security reasons, it is the government, too, that decides that, as heir to the throne, he must use the RAF Voyager – the same one used by the Prime Minister – when carrying out such overseas visits on behalf of the Queen for the country. These are often gruelling Foreign and Commonwealth Office diplomatic missions packed with scores of back-to-back engagements, important speeches and state dinners, not private sightseeing jaunts.

The official visits in which I have accompanied the prince have come at a period of subtle but still great change for the

British monarchal system, as we gradually progress from one reign to the next in the first quarter of the twenty-first century. We are, after all, at a watershed moment for the century-old royal House of Windsor, and, as heir, Charles is of course central to that ongoing transition.

The overseas visits on which I have accompanied the prince and his team have been, near as damn it, state visits, as our sitting monarch, Elizabeth II, due to her advanced age – she is both the oldest and the longest-reigning monarch in British history – no longer undertakes long-haul travel, which in this modern era is necessary if one is to be a fully active head of state. In effect, as far as the monarchy is concerned we are in unchartered waters, with perhaps two captains on the ship's deck, if not necessarily at the helm.

During the research for this book I have spoken privately and publicly to the prince and people close to him, and I believe I have, as a result, developed an in-depth appreciation of what makes this diverse character destined to be the next monarch tick. In my time as a royal correspondent – which started in 1990 – I have reported on births, deaths, marriages, jubilees, countless foreign tours and private holidays as well as the public and private lives of the main players in this story, whether for newspapers, radio, television or as an author. In that time I have been acknowledged by my peers with awards and for having broken world-exclusive stories, such as being the only newspaper reporter in history to announce the engagement of a future king (rather than the palace), when I revealed that Charles was to marry his long-term mistress Camilla Parker Bowles in 2005. I have also gained notoriety as an author writing several books, among them the No. 1 *Sunday Times* and *New York Times* international bestseller *Diana: Closely Guarded Secret*, written with the Scotland Yard personal-protection officer (PPO) of the late Diana, Princess of Wales, Inspector Ken Wharfe MVO. I have met and interviewed members of the Royal Family, too.

It is fair to say that, as a career, it has been a rollercoaster ride, echoing the vantage point of the front row of history unfolding before my eyes. But, as Philip L. Graham, *Washington Post* publisher, rightly put it, 'News is the first rough draft of history.' For some writers, that's enough, but I have always wanted to write much more than a 'rough draft' and hoped to have the chance to get closer to these historic characters and do more than just scratch the surface but to paint a portrait, not sketch a caricature. I have striven to do this both for my sake and that of the reader, and in years to come it will be for posterity and ultimately for historical record.

This book has been many years in the making. In its evolution it has had many different titles and different areas of focus. But I am pleased to say, on the completion of the first edition, there are sections in it in which I know I have managed to unearth genuinely new material; I am content with that.

Throughout this journey I have been assisted by impeccable inside sources, whom I cannot identify for obvious reasons, but to whom I am deeply indebted. With their help I have been able to unearth groundbreaking new material that goes some way to correcting past inaccuracies that, unless revised at this moment, were in danger of becoming regarded as historic record. There are those who may question my accuracy, but I am confident of my material. These so-called facts that have been reproduced since and reprinted in other books, and articles claiming to be accurate about the prince, were part of the media narrative about him at the time and, much to his understandable irritation, have never been challenged. Some of those reports, the prince told friends, were 'unbelievable and pernicious lies' that, unless corrected, were in danger of going down as 'historic fact'. I am happy to put the record straight.

I have not devoted hundreds of pages to Charles's so-called damaged childhood, his often overplayed feelings of rejection when packed off to the boarding school in Scotland, Gordonstoun, which his father attended. Nor will I devote too much space to his failed marriage to Diana, Princess of Wales, and her tragic death, or his adulterous affair with Camilla Parker Bowles, now the Duchess of Cornwall. These sorry tales are now frankly démodé and have been addressed and sensationally redrafted many times over in various other biographies. Such issues will be addressed where I believe I have uncovered valuable new material to add to or correct what has gone before.

The core of this book is about our future king, Charles, Prince of Wales, the man, husband, father and grandfather, who he is, what drives him and his raison d'être. My aim in writing this biography was to try to shed new light on the character of this man who, despite being in the autumn of his life, is still on the cusp of realising his birthright and thus cementing his place in history. I wanted to at least get close to revealing Charles's 'hopes, fears and dreams'.

The prince emerges from this book, I hope, as a deep-thinking man, one who cares passionately about our world, and who has used his position of privilege to try to make the world a better place, to work for the greater good. Of course, he has his flaws, too, and would be the first to admit them. It is easy to judge somebody, so the saying goes, until you've walked a mile in his or her shoes. I haven't done that, but I have at least followed his footsteps around the world and observed him closely. It is for you, the reader, to make up your own mind and draw your own conclusions after reading this book.

For me, this book is of special significance, too, due to the timing of its publication and its central character. It is, in effect, the culmination of my three decades of work in covering the royal story, too. For it is not simply a detailed assessment and biography of Charles, Prince of Wales, but my considered attempt to examine the modern-day unelected system of constitutional monarchy and parliamentary democracy, how it functions and an examination of its place – and the place of the heir to the throne – in today's society and political framework.

This is the first book in which I have focused on Charles, the man, his role, his work and how he will approach his future responsibilities. He has surprised me throughout this process. He is undoubtedly an exceptional man of great conviction and energy, who rightly commands fierce loyalty and demands discretion. But he is also a complex and often contradictory person. One thing he definitely isn't is dull.

Charles's views on society, education and culture tend to polarise people. In many ways he is old-fashioned, a traditionalist; in others he is a radical and dissident. The new *X-Factor* generation, desperate to be television stars or celebrities, can irritate him. 'What is wrong with everyone nowadays?' he ranted in a private memo written in 2003, continuing,

Why do they all seem to think they are qualified to do things far beyond their technical capabilities? People seem to think they can all be pop stars, High Court judges, brilliant TV personalities or infinitely more competent heads of state without ever putting in the necessary work or having natural ability. This is the result of social utopianism which believes humanity can be genetically and socially engineered to contradict the lessons of history.

This, then, leads others to call him 'elitist', which he certainly is not. Many believe his point is valid. Others feel it represents the ramblings of somebody born into great wealth and privilege who thinks he is superior but has no right to limit the dreams and advancement of others.

He is somebody who bucks trends, often on purpose flies in face of convention. He loathes the glib way experts describe the so-called advancements of the twentieth century. 'I have always wanted to roll back some of the more ludicrous frontiers of the 1960s in terms of education, art, music, and literature, not to mention agriculture,' he wrote in a private letter dated 21 January 1993.

Charles's royal rank means it has not always been easy to get close to him and those who are in his inner circle are protected by an outer layer – an elite Praetorian Guard of modern times, if you like. I have, however, done my best to do so and with some success, having had conversations with the prince personally during the course of my research and undertaken a number of off-the-record interviews with some who have served and continue to serve him.

I also, in the course of my research, read most of the many books and newspaper reports written about the prince, spanning years. I would like to thank those authors for their insight, in particular Jonathan Dimbleby, Penny Junor, the late Ross Benson and Antony Holden. I would also like to thank Sally Bedell Smith, Catherine Mayer, the late Alan Hamilton and Tom Bower, whose books I read with interest. It was odd, given his at times scathing assessment of the prince, that Mr Bower felt it appropriate to take his seat at a ceremony in Buckingham Palace in June as Charles was honouring his wife, former *Evening Standard* editor and now the Arts Council London Area chair, Veronica Wadley, with a CBE for services to the arts. I suppose if Veronica, one of my many former editors and an accomplished newspaper professional, asked him as a guest for the ceremony it was perhaps appropriate that he was there.

My view of Charles may differ considerably from that of Mr Bower and those of some other writers. That does not mean I do not respect their diligence and expertise – far from it. Every one of these tomes on Charles is revealing in different ways.

I would like to thank my publisher, John Blake Publishing, now an imprint of Kings Road Publishing, part of the international Bonnier Publishing group, for supporting this project. I would like to thank John Blake himself too, who has since left the company he established, for commissioning the project and for his many years of friendship and for supporting so many of my book ideas. Of course, I would also like to give a big shout-out too to the masterly editor of this book, Toby Buchan, for his unwavering guidance, sharp eye and editorial skill and intellect to help make this book and those we have worked on together in the past the best they can be.

I would also like to thank Inspector Ken Wharfe MVO, Ian

Walker, Arthur Edwards MBE, the late Felicity Murdo-Smith CVO, Patrick Jephson, Victoria Mendham, Richard Kay, Geoffrey Levy, the late Geoff Crawford CVO, Charles Anson CVO, DL, Colleen Harris MVO, Karen Jobson for her unstinting support and professional editing skills, Roya Nikkhah, Emily Nash, Rodney Cook of the Hearst Foundation, Bernice King, Jack Lefley, Mark Wilkinson, Doug Wills and all my friends and colleagues at the *Evening Standard*. Thanks, too, to Michael Pell, Hugh Whitfield, Jimmy Cannon, Samantha Armytage, David 'Kochie' Koch, David 'Dougie' Walters, Natalie Barr, Mark Beretta, Edwina Bartholomew, Monica Lepore and all at *Sunrise* on Australian 7 Network. I would also like to thank my colleagues who have travelled around the world with me on countless royal tours and made them fun: Alan Jones, Chris Ship, Camilla Tominey, Phil Dampier, Robin Nunn, Kent Gavin, ABC's royal producer Carolyn Durand, Chris Jackson, and Tim Rooke. I must also give a 'Trunks Up!' shout-out to all the 'Happy Elephants' – they know who they are. Cheers, lads. Thanks are also due to my mother, Jean Jobson, for inspiring my love of history, and my son Charles for being a constant source of joy and pride in my life.

Naturally, I would like to thank His Royal Highness the Prince of Wales personally for sparing his precious time to speak to me

That said, despite the amount of shoe leather I have used during the research and writing of this book, and the scores of conversations I have had, this cannot be considered in any way an official biography. Clarence House officials have not been asked to read my manuscript or to change the text in any way. I would not allow that and neither would my editor or publisher. With that in mind, however, any mistakes are therefore mine and mine alone and I will take full responsibility for correcting them in later editions. This, after all, is my assessment of Charles and mine alone, based on what I have observed for myself during my travels alongside him, and from a number of impeccable sources close to him whose views and recollections I trust implicitly.

I can only hope that my ambitions for this book have been realised and that this is an authentic, fair and honest portrayal of the man who is destined to be our next king.

ROBERT JOBSON, November 2018

## Chapter One

# A MEANINGFUL CONVERSATION

———⁓———

'I believe the world needs so desperately and so urgently a
"fair go" for people, our planet and for Nature herself.'

<small>Prince of Wales at the Queensland Governor's Reception at
Government House, Brisbane, Australia, 6 April 2018</small>

'Well, that was a triumph,' Australia's then foreign minister,
the immaculate Julie Bishop, declared enthusiastically.
She was standing in the doorway between the cabin for the royal
household and staff and the one occupied by the few media as
we flew to Cairns after a visit to Vanuatu, the string of more
than eighty islands sitting between Fiji and New Caledonia in the
South Pacific, 1,240 miles east of northern Australia. She was in
high spirits – and had good reason to be.

Known for her prowess in politics and icy stares, Ms Bishop,
then sixty-one, was buoyed, along with the rest of the delegation
aboard, by the warmth and energy of the traditional welcome we
had all received in Port Vila, the capital. Thousands had turned

out to welcome their prestigious guests, cheer and wave their flags and perform traditional, colourful dance displays. But there was more than that at stake.

The possibility of China's establishing a permanent military presence in the South Pacific on Vanuatu was potentially a big headache not only for her and her boss, PM Malcolm Turnbull, but the Trump administration in America, too. During the visit, Vanuatu's Prime Minister, Charlot Salwai, had privately told her it was not interested in hosting foreign military bases and declined, too, to hold talks with Beijing. Vanuatu, she had been assured, was a 'non-aligned country'.

We were about an hour into the Royal Australian Air Force No. 34 Squadron (VIP transport squadron) return flight aboard the chic, especially configured, twin-engined Boeing 737 Business Jet, known as the BBJ. Crewed by two pilots and four uniformed RAAF flight attendants with space for up to thirty passengers and a range of 6,800 miles costing of £2,500 per hour, it is designed to fly the Australian PM and VVIPs. I was one of just twenty-five souls on board.

Ms Bishop had just given a prerecorded television interview on the jet in the seat behind me to an acclaimed documentary film-maker, the august John Bridcut. John, like me, with his team cameraman Jonathan Partridge and sound technician Paul Paragon, had embarked on a project assiduously chronicling the seventieth year in the life of the Prince of Wales.

John wanted the perspective of the Australian foreign minister on the prince and the monarchy. He had run this by the prince's team of advisers before asking the Australian political team, and they had agreed. The interview took place in the seat behind me, and I could not help eavesdropping. When asked about the prospect of Australia's becoming a republic and another referendum on the future of the monarchy, she casually shrugged it away, suggesting such matters were a long way off. But what if Federal Labor's Bill Shorten, leader of the opposition, won the election? After all, he had vowed to make ditching the monarchy a priority. 'Bill says a lot of things,' she added dismissively.

Towards the front of the luxury jet sat a man such matters would impact on, Prince Charles – His Royal Highness the Prince of Wales, to give him his correct title – working though his correspondence in a sealed-off private section. Outside was an adjoining corridor leading to the pilots and crew at the front and the open area equipped with large, luxury, cream leather seats for the officials.

Across the table from the prince on the left sat his most senior aide for this visit, forty-year-old career diplomat Scott Furssedonn-Wood, his deputy private secretary, who had been seconded from the British Government's Foreign and Commonwealth Office. A lofty six foot four tall, the Merton College, Oxford, graduate strikes an impressive figure. His credentials are impressive, too: he is a former Deputy High Commissioner of Eastern India who had also served a five-year stint at the British Embassy in Washington, DC, where he was the Head of Strategic Threats as well working on counterterrorism and counter-proliferation issues. Later he became the head of the Political Section and was responsible for coverage of the 2012 presidential election in the US. Scott is not only charming but inescapably, extremely bright – an essential quality when working for somebody as perspicacious as the prince. The two of them were running through the schedule for the remainder of the visit. There were still three days of the Australia tour left to run and the prince, as ever, wanted to ensure he was across every detail, no matter how small.

The Prince of Wales had been the headline act during the flying visit to Port Vila, not Australian foreign minister Julie Bishop, who had accompanied Charles as he is still heir to the throne of the realm of Australia. It was an important visit for both of them: Charles, by his presence and taking part dutifully in key ceremonial events, and Ms Bishop, with the odd quiet word here and there. Both were able to remind the leader of the South Pacific nation who its true friends really were.

It had been Prince Charles, after all, who had insisted on including Vanuatu – discovered in 1774 by Captain James Cook, who had named the islands the New Hebrides, a title that would last until independence in 1980 – into his packed schedule. It had been the proposed destination to host the summit known as the Commonwealth Heads of Government Meeting (CHOGM) at the end of 2017, but the venue was moved to London and Windsor in the United Kingdom because Vanuatu was no longer able to host the event due to the damage done by Cyclone Pam to the island nation's infrastructure.

Charles may not have godlike status like his father, the Duke of Edinburgh, who is treated as a 'divine being' by a cult on one of Vanuatu's tiny islands, Tanna, but he was given a most spectacular and uproarious welcome, befitting a king, much as his mother and father had been forty-four years earlier. Greeted by the locals in traditional dress and with painted faces, he smiled and waved as he walked across woven red ceremonial mats, a profoundly respected local tradition. After meeting with

Vanuatu's president and being given the first of many traditional garlands, he went shopping at the Haos Blong Handikraft market with the Pacific as the backdrop, admiring local handicraft.

'They do make such wonderful gifts, don't they?' he quipped, snapping up a bag for 6,000 vatu handed to his aide, Scott, by the British High Commissioner, David Ward, who looks after the Solomon Islands as well as Vanuatu. When the prince finally emerged, he was greeted by loud cheers and went on to shake hundreds of hands. At the final stop, Charles, as ever, gamely donned a grass skirt, to the delight of the travelling photographers. These included the exuberant professional photographer Tim Rooke of the international picture agency Shutterstock and Steve Parsons, a photographer from the UK's 150-year-old agency the Press Association. Both went into overdrive taking a series of brilliant shots of the historic and colourful scenes unfolding before them at the Nakamal, a traditional meeting place for tribal chiefs.

Others may have been reduced to fits of the giggles at the absurdity of it all, but not Charles. After a sip or two of special kava, known as Royal Kava, a powerful concoction reserved for special occasions, he seemed genuinely touched and humbled by the welcome and its attention to detail as he stood with a huge palm leaf up his back and a grass skirt over his lightweight suit, and splendidly bedecked with a white salusalu (garland) made from from indigenous natural rope fibres, leaves and flowers around his neck.

The Malvatumauri Council of Chiefs had honoured Charles, making him 'Chief Mal Menaringmanu'. With the Queen's Royal Standard, the official flag of the reigning British sovereign, fluttering on his chauffeured car, there was an easy symbolism in the heir to the throne being made 'paramount chief'. At long last he had been given a coronation of sorts. Indeed, he had been touched at the opening ceremony of the Commonwealth Games on the Gold Coast a few days earlier, when the entire Vanuatu team stopped in front of the of the royal box and bowed deeply in his honour. Charles in turn delighted the crowds, who had turned out in their tens of thousands, many in traditional dress-fibre skirts for women and loincloths for men, as opposed to Western-style clothing worn in the city during the Port Vila visit.

'Halo yufala euriwan,' Charles said from the podium (a rough translation being 'Hello, everybody'). 'My visit, while far too brief, has nevertheless allowed me to experience for myself the warmth, generosity and spirit for which the people of Vanuatu are so justly famed.' He added, 'Vanuatu, you are number one!' More deafening cheers followed. 'I am deeply touched by the generous welcome shown to me today and by the very great honour you have bestowed on me in granting me the chiefly title of Mal Menaringmanu. I know that chiefly titles are rarely given, and that to bear one is both a great privilege and a great responsibility. I can only say that, as Chief Mal Menaringmanu, I will do my very best to honour the four dual principles upon which the Law of the Malvatumauri Council of Chiefs is based – namely, love and happiness; respect and honour; goodness and peace; and goodwill and service,' he said sincerely.

Back in the chic surrounding of the BBJ, where I was the only 'Fleet Street' correspondent on board, I was tucking into some freshly prepared sandwiches and a glass of Australian Sauvignon handed to me by the RAAF uniformed crew. I was beckoned forward into the middle section of the plane where the Royal Household (Charles's staff and travelling team) were all seated by his communications secretary Julian Payne. The prince, he said, would be very happy to have a conversation with me for a few minutes. I was elated that he had accepted my request and even more so when that brief audience turned into twenty-five minutes of what was for me an absorbing conversation.

It seems a little absurd to me for a writer to pen a fair and contemporaneous biography about a living person without actually having met that person, or at least watched them at close quarters. It is different for historians: short of inventing a time machine, what other options are open them apart from digging deep and relying on sourced material they unearth? To claim to get some idea of the person's real character from just second- or third-hand accounts is implausible.

Charles is complex. As he himself said in an interview with his biographer Jonathan Dimbleby in 1994, 'I am one of those people who searches. I'm interested in pursuing the path, if I can find it, through the thickets.' It is Charles's character – that of a man who admits to getting carried away by enthusiasm in his bid to try to improve things, not just his position in society and royal status – that makes him interesting to write about.

During my work I have, of course, met and chatted with the prince on numerous occasions over the years that I have chronicled the Royal Family as a royal correspondent, at receptions and as I have followed him at home and abroad. He collected a special Londoner of the Decade award at the Evening Standard Progress 1000 party honouring the capital's innovators in 2016, an idea I put to the editor, and I was on hand as owner Evgeny Lebedev presented him with the special front page. Charles jokingly described it as 'one of your better front pages'.

Charles and Camilla also visited the *Evening Standard* offices in February, 2015 when the owner and then editor Sarah Sands escorted the prince, and I was on hand to show Camilla around along with the then deputy editor, Ian Walker. The prince was in fine form. When Ian was introduced to Charles on arrival in the entrance hall, he joked as they shook hands, 'I'm only the deputy,' to which the prince, quick as a flash, responded, 'There are rather a lot of us.'

In turn I have visited his home, his beloved estate, Highgrove, in Gloucestershire, which he bought, with Camilla's encouragement, back in 1980. Ever since then, he has poured his heart and soul into transforming its 25 acres into his sanctuary; it is his beautiful, eclectic garden, where he insists on applying his principles, which are strictly organic. There is a sense of bohemian, hippy, shabby chic about it that bizarrely, considering his place in the established order, reflects its owner's character. The two are intrinsically linked, it seems. And he seems to agree.

He said when he took over Highgrove it was practically a spiritual experience. He developed an almost unconscious train of thought that seemed to him like some 'powerful echo that arose, inexplicably, from within'. Entering the garden through a pair of carved Indian wooden door panels – a present to Charles from his late brother-in-law, Mark Shand – one is transported into another, magical world. On the wall beside them was the headless carved bust of a topless Indian lady, another Shand present to welcome attentive gardeners. On the garden's wall stands the scented modern English rose Jude the Obscure, and nearby chairs and seats have been painted a bright canary yellow to bring more light into the green surrounds.

No photographs can do justice to the famous stumpery laid out for the prince in imitation of an old Victorian idea – a modern variation of the practice of planting ferns among tree stumps. Work on this started in 1996, when a trailer arrived from the Scottish Highlands carrying 40 tons of petrified wood. Shortly afterwards, Charles took a delivery of giant roots from fallen sweet chestnut trees. 'I happily talk to the plants and the trees, and listen to them. I think it's absolutely crucial,' Charles said to gardener and presenter Alan Titchmarsh during a documentary screened in 2010.

On a wall leading into the big kitchen garden, there are sculpted portrait busts of 'worthies', people of special importance to Charles, among them Miriam Rothschild, champion of meadow wild-flower gardening and kindred spirit, and Vandana Shiva, the great environmentalist from India. He finds India, with its 'functioning chaos' and 'unending crowds', irresistible and has visited officially many times. However, he longs to return there privately so that he can avoid what he has described as 'the excessively dreary calls' on politicians and others 'who seem incapable of behaving as reasonable human beings'. A friend and mentor to Charles, the late Laurens van der Post (whom we'll meet later), is not visible, but the Bishop of London is. Carved on the gateway in Egyptian hieroglyphics is an inscription that reads poetically, 'The stars in the sky are represented by the flowers of the earth.' He even has four busts of himself, cast and given to him at different stages of his life, inset in alcoves.

'Did you notice the busts of me?' he asked one his team once.

'What did you think?'

'Very good likenesses, sir,' the nervous retainer responded.

'Yes, but they always get one thing right: my bloody ears,' he bemoaned with perfect comic timing.

On board the Australian Government's BBJ aircraft somewhere over the Coral Sea, however, I had my first meaningful one-to-one conversation with the heir to the throne, and it was certainly helpful with his project in mind. Having listened to the voice of the prince reading his book in the audio version of *Harmony* (essentially a distillation of his beliefs about nature, spirituality and the allure of life) several times driving in my car while I carried out research for this book, it seemed perfectly natural, oddly, to be sitting opposite him and striking up a conversation about the trip and all sorts of issues he cares deeply about. It helped, too, because I felt I had a good grasp of his thoughts on key issues as the conversation ebbed and flowed.

Inside his section of the plane, with its luxury fittings resembling the inside a top-of-the-range Jaguar car, the prince was sitting at his desk in a comfortable, dark-grey leather chair surrounded by papers and his handwritten letters. One of them, sealed in an envelope, was addressed to his ninety-six-year-old father, HRH Prince Philip, the Duke of Edinburgh, who was recovering in hospital after a hip-replacement operation. We were joined in the room by Julian, Charles's eyes and ears when it came to the media, who sat on my right; the prince was opposite me. Scott, his private secretary, collected his papers and duly left.

We shook hands and I told the prince honestly that, in my view, I felt his visit to Vanuatu had been a 'triumph' (shamelessly stealing Julie Bishop's phrase). The prince, sitting in his seat with his lightweight-wool Anderson & Sheppard tailored suit and silk tie still on, doesn't seem to take praise that well, but actually my comment seemed to please him. He smiled warmly and said, 'Yes, I was very touched by the warmth of the welcome.' It had, he added, felt like something from 'history, from another time'. He was right. At times the power of the energy created by the hundreds of dancers, the men with bare backsides and penis sheaths and the bare-breasted women in grass skirts performing a kastom dance, had seemed almost hypnotic and overwhelming to one watching for the first time.

We chatted for a few minutes about the Great Barrier Reef and I showed him a picture I had snapped of a giant loggerhead turtle that had poked out its head as his glass-bottom boat went by. 'Really,' he said, 'I never seem to see anything when I go out on those boats.' Suntanned, his skin was perhaps a little reddened, his hands slightly swollen, and he seemed a tad weary from his relentless schedule. But there was a genuine warmth about him. 'Imagine what it would be like coming into that harbour [Port Vila] aboard the Royal Yacht *Britannia*, with all the small craft to greet us,' he said, bemoaning, but without bitterness, the loss of that vessel.

He had a valid point. It was not as if the Royal Family were all going off on junkets all the time on the yacht, using it as a private craft. It was, Charles felt strongly, part of the process of trying to represent Britain abroad, 'entirely motivated by a desperate desire to put the "Great" back into Great Britain', as he puts it. What truly concerns him, however, is the erosion of Great British values by deliberate cynicism and ridicule.

One could immediately envisage the advantages of such a

vessel: hosting leaders on board, being able to spend more time in the region, having more time to recover and recharge fully, instead of charging around in jets from one engagement to the next. But it was more than that. It was what this ocean-going palace could achieve for the greater good that interested the prince. 'It really did have great convening power,' I said, 'and helped raise billions' for the UK economy, referring – like the former Foreign Secretary, Boris Johnson – to the clear 'soft power' benefits of such a yacht.

*Britannia*'s pulling power, after all, was the stuff of legend. We recalled how one could invite the world's busiest and most powerful business leaders to breakfast, lunch or dinner in the swankiest restaurant and you might get a handful of takers; or, in the case of this trip to Lady Elliot Island on the Great Barrier Reef, for a round-table meeting with big-business CEOs to thrash out challenges facing the world's reefs, and they'd all come. Sadly, as the prince noted, although the meeting had been overwhelmingly positive, senior representatives from Australia's mining industry had failed to show up despite saying they would come; and other industry leaders sent more junior executives to represent them at the table. He was clearly a little peeved about it, but had soldiered on regardless.

That wouldn't have happened if the meeting had been aboard *Britannia*, we both agreed. Invite anyone – top bankers, presidents, billionaires – aboard for a drink on the Royal Yacht and there would be a 100 per cent 'Yes, please!' That was when *Britannia* did not even have a member of the Royal Family on board, as on one occasion in 1993 when she staged a trade day in what was then known as Bombay and contracts worth an incredible £1 billion were signed. When she was due in port carrying the Queen or the Prince of Wales, the British Ambassador was suddenly the most popular person in the entire country.

'Sadly, the Treasury did not seem to think so,' the prince said. 'And, what's more, the Royal Navy didn't want to pay to staff it, either,' he added wryly.

Surely, a solution could be found just as the RAF had done with the RAF Voyager, the so-called 'Cam Force One' (Britain's equivalent of the US's presidential jet, Air Force One). This is typically used as a refuelling and transportation jet, but also used by the prince or senior royals such as the Duke of Cambridge when representing the Queen abroad and the Prime Minister for international travel, I suggested.

'You would have thought so,' Charles said. He clearly likes Boris Johnson's idea for a privately backed investment for a new royal yacht that would add greatly to the soft power of this country. Charles believes that a new yacht like *Britannia* would be a statement of serious intent as well as a floating embassy-cum-trade platform, instantly recognisable and sleek, without being ostentatious. The old lady HMY *Britannia* is now a tourist attraction docked in Edinburgh, something lamented by the man who will be the only British king since Charles II not to have a royal yacht.

'Blair and Brown. . .and the Treasury simply wouldn't have it, so there we are,' he said, with an air of resignation in his voice. He wasn't being controversial, just stating a fact. Prince Philip was adamant this was the wrong decision, too. In a forthright interview to mark his ninetieth birthday, he said as much: 'She should have had her steam turbines taken out and diesel engines put in. She was as sound as a bell and she could have gone on for another fifty years.' Bizarrely, then PM Tony Blair himself says he regrets the decision. 'I think if it had happened five years into my time [as Prime Minister], I would have just said "no",' he said some years after *Britannia* was decommissioned.

'Were you with us in Hong Kong for the handover?' Charles asked me. This was the transfer of sovereignty over Hong Kong from the United Kingdom to China on 1 July 1997, HMY *Britannia*'s last foreign mission. It was to convey the last governor of Hong Kong, Chris Patten, and the prince back from Hong Kong before being decommissioned in front of a tearful Queen and Royal Family on 11 December 1997.

'I wasn't, sir,' I responded.

'This is exactly where it could be used to great effect,' he went on, 'and in places like the Solomon Islands.'

I couldn't help but agree.

Talk of the handover shifted his thought process to another bugbear of his – China. The Communist regime and its continued grip on our world – particularly on emerging nations – with its financial clout clearly troubles him. He has often spoken privately of what he calls the 'awfulness' of the Chinese Communist government and its 'monstrous' treatment of its Tibetan and Muslim minorities.

Unlike the Queen, and his eldest son, William, the Duke of Cambridge, Charles has yet to set foot on the soil of mainland China and is clearly still not enamoured of the Communist regime led by its president for life – and, effectively, the new Chinese 'Emperor' of the modern age – Xi Jinping.

'They [the Chinese] are investing everywhere,' Charles said, with a slight note of alarm in his voice. We both acknowledged the two ugly blots on the landscape concrete-block buildings in Port Vila, funded by Chinese investment. 'Indeed,' he said, 'they [the Chinese investors] are everywhere,' his brow furrowing further.

The prince believes the UK and the leading Commonwealth nations, the financial powerhouses of this old club – the UK, Australia, Canada, New Zealand – are missing a trick. They should, he feels, be combating this issue head on together, putting on a united effort funded with a proper, all-encompassing united financial institution. 'We should form a Commonwealth Bank,' he said, a radical idea he had clearly been mulling over for some time. This way, he said, together we could unite in the fight against outside influences and support small Commonwealth nations such as Vanuatu, ensuring too that they know which side they are on when others come to use them for strategic or military reasons. That way our influence as a united Commonwealth club banded together in the fight for the greater good would be real and dynamic. Doing it bilaterally, he felt, was self-defeating, tied up in red tape.

The Commonwealth would not be so easily dismissed, as it so often is, as just a talking shop made up of Britain and its former empire, but active on the ground in countries where it really matters. The prince is clearly passionate about the Commonwealth, and now he is confirmed as its next head, albeit a titular one, he can slowly begin to put his own stamp on it. One way he has always tried to promote the Commonwealth, as well as by military links in the past, is, where possible, by meeting senior officers of Commonwealth army regiments, such as those in India, which are affiliated to some of his regiments in the UK. However, he has encountered problems doing this in the past, with bureaucrats and politicians suspicious of his motives. 'Seemingly, old Soviet-learnt habits die hard in Indian officialdom,' he quipped to a friend.

His is the sort of free, forward-thinking leadership that this unique voluntary club of fifty-three nations will benefit from a force to take it to another, more effective level. One feels such action and innovative ideas are something he will suggest and push for in conversations with leaders. After all, Charles is not the kind of person just to rubber-stamp decisions after they've been discussed around the table: he is one who would want to be at the table too, as a high-level source close to him pointed out to me.

After all, its membership is almost entirely made up of English-speaking former colonies that share similar legal systems and very often a constitutional framework that mirrors that of the United Kingdom, with so many professional, trade, sports, educational and cultural associations – eighty in all. It means so much can actually get done and lobbied for outside government circles.

The Commonwealth talks in high ideals but trades in a much more compromised reality. It confers no trade privileges, has no influence on defence or economic policy, no executive authority and no sensible budget to play a global role. Thus, it remains, those who criticise it say, a glorified global debating society, at best, and, at worst, a costly junket.

A dynamic central Commonwealth Bank would actually make a real difference where it matters in the world. Such an organisation, Charles believes, would be able to help and fund the indigenous people whose world, like that of the people in

Vanuatu, was sinking and being submerged amid great population growth (at the last count in 2018, Vanuatu had a population of 282,117 with more than 2.2 per cent annual change).

'How on earth are they going to live or feed themselves?' he said.

Charles was, of course, right and his point was a serious one. One could feel his deep concern coupled with a sense of growing frustration.

Our conversation was wide-ranging. One minute we were discussing climate change, the next the built environment and Poundbury, his visionary traditionalist village in Dorset. This is so often unfairly mocked as a 'feudal Disneyland', but a growing and diverse community has settled there and developed over time, suggesting it has achieved its objective.

Had I been, Charles asked me. I nodded in the affirmative and expressed my genuine approval. I had, in fact, visited Poundbury three times on media days arranged by his Clarence House office and, essentially, agreed with the concept.

When we moved on to the subject of London's scourge of knife crime and violence on our capital city's streets. The prince was quick to point out that his 'causes' are all linked and stressed he does not blindingly leap from one subject or concern to another, as some have suggested. He reminded me that crime and the built environment are intrinsically connected, and lamented the fact that developers and council planners had failed to grasp it, either deliberately or through ignorance. He believes London is a unique 'city of villages' now under assault from 'faceless' towers, and is 'poorly conceived' – so-called mega-developments.

He said of architecture as far back as 1987, 'In the space of a mere fifteen years in the sixties and seventies. . .the planners, architects and developers of the City wrecked the London skyline and desecrated the dome of St Paul's.' His opinion hasn't changed.

Retaining London's squares was important, he said, because in this way people get to know their neighbours and ultimately develop a sense of community and of responsibility for that community and the people within it. As a result, people living there would, ultimately, as they had in the past, largely 'police themselves'. He told me he had spoken at length with the UK capital city's elected Labour mayor, Sadiq Khan, about it. 'I can't seem to get through to him,' said the prince.

Prince Charles's thoughts on architecture and the built environment have long been contentious, but have merit and widespread support among the general public. He believes developers, architects and town and city planners must go back to the drawing board and look again, to see the advantages of the traditional mansion blocks, no more than three storeys high, along with those classic Georgian and Victorian squares and crescents of central London, as inspiration for forms of housing that perfectly meet London's needs.

My conversation with the prince was not exclusively serious. There was humour, too – with Charles that is almost inevitable. He is a very funny man, with a quirky sense of humour formed from his love of Spike Milligan and *The Goons*. When I commended his amusing speech at a governor general's reception in Brisbane, where he had his audience in stitches, he was typically humble. He had joked that he would never again fit into a pair of skin-tight 'budgie smugglers' and said, somewhat alarmingly, that his advancing years coincided with 'bits falling off'. What was so refreshing was the self-deprecating tone in his speech. For years, when forced to travel alone, he was less positive and would moan about struggling to make a difference when talking to world leaders. He described them to friends as 'silent cronies' for just sitting there during meetings and paying him lip service. It made him feel 'worryingly decrepit'. He would also tell friends how he always liked staying in the 'old house' because of its 'particularly comfortable bed'.

'You're very kind,' he said with a smile, before adding, 'But I've never even owned a pair of budgie smugglers in my life,' with perfect comic timing. Even the way he put emphasis on the words 'budgie smugglers' made one chuckle.

My five-minute 'brush-by' had turned into twenty five minutes of intriguing, enlightening and meaningful conversation with the future king. I returned to my comfortable seat for the remainder of the two-and-a-half-hour flight, sipped a perfectly chilled glass of Australian Sauvignon Blanc and made contemporaneous notes of our conversation on my Apple Mac.

The prince continued with his work, prepping for his next engagement, a church service at St John the Evangelist Anglican Church in Cairns, Queensland. It would be a Sunday service, where he would be greeted by the Bishop of North Queensland, Bill Ray, and the Rev. Rod Gooden. He had short biographies to read on all the people he would meet. Nothing is left to chance. No wonder Charles had expressed regret over the loss of HMY *Britannia* during our exchange: the pace of this visit to Australia and Vanuatu, in and out in just a few hours, was truly relentless and would have left a man half his age drained.

'It's going to be even hotter in Cairns,' he reminded me, as I stood by the door of his office in the air.

'I don't know how you remain looking so cool,' I admitted.

'I don't,' he said with a smile.

His secret, I was told later by one of his household, was always being rapidly hydrated with still water between engagements inside the air-conditioned vehicles or rooms he occupied usually.

## Chapter Two

# ICH DIEN – 'I SERVE'

———◇———

*'Not all the water in the rough rude sea*
*Can wash the balm from an anointed king'*

WILLIAM SHAKESPEARE, RICHARD II

Lurking in the shadows throughout time, but just markedly below the rank of a monarch, is the male heir to the throne, sometimes known as the Crown Prince. In the British hereditary monarchal system, he is often, but not always, given the title 'His Royal Highness the Prince of Wales'. Just twenty-one men have held that coveted rank. History has shown the majority of them who bore the title to be great supporters of, and impeccable servants to, their sovereign. In a few cases, the skulking heirs have been more trouble than they were worth. Among the unscrupulous few are those who secretly plotted to overthrow the reigning monarch in a bloody power grab. In other cases, such unfitting behaviour has gone so far as to undermine seriously the sitting monarch.

The title 'Prince of Wales' is one of the great continuities of English and Welsh and, latterly, British, history. The incumbent has no formal public role or responsibility legislated by Parliament, but the bearer of the title is usually the next in line to the throne or heir apparent. The title, which is within the gift of the reigning sovereign, is granted to the heir apparent as a personal dignity and the title Earl of Chester has always been bestowed upon the recipient in conjunction with it. It is not automatically given, and the title not heritable, either. It is seen as a great honour. But it can be, as history has shown, a poisoned chalice too, a role immersed in bloody intrigue, peril and even murder.

What links all these men, other than the title of Prince of Wales, is that each of them at the time of being given the title was heir to the throne of England (prior to 1707, that is, and the implementation of the Act of Union with Scotland, and of Great Britain ever since). There is, however, little affiliation other than that. Ten of the twenty-one were created Prince of Wales as adults or youths and eight as children. Only a select few have held the title for more than a decade with a couple holding it for barely a year. Nor has being given the title guaranteed reaching the throne. Of the eighteen English Princes of Wales, only ten lived to be king; seven failed to get there. The current incumbent, Prince Charles, the man who has held the title longer than any of those before him, is still waiting for the top job having long passed the accepted retirement age.

The title 'Prince of Wales' (Tywysog Cymru) was originally granted to princes born in Wales itself from the twelfth century onwards; the term replaced the use of the word 'king'. One of the last Welsh princes, Llywelyn ap Gruffudd, was killed in battle in

1282 against English King Edward I, dubbed Edward Longshanks and the Hammer of the Scots, who was the tyrannical monarch from 1272 to 1307. He may have been lauded for hammering the Scots, but he did a pretty effective job at pulverising the warring Welsh too and keeping them at bay. To further stamp his authority, he made his son, Edward of Caernarfon – born at the castle bearing his name in Wales – the first English Prince of Wales in 1301 at the age of sixteen. He held the title for six years before ascending the throne as Edward II.

Edward III's son, Edward of Woodstock, was created Prince of Wales at just twelve in 1343. Known as the Black Prince, the feared soldier held the title for thirty-three years until his death in 1376, just a year prior to his father's passing, not having ascended the throne. The Black Prince's own son held the title for less than a year. Richard married twice but produced no children and was deposed by Henry IV, who moved quickly to make his son, Henry of Monmouth, Prince of Wales at the age of thirteen. Henry V died in 1422 and his son, another Henry, succeeded to the Crown aged nine months. When Henry VI took control of the monarchal system, it had lost its shine and much of its power. His son, Edward of Westminster, was created Prince of Wales five months after his birth and held the title for seventeen years. The Duke of York's son, however, took the title Edward IV and deposed the king in 1461, and the Prince of Wales, rather than inheriting the throne, became a fugitive for a decade. He was finally killed in the bloody Battle of Tewkesbury in 1471 following his father briefly reclaiming the throne the previous year.

Edward IV's son, known as 'Edward of the Sanctuary', was created Prince of Wales immediately on the death of his predecessor. On his father's death in 1883, he was created Edward V, but weeks later was denounced as a bastard by his uncle, Richard of Gloucester, who seized the Crown as Richard III and imprisoned him and his younger brother Richard in the Tower of London. In one of the great royal mysteries, 'the princes in the Tower' disappeared and were presumed murdered. Richard III then made his son, Edward of Middleham, Prince of Wales.

When Richard was overthrown and killed at the Battle of Bosworth Field in August 1485, Henry Tudor became Henry VII and his eldest son, Arthur, just three, took the title Prince of Wales. A frail youth, Arthur died at Ludlow in April 1502, leaving Catherine of Aragon, the devout Roman Catholic Spanish princess to whom he was betrothed, free to marry his younger brother, Henry, Duke of York, who also inherited his brother's title once it was clear Catherine was not pregnant with his brother's child. The whole Tudor dynasty ended in 1603 with no further claimant of the title, as Henry VIII didn't ever make his legitimate son, Edward VI, the Prince of Wales. In fact, there was a hiatus for the title until James I – the first Stuart king – gave the title to his son, 'Renaissance man' Henry Stuart, in 1610.

Since 1714, the title of Prince of Wales has carried no formal responsibilities in the principality and has only an honorary association with Wales. When the future George II was created Prince of Wales after a lapse of some years, a special Parliamentary Act was needed to ensure he received the revenues that went with the title. Frederick, his son, was given the title in 1729 and his son George, later 'mad' king George III, in 1751. From 1727 onwards, all Princes of Wales relied on the Civil List for their income except when they have also been Dukes of Cornwall.

('In the United Kingdom, the Civil List was, until 2011, the annual grant that covered some expenses associated with the sovereign performing their official duties, including those for staff salaries, state visits, public engagements, ceremonial functions and the upkeep of the royal households.' – Wikipedia) King George III found it difficult to run his household within the limits of the Civil List and went cap in hand to Parliament for more money to clear his debts.

George's gaudy eldest son – known popularly as 'Prinny', later Prince Regent and eventually King George IV – strove to fashion an idealised image of himself that increasingly bore little relation to reality. It was he who, having been made Prince of Wales in 1762, lived a life devoted to excess and seemingly found it impossible to live within his means, and ran up huge debts in his lifetime. He once bought eighty-three pairs of boots and seventy-four pairs of gloves on a single shopping expedition and lived his entire adult life in massive debt, becoming the biggest spender in Britain's royal history by squandering a fortune. No matter how much money Parliament awarded him, George always needed more. His extravagance was legendary. When he was a teenager, his tutor had complained that the prince 'could never be taught to understand the value of money'. Half his income disappeared in the upkeep of his horses; he also employed a private band of forty-two musicians.

The spendthrift George collected everything from walking sticks and handkerchiefs to kangaroos for his private zoo. Also known aptly as the 'Prince of Pleasure', George was a dandy and a drunkard. Debauched and dissolute, selfish and self-indulgent, he had many mistresses. Rumours of illegitimate children circulated during his lifetime, and after his death, too. Debt was a recurring theme for the House of Hanover and George also needed a special Act to rescue him. Among the many debts he owed was £947 (a sizeable sum in today's money of more than £100,000) to a Windsor apothecary for medicines purchased for treatments for a venereal infection.

George was a man of superhuman appetite, too. A lifelong hypochondriac who nevertheless ate and drank with gusto, he often shamelessly appeared in public befuddled with drink. Suffering from gout, arteriosclerosis and possibly the porphyria that sent his father mad, he took up to 250 drops of laudanum a day. Depressed by his evident failure to reinvent himself as monarch (1820–30), the ailing king simply withdrew into a fantasy world of laudanum and alcohol. It was a toxic cocktail and it finally took its toll on 26 June 1830, when George IV died at sixty-seven. Never in modern times has a sovereign died so unlamented and his contemporaries shed few tears for this spendthrift playboy. *The Times* commented, 'There never was an individual less regretted by his fellow-creatures than this deceased King.'

There was another lengthy space in time after George IV's ascension in 1820 before the next Prince of Wales. Queen Victoria's son, the future King Edward VII – Albert, known to the family as Bertie – held the title for more than fifty-nine years before ascending the throne, longer than anyone else until Prince Charles, who surpassed the record held by his playboy great-great-grandfather on 9 September 2017. Denied involvement in many matters of state by his ageing mother, Bertie became a devoted leader of society, gaining a louche reputation for his hedonistic lifestyle, enjoying a number of celebrated extramarital affairs. He didn't let his marriage to Danish Princess Alexandra cramp his style. In his own way, he apparently loved her. 'She is my brood mare,' he used to say. 'The others [his scores of lovers, including prostitutes, society women and professional beauties] are my hacks.' Loving and loyal, Alix, as she was known, was totally devoted to her Bertie, indulging his public infidelities. 'Edward the Caresser' – another of his nicknames – clearly believed his philandering almost as his right. Several illegitimate children were attributed to him, although not proven.

He partied, ate and gambled to excess, never read books, apart from the odd novel, and had the reputation of a complete vulgarian. His antics left his mother, Queen Victoria, exasperated. He was, in her view, the complete antithesis of her late beloved husband Albert, whom she idolised. She even blamed the unfortunate Bertie's bawdy behaviour for his father's premature death. (He caught a cold travelling to Cambridge to admonish his son, which speedily developed into pneumonia.)

When the overweight, scandal-prone waster Prince of Wales finally got the top job, he was fifty-nine and, in his own view, washed up. 'It has come too late,' he said, in German, to his wife, as she knelt and kissed his hand beside his Empress Victoria's deathbed after the old Queen had died. Nobody expected too much of him. The story of his reign – like the reign itself – was too little, too late. Perhaps the long waiting game and the fact that his mother refused to allow him access to government papers and responsibility belied his many talents. During his short reign (1901–10) he proved a guileful diplomat and was astute at handling his personal public relations. As king, he is best remembered for improving Anglo-French relations with the so-called 'Entente Cordiale'. Perhaps his greatest achievement was his closeness to his son and heir, for, unlike his own relations with his parents, Edward enjoyed a loving bond with his second son George (later George V), whom he created Prince of Wales in 1901.

Until the sudden death of his elder brother, Prince Albert Victor, Duke of Clarence, in 1892, aged just twenty-eight, Prince George had no expectation of inheriting the Crown. He had a second-rate home education before entering the Royal Navy when still a child. He was, at best, conscientious but, at worst, tense when forced to make important decisions. Early in his reign he faced the most testing domestic challenges of any monarch in recent history.

First, in 1910–11, there was the constitutional crisis caused by the veto pronounced by the Tory-dominated House of Lords over the Liberal government's legislation. Then in 1913–14, there was the furious controversy over Irish home rule, which many observers expected to end in civil war. Like his father, George V believed he had to be seen by the people to be loved by them. His provincial tours, and visits to hospitals and factories, unprecedented in number, started early in his reign in a bid to bring the Crown closer to its people.

In his reign, the UK became, for the first time, united. As king after 1918 he presided over the transition to full adult suffrage, and reconciled the Labour Party to constitutionalism. Although he favoured the Tories, Labour's Ramsay MacDonald became his favourite prime minister.

As a devout Anglican, he read the Bible every day without

fail. He was an authoritative yet mollifying public speaker. His first Christmas radio broadcast in 1932 – written by the brilliant Indian-born writer of the empire, Rudyard Kipling (author of *The Jungle Book* [1894], *Kim* [1901] and many short stories, including 'The Man Who Would Be King' [1888] – was greeted as a great triumph by the public and commentators alike. In his Silver Jubilee celebrations of 1935, his people turned out in their thousands to cheer him and praise him for his dutifulness and paternalism.

The first monarch since 1714 not to speak fluent German, George preferred the English-speaking Empire to the 'foreigners' of Europe and mistrusted what he dubbed 'abroad'. After the Great War (1914–18), which saw the end of the reigns of five emperors, eight kings and eighteen minor royal dynasties, the old 'cousinhood' monarchy of Victorian times became imbued with a narrower sense of national identity. George disliked foreign travel and, apart from the celebrated Imperial Indian Durbar of 1911, which became known as the 'Delhi Durbar', he made only three state visits during his reign: to Paris in 1914 and to the kingdoms of Belgium and Italy in 1922–3. His pet hates included: trendy new or foreign music fashions and new dances such as the slow waltz or more gaucho-style tango; girls who used nail varnish or did not ride horses side-saddle; Communists, Fascists, submarines and chemical warfare. He would find fault in them all. He shook his stick at a Cézanne in the National Gallery, to whose director he declared, 'Turner was mad. My grandmother always said so.'

As a father, George was an authoritarian, browbeating bully and was both physically and orally abusive to all of his sons. George made his eldest son, the hugely popular and charismatic David, Prince of Wales in 1911, when he was sixteen. He held the title for fifteen years and did a first-class job in the role, becoming the Royal Family's first truly global superstar. His charm, however, did not compensate for the lack of steadfastness and moral fibre that his father possessed. The latter is reported to have told his then prime minister, Stanley Baldwin, 'After I am dead, the boy will ruin himself in twelve months.'

David ascended the throne in 1936 as Edward VIII, but his reign soon collapsed, ostensibly over a damaging constitutional battle concerning his desire to wed twice-divorced American socialite Wallis Warfield Simpson, with the same Baldwin playing a central role. Since the monarch was also head of the Church of England and Defender of the Faith, a conflict of interests was obvious and imminent. The king decided he should abdicate rather than create a constitutional crisis.

On 10 December 1936, Edward signed the Instrument of Abdication at Windsor, which was witnessed by his three brothers. On the evening of 11 December, Prince Edward made a radio broadcast to the nation, stating, 'You must believe me when I tell you that I have found it impossible to carry the heavy burden of responsibility and to discharge my duties as king as I would wish to do, without the help and support of the woman I love.' Edward was never crowned and reigned for just 325 days.

He was succeeded by his brother, Albert, Duke of York, who chose to reign as George VI, to mark the continuity with his father's reign. One of his first actions was to create his brother Duke of Windsor. He eventually did marry Mrs Simpson in a civil ceremony at the Château de Candé, near Tours in France on 3 June 1937 and remained in exile in France, regarded as a virtual outcast by the rest of the Royal Family. The marriage produced no children and his brother, the new King George VI, continually refused to grant the Duchess of Windsor the style of Royal Highness, which became a lasting source of friction between the brothers.

Years later the current Prince of Wales's mentor and great-uncle, Earl Mountbatten of Burma, who was a lifelong close friend of the ex-king, pleaded his friend's cause with the young and impressionable Charles. He tried to explain the complexities of his case and the abdication from another perspective to the new Prince of Wales. The wily aristocrat hoped to persuade Charles to lobby his family, particularly the Queen and the Queen Mother, to secure an invitation for the exiled duke and his wife to return to Britain and to live out the rest of their lives peacefully and reconciled with the royal family.

Charles, perhaps fuelled by the naïveté of youth and blinded by his devotion to the wily Mountbatten, was essentially on side. 'I, personally, feel it would be wonderful if Uncle David and his wife could come over and spend a weekend. Now that he is getting old he must long to come back and it would seem pointless to continue the feud,' he noted. The prince boldly even took the case to his other champion, the Queen Mother, but received an ice-cold response. He soon realised she was not about to do a *volte-face* on the matter under any circumstance. Queen Elizabeth (the Queen Mother) bluntly stopped her grandson in his tracks and made it clear that the idea was a nonstarter. She made it transparent that she regarded her brother-in-law as a weak man who had been led astray by 'that woman' – she wouldn't even use Wallis's name – and was always convinced that her beloved George's life was shortened by the stress caused by stepping in for his older brother and becoming king. The idea was shelved and Charles never even put it to his mother.

Charles did, however, make a private visit to France and arranged to meet his great-uncle, David – and the previous holder of his title the Prince of Wales – for the first time. 'Upon entering the house I found footmen and pages wearing identical scarlet and black uniforms to the ones ours wear at home. It was rather pathetic seeing that,' he wrote. 'The eye then wandered to a table in the hall on which lay a red box with "The King" on it,' he wrote in is diary. He found that the old Duke was on good form, although bent and using a stick, Charles noted. He had one eye shut most of the time due to his cataract operation and used 'expansive gestures' while clutching an enormous cigar. 'We got onto the subject of his relationship with his father,' Charles wrote,

> and he said he had had a very difficult time with him and that Gan-Gan [Charles's great-grandmother, Queen Mary, the consort to George V] was a hard woman and he had been brought up extremely strictly, which had led to his harsh feelings against older people and traditions of all sorts. While he was talking the Duchess kept flitting to and fro like a strange bat. She looks incredible for her age and obviously has her face lifted every day.

Charles noted that Wallis struck him as a 'totally unsympathetic and somewhat superficial' person. All that she talked about was whether she would wear a hat at the Arc de Triomphe de l'Étoile the next day, he said. When asked if he would like to return to England for the last years of his life, the duke half-jokingly responded that no one would recognise him. 'The whole thing seemed so tragic, the existence, the people and the atmosphere, that I was relieved to escape it after 45 minutes and drive round Paris by night,' Charles candidly wrote.

Eight months later the former king was dead. Charles cut short an official visit to Malta to fly home for the old king's funeral and attended a dinner at Buckingham Palace with the Queen and the duchess. It was the first time the duchess had been to the palace since the abdication of 1936 and the first time the Queen had shown her any form of recognition. After dinner they were joined by other members of the Royal Family to watch Mountbatten's tribute to his late friend on television. Loyally, Charles accompanied Lord Mountbatten to St George's Chapel, Windsor, the following evening, where the duke was lying in state.

The duke's widow had not been well that day, her mental as well as physical frailties exposed, and had to be supported by Lord Mountbatten. As Charles stood there he watched her as she appeared to be admonishing herself and repeating the words, 'He gave up so much for so little.' Once inside the ornate fourteenth-century chapel for the service, Charles was overcome, his eyes brimming with tears as he followed the coffin into the nave. 'Somehow I felt deeply moved by the whole experience and felt that it was right that we were honouring uncle David like this . . . The service was simple, dignified to perfection, colourful and wonderfully British,' he noted.

The current incumbent of the title Prince of Wales lives a life a world away from all twenty men who have held the title before him. His mother was already married and had given birth to him and his sister, Princess Anne, when she came to the throne in 1952. On 26 July 1958, the headmaster of his prep school at Cheam, Peter Beck, summoned a group of boys to his sitting room; Charles was amongst them. The last days of empire had already become a distant memory and the bright new Commonwealth Games in Cardiff were being broadcast on the BBC. The boys were allowed to watch the closing ceremony on his television. It was announced that, while the Queen was unable to attend, she would address both the packed stadium and the television audience in a recorded message.

The serene figure of Charles's mother then appeared on the screen and read out a simple, but, for Charles, life-changing message: 'The British Empire and Commonwealth Games in the capital . . . have made this a memorable year for the principality. I have therefore decided to mark it further by an act that will, I hope, give much pleasure to all Welshmen as it does to me. I intend to create my son Charles Prince of Wales today. . . When he is grown up, I will present him to you at Caernarfon.' His friends turned to the young prince and offered their congratulations on his elevation in status, much to his discomfort.

He later recalled the announcement at a dinner in Caerphilly Castle in July 2008 to celebrate his half-century as the Prince of Wales. 'I remember with horror and embarrassment how I was summoned with all the other boys at my school to the headmaster's sitting room, where we all had to sit on the floor and watch television. To my total embarrassment I heard my mama's voice – she wasn't very well at the time and could not go. My father went instead and a recording of the message was played in the stadium saying that I was to be made the Prince of Wales. All the other boys turned around and looked at me and I remember thinking, "What on earth have I been let in for?" That is my overriding memory.' The prince said later it was one of the greatest privileges possible to be the twenty-first Prince of Wales. 'I have tried my best – it may not be very adequate to live up to the motto of my predecessors, "*Ich Dien* – I Serve",' he said.

Eleven years later at Caernarfon Castle at an investiture modelled on the one for his great-uncle David in 1911, he was sworn in as the Prince of Wales. On the eve of the initiation Charles boarded the royal train with his parents bound for north Wales. They knew that the pageant had to be perfect and hoped for a positive response. They had no choice but to trust in the security already in place. Fanatics had formed what they called the Free Wales Army and had finally won the attention of the police and security services after an RAF warrant officer was seriously injured in an incident. Then the gang planted a bomb that destroyed the Temple of Peace in Cardiff. Another bomb was found in the lost-luggage department of the railway station. Anonymously, too, it was announced that the Prince of Wales was on their target list. Charles was understandably uneasy.

After four terms at Trinity College, Cambridge, the prince was sent to the University College of Wales at Aberystwyth in order to learn Welsh before his formal investiture as the Prince of Wales. This was a political decision rather than a cultural one, amid a revival of nationalism in Scotland and Wales. Just before his departure to the Welsh college, Charles recorded his first radio interview and, not surprisingly, he was asked about his attitude towards the hostility in the principality. 'It would be unnatural, I think, if one didn't feel any apprehension about it. One always wonders what's going to happen . . . As long as I don't get covered in too much egg and tomato I'll be all right. But I don't blame people demonstrating like that. They've never seen me before. They don't know what I'm like. I've hardly been to Wales, and you can't really expect people to be overzealous about the fact of having a so-called English prince to come amongst them,' he said.

To cancel the university term in Wales would have been a public-relations disaster for the government and indeed for Charles himself. It was decided it would be a weakness to bow to extremist threats. So they went ahead regardless. Upon his arrival at Pantycelyn Hall, where he would share accommodation with 250 other students, Charles was met by a 500-strong cheering crowd. He was deeply touched. In the end the prince enjoyed his time there and was treated kindly in Aberystwyth. His period of study there passed without incident.

He wrote to a friend,

If I have learned anything during the last eight weeks, it's been about Wales. . .they feel so strongly about Wales as a nation, and it means something to them, and they are depressed by what might happen to it if they don't try and preserve the language and the culture, which is unique and special to Wales, and if something is unique and special, I see it as well worth preserving.

Years later he said the time he spent studying there were among his fondest memories of times he has spent in the principality. He recalled with pleasure the 'memorable times spent exploring mid-Wales during my term at Aberystwyth University and learning something about the principality and its ancient language, folklore, myths and history.'

More bombs were promised by the militant Welsh for Caernarfon on the actual day of his instalment as the Prince of Wales on 1 July 1969. Charles was driven through the town in an open carriage on his way to the castle past cheering crowds. As the guests and choir sang 'God Bless the Prince of Wales', he was conducted to the dais and knelt before the Queen. He would later write that he found it profoundly moving when he placed his hands between his mother's and spoke the oath of allegiance.

The Queen then presented the prince to the crowd at Eagle Gate and at the lower ward to the sound of magnificent fanfares. After that he was again paraded through the streets before retiring aboard the Royal Yacht at Holyhead for a well-deserved dinner, an emotionally exhausted but very happy prince. Buoyed by the experience, the prince noted, 'As long as I do not take myself too seriously I should not be too badly off.'

The next day Charles set off without the rest of the family to undertake a week of solo engagements around the principality. He recalled being 'utterly amazed' by the positive reaction he received. As the tour progressed south, the crowds grew even bigger. At the end of it, Charles arrived exhausted but elated at Windsor Castle. He retired to write up his diary, noting the silence after the day's cheers and applause, reflecting that he had much to live up to and expressing the hope that he could provide constructive help for Wales.

Unlike previous bearers of the title, Charles has chosen to cultivate close contacts within the principality. He is by no means obliged to do so, and indeed none of his immediate predecessors did nearly as much. He purchased a 192-acre estate near the village of Myddfai, Llandovery, Carmarthenshire, through his Duchy of Cornwall trust, called Llwynywermod, also known as Llwynywormwood, just outside the Brecon Beacons National Park. Adapted from a former model farm in Carmarthenshire, it bears witness to his philosophy of sustainable building with a structure traditionally made from existing and locally sourced materials, an ecologically sound heating system and elegant interiors that harmonise perfectly with the architecture.

He uses it for meetings, receptions and concerts, and as the base for his several yearly visits to Wales, including the annual week of summer engagements, known in his annual schedule as 'Wales Week'. He says he wants it to be a 'showcase for traditional Welsh craftsmanship, textiles and woodwork, so as to draw attention to the high-quality small enterprises, woollen mills, quilt-makers, joiners, stonemasons and metalworkers situated in rural parts of Wales'. It enables him, he says, to feel part of the local community. To him, he says, preserving this sense of community 'is timeless'.

When asked, how important it was for him to have a retreat in Wales, Charles said, 'Very important! Having been as Prince of Wales for fifty-five years [at the time of the interview], it enables me, on various occasions, to be part of the local community around Llandovery and to have a base for entertaining and meeting people from throughout the principality.'

He went on, 'Wales has still preserved its wonderful sense of community, particularly in the rural areas, and Llandovery, an old sheep drovers' town, somehow maintains those priceless assets of its own community hospital, family GPs, a rugby club [of which I am proud to be patron], a railway station and a strong connection with the family farming communities in the surrounding countryside. Some may say this is old-fashioned, but to me it is timeless; the bedrock of our humanity in a profound relationship with nature and the very heart of Wales's cultural, social and spiritual heritage.'

During Wales Week of 2018, he attended an important birthday party to celebrate the National Health Service turning seventy just four months before he would himself. He opted to celebrate the occasion at a garden party in Ysbyty Aneurin Bevan, a 107-bed hospital that opened in 2010 and was named after the founder of the NHS, the Labour politician Aneurin Bevan, who is credited with establishing free healthcare in the UK, the guiding principle of the NHS.

He also made a group of women laugh when he asked if they all had their babies here. 'Oh, no, sir, we're all in our fifties!' one chuckled. The group told him they worked in the mental-health department, and he complimented them on 'a fantastic job'. Strolling past the minor-injury department, the future king came face to face with a skeleton known as 'Elvis the Pelvis'. 'What have you done to this?' he joked as he pointed at the bones. It is typical of the relaxed manner with which he conducts himself on such public engagements, putting those he meets, who are usually very nervous, totally at their ease. He was in Wales as part of a week of events that included having a bridge named after him and joining in the summer festivities in a tiny riverside village with his wife Camilla.

The bridge naming had been controversial. Not everyone in the principality, it seemed, had warmed to the government-backed decision to rename the Second Severn Crossing the Prince of Wales Bridge. In fact, it was roundly criticised by politicians on the left and Welsh nationalists when it was announced. Secretary of State for Wales, Alun Cairns played down the negativity, saying he was not surprised, and insisted, probably with confidence, that the 'wider, silent majority is absolutely with us'. He urged 'republicans' disliking the plans to 'respect' the prince because of the work he had done in the community over many years. It marked Charles's being given the Prince of Wales title sixty years ago, he said, and his turning seventy, and the decision that had been sanctioned by the Queen and Prime Minister Theresa May would stand. It all went on above Charles's head and, on 2 July, the prince and the duchess stopped off at the Second Severn Crossing to unveil a plaque to mark the new name.

Alun Cairns said afterwards he was delighted by the naming ceremony, which he said marked the start of a new era of cross-border opportunity. As for the controversy, Mr Cairns had said the silent majority backed the plan and respected the prince for the work he did in the community.

He went on, 'I know some republicans who absolutely strongly support the charities that he stands for – the Prince's Trust, PRIME Cymru, Business in the Community – and the fantastic work that they do. And I would hope that they would at least look at the work of those charities and recognise that this is a fitting title for that work, if nothing else.'

This Prince of Wales, the twenty-first to hold the title, perhaps due to the length of time he has occupied the role and the epoch of his stewardship, is different from those who have come before. Throughout his life he has confronted orthodoxy head on, no matter the personal cost to him or his reputation. A pioneer, he has demonstrated his belief in the progress of mankind – but certainly not at any cost.

He asks only that progress be touched with humanity and be guided by the gentler side of the human spirit. Progress can only be *real* progress, he believes, if it embraces the harmony of nature and that the earth's natural balance is not destroyed in the process. Nature – indeed, our earth itself, according to the prince – is there to guide, enhance and teach us not to be drained or used as a resource. He believes it is nature that embraces diversity. 'Our ability to see beauty in nature is entirely consequential in our being a part of nature itself,' he insists. 'Nature is the source, not us.'

The prince maintains that we all have a personal responsibility to avoid draining our natural environment of resources, even if it leaves him open to looking just a little absurd. On one occasion the prince insisted on returning to Balmoral Castle whilst on a break at the Queen's estate in the Scottish Highlands after a long drive through the estate in Range Rovers, complete with his entourage of PPOs and some gillies – because he had left his bathroom light on. When it was suggested to him that the police simply radio back and ask a housemaid to turn off the light, he insisted, 'No, no, I can't do that, I have a personal responsibility.' The entire party, Range Rovers and policemen, had to return to the castle so the prince could turn the light off.

Charles can be amusing when he is not aware of it. On another occasion at Balmoral he was with a group fly fishing on the River Dee. He had caught nothing all morning while his guests seemed to be hauling out fish for fun. In the afternoon he decided to move to their spot while they went to his. The same thing happened, with the prince again out of luck. His gillie was getting more and more tense as the hours went by. Eventually, when he emerged from the river in his waders and called it a day, there was the delicate matter of tipping the gillie. 'How much should I give him?' the prince asked his policeman, only to be heard saying loudly, 'Fifty pounds. . .that does seem rather a lot, I didn't catch a thing.'

In another instance he advised Camilla to stop wasting energy by heating her swimming pool at Ray Mill House near the picturesque Wiltshire village of Lacock during winter. She had rightly been advised to keep it on to avoid the pipes freezing and bursting and causing damage to the pump, which is exactly what happened, costing thousands of pounds to repair.

A man most at home in the English countryside at his beloved Highgrove estate in Gloucestershire, Charles appreciates that, for mankind to have a future, humanity – the dominant and most destructive species – must learn to coexist with its natural environment, crucially in harmony with other species and the kingdom Plantae all around us. His bugbear is humanity's irresponsible destruction of the world's rainforests, which he often describes in his speeches as 'the earth's lungs'. 'The Earth is under threat. It cannot cope with all that we demand of it,' he writes with conviction in his provocative book *Harmony*. 'It is losing its balance and we humans are causing this to happen.'

Cities and towns must not, he insists, be solely about construction – a mass of high-rise buildings, glass structures, roads and infrastructure – but must be designed for the sake of those who live and work there. The prince maintains that we all need a sympathetic landscape, one that embraces the emotions and character of its inhabitants, so that they can live in concord with the environment they find themselves in. When we achieve this equipoise he calls it 'active but balanced state harmony'. He writes in *Harmony*, 'The active state of balance… is just as vital to the state of the natural world as it is for human society,' he writes.

The prince predicted the devastating housing crisis that caused so many difficulties in the United Kingdom in the early part of the twenty-first century. He championed the production of real, properly sourced, organic food when so many scoffed at him. He has reminded us too that the future must have a relationship with the past and that not all change for the sake of it is good.

What is exciting about Charles is that he is a trailblazer, that he is not a figurehead who jumps on bandwagons when they become trendy. He has been delivering speeches for decades on his core subjects such as climate change and polluting our planet. Way back on 6 March 1989, he was addressing delegates at the Saving the Ozone Layer World Conference, where he spelt out the doomsday scenario we faced then when few wanted to listen. 'Since the Industrial Revolution, human beings have been upsetting that balance [of nature], persistently choosing short-term options and to hell with the long-term repercussions,' he said. Indeed, he faced an avalanche of criticism in the 1970s for even daring to raise these heartfelt concerns. But raise them he did.

'Most critics imagined that I somehow wanted to turn the clock back to some mythical golden age when all was a perfect rural idyll. But nothing could be further from the truth,' he wrote in his tome *Harmony*.

Nearly thirty years later, he is still using his influence to urge mankind to take effective action to save our sick planet before it is too late; this has been one of the core causes he has championed. Through the tireless work of his charities, in particular the Prince's Trust, Charles has encouraged social cohesion and social mobility, changing the lives of thousands of young people for the better. He is one of the most successful charitable entrepreneurs of his time.

Over the course of his lifetime, the Prince's charities have raised billions of pounds and transformed lives for the better. His seventieth birthday on 14 November 2018 sees him already as Britain's longest-serving heir to the throne. When he eventually ascends the throne on the death of his mother, he will be the oldest person ever to become our monarch. None of this concerns him, or, for that matter, ever has. He has always said his getting the 'top job' is 'in the lap of the gods'.

Some close to the monarch say that, if she reaches the age of ninety-five, she will make a monumental decision and choose to officially allow Charles to take over the stewardship of her reign. She will, they say, officially transfer all executive powers to him as Prince Regent until her death, when he will become king. This would enable her to fudge the issue of her not fulfilling her Coronation Oath to God and her people to serve as queen regnant until her death. Others, who claim to be equally well informed, say that such a move or use of the 'Regent' title is not really necessary. After all, the Queen made it clear to the unassuming 103rd Archbishop of Canterbury, Dr George Carey, when he went to see her when he resigned in her Golden Jubilee year of 2002, 'That's something I can't do.'

Times, however, do change. Since then the monarch has marked her Diamond and Sapphire jubilees. She has already surpassed her great-great-grandmother, the Empress of India, Queen Victoria, and become the oldest and longest-reigning monarch. In truth, with the Queen now well into her tenth decade, senior officials within the Royal Household confirm that Prince Charles is, effectively, already our 'Prince Regent', a king in all but name. He already takes on many of her responsibilities and, now that she does not travel overseas, his royal tours representing her across the globe are state visits. It is, in effect, a job-share monarchy, with the heir leading the way for the House of Windsor, not following.

The sudden abdication of King Juan Carlos of Spain in favour of his son, the new King Felipe, in 2014, after thirty-nine years on the throne, led to a familiar chorus: 'It will never happen here.' For some reason commentators assume that Elizabeth II will just go on and on even though we are already sailing in new waters. Granted, Her Majesty is a consecrated monarch who pledged in her Coronation Oath to serve throughout her life. But can she seriously remain as head of state if she lives to be a centenarian like her mother?

Unlike in Spain, where politicians had to amend the constitution to accommodate Juan Carlos's decision, in the UK we already have the Regency Act enshrined in law. The last time such provisions were used was in 1810 during the reign of George III, when the monarch became permanently deranged. It meant his eldest son assumed the title Prince Regent for ten years until, on his father's death, he became George IV.

The Prince of Wales has always felt aggrieved on behalf of his infamous relative. In a foreword for a biography of King George III, he wrote in 1972, 'As human beings we suffer from an innate tendency to jump to conclusions; to judge people too quickly and to pronounce them failures or heroes without due consideration of the actual facts and ideals of the period.'

Queen Elizabeth II has enjoyed remarkably good health, both mental and physical, and there is nothing to suggest that a regency would be necessary in the way that it was for George III. Behind palace gates, however, preparations have been made in recent months for all eventualities with Her Majesty's blessing.

Charles has always been consistent about his position. His ascension is in the 'lap of the gods', he has said. In 1994, talking about becoming king one day, he told Jonathan Dimbleby, 'Sometimes you daydream about the sort of things you might do . . .I think you could invest the position with something of your own personality and interest but obviously within the bounds of constitutional propriety.'

The only time he went further was in 1998, when he was forced to react to claims that he would be 'pleased' if the Queen abdicated. Irritated at the impertinence of the suggestion in the tabloids, he stated, 'I begin to tire of needing to issue denials of false stories about all manner of thoughts which I am alleged to be having.'

In fact, in the aftermath of his divorce, he grew increasingly embittered towards the tabloids, although in recent years his relationship with the press has improved. Back then, he regarded them not only as his enemies but as the enemy of the people. For a considerable time aides would have to listen to his rants about how the 'poor brainwashed' country is controlled by the tabloid press, who actively sought to make him look 'truly absurd' whenever the opportunity arose. He dubbed the *Mail on Sunday*, at the height of the so-called 'war of the Waleses' of a few years back, the organ of 'depravity and deception' that poisons society. (Ironically, under the stewardship of editor Geordie Greig from 2012 to 2018, the *Mail on Sunday* was largely supportive of the prince. In September 2018, Greig replaced long-serving editor Paul Dacre as editor of the *Daily Mail*.) 'There was nothing one could say or do to alter his view at that time,' said one former member of his team. 'Thankfully, with time he has mellowed and his relationship improved.'

The left-leaning *Guardian* newspaper in the UK reported in March 2017 that, for years, arrangements have been in place by the palace and government for the death, funeral and internment of the Queen. There is even a codename to be used in the event of the inevitable eventuality: Operation London Bridge. I was among a group of media representatives given such a detail off the record by palace officials; the *Guardian*, which did not send reporters to the palace briefings, was not. The editor, however, after the Queen's serious bout of ill health over Christmas 2016, commissioned an article on the 'secret plans that exist for the death of the Queen'. Journalist Sam Knight made a good fist of it, basing much of it on what happened on the death of the last monarch, George VI. But he had the codename for Elizabeth right and much of the detail was fairly accurate, too.

The Prince of Wales, as her heir, will be the first to know of his mother's passing. He will probably be at her deathbed, unless the monarch dies suddenly or unexpectedly. On his mother's death, Charles will be king immediately. His siblings and children will kiss his hands. Then constitutional government will kick in. The Prime Minister will need to be informed immediately of the passing of the head of state.

That job will now fall to Sir Edward Young, Lord Geidt's successor as the Queen's current private secretary, who will then go to a secure telephone line and tell the PM 'London Bridge is down'. Then, from the Foreign Office's Global Response Centre in London, the news will go out to the fifteen governments, directly to the respective prime ministers, outside the UK where the Queen is also the head of state, and the thirty-six other nations of the Commonwealth for whom she has served as a figurehead. For a time her subjects will not know she is dead and that the throne has passed to her eldest son. But in the world of twenty-four-hour news it will not stay secret for long. Governors general, ambassadors and prime ministers will learn first. But, as more people are told, the more likely there would be a leak of the monumental news.

Nothing will be left to chance. If the Queen dies abroad, a BAe 146 jet from the RAF's No. 32 squadron, known as the Royal Flight, will take off from Northolt, at the western edge of London, with a coffin on board. The royal undertakers, Leverton & Sons, keep what they call a 'first-call coffin' ready in case of royal emergencies. If the Queen dies on the Sandringham estate in Norfolk, her body will come to London by car after a day or two.

The most elaborate plans are for what happens if she passes away at Balmoral, where she spends three months of the year.

First, the Queen's body will lie at rest in her smallest palace, at Holyrood House in Edinburgh, and will be guarded by the Royal Company of Archers. Then the coffin will be carried up the Royal Mile to St Giles's Cathedral, for a service of reception, before being put on board the Royal Train at Waverley station for a sad progress down the East Coast Main Line. Crowds are expected at level crossings and on station platforms the length of the country. 'From Musselburgh and Thirsk in the north, to Peterborough and Hatfield in the south – to throw flowers on the passing train. (Another locomotive will follow behind, to clear debris from the tracks)' Knight reported.

This is, however, jumping the gun. Given the Queen's history of robust health, perhaps a far more likely scenario is that her great age will mean she herself will trigger a period of regency, thus ensuring safe stewardship of the great office she has held and worked so hard to secure. Senior former members of her household believe the Queen will grant her eldest son and heir the full power to reign while she still lives because of the respect she holds for the institution of monarchy.

One senior aide told me that the Queen has given the matter of her passing years considerable thought and believes that, if she is still alive at ninety-five, she will consider passing the reign to Charles. Abdication, however, is not even a consideration.

One senior aide admitted to me the 'dusting off' of the Regency Act. My understanding is that senior figures, with the Queen's blessing, have been examining various scenarios. Before his unceremonious departure, the Queen's private secretary, Sir Christopher Geidt, was awarded a second knighthood for, according to the citation, 'a new approach to constitutional matters. . .[and] the preparation for the transition to a change of reign'. This was interpreted as the clearest sign yet that the Queen was getting ready to pass on the mantle.

Strangely, until 1937, our constitutional law had no permanent provision for a regent to cover the situation of a monarch being incapable of performing his or her duties. It was the debilitating illness of the Queen's grandfather, George V – who suffered from chronic bronchitis from 1935 until his death – that led to the reformed Regency Act. Since then, no statutory regency has been created. A statutory regency would be established if the person inheriting the throne were under eighteen or if the monarch were, 'by reason of infirmity of mind or body', incapable of performing the royal functions. But there is an intriguing additional ground within the drafting of Section 2 of the Act. This says that a regency arises if 'the Sovereign is for some definite cause not available for the performance of those functions'. It is not clear what situations this covers. Perhaps it is vague enough to allow the monarch simply to pass the baton to her heir and effectively retire – thus effecting the smoothest of successions with the minimum of fuss.

The Queen is *au courant* with the passage of time, and how her age impacts on the institution she serves. She has, impeccable sources have told me, already drawn a line in the sand, a date when, like Prince Philip, she will effectively retire from public life. Another former senior courtier said, 'Her Majesty thinks long and hard about this issue. She would never want to do anything, or be seen to do anything, that would harm the monarchy, and that includes going on too long. If she felt her age was in any way damaging the monarchy, she would act accordingly.'

Nobody has a crystal ball. But my knowledge of the monarchal system leads me to believe that, whatever happens, it will unfold naturally. It will, when that happens, be seamless. It is clear, however, that Charles's position as the driving force of the institution in the second decade of the twenty-first century, as he approaches his seventieth birthday, is indisputable. He, not the Queen, is the firm hand on the tiller.

## Chapter Three

# SHADOW
# KING

———~———

'I think it's something that dawns on you with the most
ghastly inexorable sense. I didn't wake up in my pram and say:
"Yippee, I. . ." But I think it just dawns on you slowly that
people are interested in one and slowly you get the idea that you
have a certain duty and responsibility.'

THE PRINCE OF WALES TO BRITISH JOURNALIST AND RADIO PRESENTER
GIOVANNI BATISTA 'JACK' DE MANIO, MC AND BAR, IN 1969, WHEN ASKED
WHEN HE FIRST REALISED THAT HE WAS HEIR TO THE THRONE

Head bowed, His Royal Highness Prince Charles, the
Prince of Wales, heir apparent to the British throne,
Field Marshal in the British Army, Admiral of the Fleet of the
Royal Navy and Marshal of the Royal Air Force, stood bolt
upright. His job that cold November morning was simple
enough: to lay a wreath, or in his case two. Pristine as always,
he was wearing his ceremonial uniform of an RAF Air Marshal
with his large medals pinned to his chest, but hidden under his

heavy blue-grey greatcoat. He had performed this solemn duty many times before, but today was special.

Right on cue, the heir to the throne would lead the nation in commemorating our war dead on Remembrance Sunday. This time it fell to him, not his mother, Elizabeth II, to lay the first wreath – the nation's wreath – of red poppies at the foot of the Cenotaph memorial in Whitehall. This time, the sovereign, our once ever-present Queen, would not be on duty or the star performer, but *he* would be. The man who will be king and commander-in-chief of the UK's armed forces then snapped a salute to the fallen. As ever, he had performed his duties with aplomb but, unequivocally, this was a watershed moment in his developing royal journey.

A few minutes earlier he had led out seven members of the Royal Family all bedecked in military uniform. His sons, William and Harry, his siblings Anne, Andrew and Edward, and his mother's first cousin and grandson of King and Emperor George V, the Duke of Kent, dutifully followed him and then stood in silence. Charles, in front of them, waited patiently for his signal to perform. The unmistakable chimes of Parliament's Big Ben and a gun salute marked the beginning of the two-minute silence. Another gun salute, followed by the Reveille played immaculately by nine white-gloved buglers of the Royal Marines' Portsmouth Band, bedecked in Number 1 Full Dress of full-length, dark-blue greatcoats with the white Wolseley-pattern helmets, signalled that the impeccably observed silent tribute was at an end.

Queen Elizabeth II's equerry, Major Nana Kofi Twumasi-Ankrah of the Blues and Royals, stepped forward with the sovereign's wreath and handed it to Charles. He held it firmly in his right hand and then, with his left hand holding the hilt of his sword, walked forward and placed it in pride of place at the foot of the Cenotaph before walking backwards whence he had come.

It was 12 November 2017 – the day after Armistice Day and just two days shy of Charles's sixty-ninth birthday and the start of his milestone seventieth year.

Without doubt it was going to be a momentous twelve months for the man who is now the longest-serving heir to the throne in the British monarchy's history. Less than a hundred metres away on a Whitehall balcony, the Queen, wearing a spray of poppies held in place by Queen Mary's gleaming Dorset bow brooch, keenly observed proceedings, watching her eldest son's every move with a sharp eye. Alongside her, in his uniform as Lord High Admiral, was World War II veteran Prince Philip, then ninety-six, protected from the autumn chill by his heavy Royal Navy winter greatcoat. Next to the royal couple stood Prince Charles's second wife, all in black, the seventy-year-old Duchess of Cornwall.

From her vantage point the Queen surveyed the solemn scene: the one time of the calendar when all the Royal Family, all the party leaders, all former prime ministers and representatives of every Commonwealth nation gather in London. Although on six previous occasions she had been absent from the parade in her sixty-five years on the throne (during her pregnancies with Prince Andrew in 1959 and Prince Edward in 1963, and on four other occasions when she was on overseas visits in 1961 in Ghana, in 1968 in Brazil, in 1983 in Kenya and in 1999 in South Africa), 2017 was much more significant. After all, she had always been centre stage, not an observer, as in this case.

It was also a definite move to authorise her heir to carry out the job and it was certainly not a decision taken lightly. As she watched on, some reporters insisted they had seen the Queen wipe away a tear, but it seemed unlikely from such a stoic character and was more likely the effects of a bracing northwesterly wind in a November cold snap that chilly morning.

In the months leading up to this symbolic moment the Prince of Wales had slowly but surely been taking on a number of the Queen's more physically taxing engagements at her request. In 2017 the prince clocked up 374 UK engagements and 172 abroad, making him the busiest member of the Royal Family with a grand total of 546 engagements. He did the most travelling, too. For the prince in the coming years it was going to get busier as more and more he did the heavy lifting for the ageing sovereign. As ever, he carried out his duties with the minimum of fuss. It was, as he saw it, his duty to do so as her 'liege man', as he had sworn to be before four thousand guests inside the medieval walls of Caernarfon Castle at his investiture as Prince of Wales in 1969. Back then he had received the insignia as the twenty-first Prince of Wales and, along with it, the right to use the heraldic badge of the title that bears motto, '*Ich Dien*' – 'I Serve' in German – on the ribbon below the coronet and his feathers.

This engagement at the Cenotaph was perhaps the most 'kingly', perhaps too the most piquant. It was visually regal without doubt. Charles was surrounded by the political, military and religious establishment and with millions watching the broadcast live on BBC television around the country. What unfolded was an unmistakably historic image, the clearest visual sign to date that the British monarchy was undergoing a seamless transition from its ageing monarch to her eldest son. It is also an emphatic nod to the future, with the ancient institution's dutiful steward ensuring continuity at the end of her record-breaking long reign.

Prince Charles will in this interim period before his ascension to the throne enjoy playing a dual role, standing in and covering for the monarch where necessary, as well as fulfilling his own public obligations. This dual role was perhaps shown most visibly on this day when he became the first person to lay two wreaths in a single Remembrance Sunday service. As soon as the Duke of Edinburgh's equerry, Captain Ben Tracey of the Grenadier Guards, had laid the Duke's wreath on his behalf, Charles was tasked with returning to the foot of the Cenotaph to pay tribute all over again, this time placing his own wreath of his unmistakable Prince of Wales feathers next to his father's wreath.

Then followed the Duke of Cambridge, Prince Harry, turning up to the service sporting a beard amid false claims that he had broken military rules, his critics forgetting he was exempt as he left active service in 2015; and the Duke of York, who had also served in combat in the Falklands conflict. Then came the last of the royals, the Earl of Wessex, the Princess Royal and the Duke of Kent, at eighty-two the only royal on parade of the World War II generation. Prince Philip appeared to be propping himself up as he stood on the balcony, while at other points he seemed to be leaning on a wall to support himself. The Queen appeared to suggest Philip sit back down again during the service. He ignored her. Following the playing of the national anthem, the Queen, perhaps for her husband's sake, moved swiftly inside to the warmth of the Foreign Office; the duke, clearly feeling the effects of the cold, puffed out his cheeks, perhaps in relief that this public duty was all over. Ever the gentlemen, however, he insisted that his daughter-in-law, the Duchess of Cornwall, go inside first before following on.

The other VIPs withdrew, clearing the path for the Royal British Legion parade. More than 10,000 people from over 260 organisations proudly marched by the memorial. Several old comrades had elected to be wheeled around the same route. Victoria Cross recipient, Grenadian-born Lance Sergeant Johnson Beharry of the 1st Battalion, Princess of Wales's Royal Regiment, was there too. The thirty-eight-year-old had been awarded the highest honour for gallantry in 2005 after his incredible heroism helping save the lives of his colleagues on two separate occasions whilst driving an armoured vehicle under heavy enemy fire in the Iraq war in 2004. On this, he elected to parade with Chelsea Pensioners, pushing one old solider in his wheelchair. Charles's sovereign moment was over in a matter of minutes. He had, as ever, performed his duty with equanimity.

Announcing the decision to entrust the job to Prince Charles a few weeks earlier, Buckingham Palace had said the reason was that the Queen wished to be by her husband's side on the balcony and had asked her heir to lay a wreath instead. (The Queen does not suffer from bathophobia, but she had privately expressed concern about walking backwards and going up and down steep stairs, and this engagement involved both.) Make no mistake, however, that what we have been witnessing in Charles's seventieth year is a gradual transfer of monarchical responsibility from the reigning queen to the heir apparent.

Buckingham Palace officials had been for weeks at pains to

stress that this engagement should not be interpreted as a transfer of sovereign power. That word 'power' rankles with them, and perhaps even with the Queen herself. Indeed, those close to the monarch have made it clear to me that, whilst the Queen lives (and is in good physical and mental health) she remains in full charge, presiding over her people as monarch until her last breath. She is still the authority, they assert.

That may well be the official line and it is true that monarchy has a logic-defying resilience founded on appearances. Appearances, after all, can be deceptive but, as far as the paying public is concerned, seeing is believing. It was clearly a passing on of obligation, if not power. Inevitably, with such designated responsibility – whether Buckingham Palace and the monarch like it or not – comes at least the perception of power and an expectation of a new leader waiting in readiness in the wings.

## Chapter Four

# 'YOUR MAJESTY,
# MAMA, MUMMY'

───────◦───────

*'She shall be, to the happiness of England,*
*An aged princess; many days shall see her,*
*And yet no day without a deed to crown it.'*

THE PRINCE OF WALES READ THIS EDITED PASSAGE FROM
WILLIAM SHAKESPEARE'S *HENRY VIII* ON THE BBC AS A TRIBUTE
TO THE QUEEN ON HER NINETIETH BIRTHDAY

T he only time she reached for her handkerchief to dab her
moistening eyes was when watching the footage of her
family aboard the Royal Yacht *Britannia*. Her Majesty and the
Prince of Wales sat in the elegant White Drawing Room at
Buckingham Palace watching prepared footage clips of days gone
by. As they were doing so, their reactions were being recorded by
John Bridcut's documentary crew for the film *Elizabeth at 90*.

Bridcut had hit upon the idea of getting members of her
family to sit and reflect upon archived and personal cine film,
the term commonly used in the UK to refer to the 9.5mm,

16mm, 8mm and Super 8 motion-picture film formats. The royals had always been ahead with technology and been using such cameras long before it was commonplace. The prince liked the idea and Bridcut granted special access to the complete collection of the Queen's personal cine films, shot by the Duke of Edinburgh and the Queen herself, as well as by King George VI and the Queen Mother.

His film was a triumph, not least in demonstrating the warmth that exists between mother and son as they chatted informally over footage that chronicles their life's journey.

The film might not have made the cut if Charles had not persisted and actively intervened. When the idea was first proposed by Clarence House to the Queen's communications secretary, Sally Osman, she said the Queen would never do it and rejected it. It was only when the prince was urged to take it up with his mother personally over Christmas lunch at Sandringham that the project was revived.

The film, narrated by Charles, won widespread acclaim, with Sam Wollaston, writing in the *Guardian*, likening it to a royal version of the popular UK television show *Gogglebox*. He wrote, 'Charles says "wonderful" a lot, the Queen says very little... In some ways, as her eldest son says, the birthday girl's life has defined our age.' The *Daily Telegraph*'s Gerard O'Donovan felt that it was 'a triumph from start to finish. I cannot recall ever seeing a more charming, warm and – dare I say – human portrait of the Queen than this one.'

Occasionally, Charles would jog his mother's memory but most of the time her recall of what was being shown was excellent. Much of the footage had never been seen publicly before. It was not limited to Charles and the Queen, but various members of the Royal Family were filmed watching the private footage and contributing their own personal insights and their memories of the woman they knew both as a member of their own close family and as Queen, including the Duke of Cambridge, Prince Harry, the Princess Royal, the Duke of Kent and his sister Princess Alexandra, who had never before given any interviews.

Two years later, Charles was again leading the tributes to his mother. For when the prince took to the Royal Albert Hall stage the evening's performers, Tom Jones, Kylie Minogue, Sting, Shaggy and Craig David, joined him to a rousing reception. At first he respectfully and properly called her 'Your Majesty' throughout, but then decided to get a little too personal, calling her 'Mummy'. At that precise moment, Queen Elizabeth's eyes grew extremely wide, drawing huge laughs from the crowd.

Charles, with his perfect comic timing, knows exactly how to play an audience, and so does the Queen. She may well have anticipated that his 'mummy' quip was coming and prepared her response – after all Charles had used it many times before, notably in his speech at the pop concert at Buckingham Palace gardens to celebrate her Golden Jubilee. It always got a laugh.

Despite reams of paper devoted to the apparent frostiness of their relationship, especially when he was a youngster and public duty meant she had to put some motherly duties second, there is indelibly a deep love between them. Charles, of course, deeply cares for, loves and respects his mother. Whenever he hosts an event or dinner to celebrate another milestone in her incredible life and reign, he demands absolute perfection.

On the Queen's eightieth birthday, for example, he, with

the help of the fastidious factotum Michael Fawcett, arranged a magical evening of celebration at Kew Palace, where she arrived to the strains of Bach, Wagner and Donizetti, played by a harpist and flautist. The music played as the light began to fade in the exquisite Royal Botanic Gardens that surround the palace, and the family progressed through the Queen's Boudoir, known as the Sulking Room, and on into the King's Drawing Room.

The table was set to perfection too, bathed in the soft light of a myriad candles. Spring blooms brought fragrance and colour to the room; silverware placed with military precision shone; glassware gleamed. Appropriately for a woman proud of her Scottish ancestry, the menu included a starter of timbale of organic Hebridean smoked salmon. There was juniper roast loin of venison from the Sandringham estates served with a port-wine sauce, steamed young cabbage and spring vegetables; and fruits from Charles's Highgrove estates were used in the dessert.

It was a day and an evening that would live long in the memory of all who were there. It was truly special, exactly as the prince had wanted it.

Change was clearly coming even back then. The cogs of the transition to the reign were turning quietly as the royal machine prepared for a smooth gear change. The key to the monarchy and an effortless passage from one reign to the next is that nobody sees the joins.

Even back then the Queen was making moves into semi-retirement, her place in history already assured. A handover of power is happening right before our eyes; the changes are subtle but seismic. Nothing has been left to chance. It never is. It is no coincidence that the Queen has been spending more and more time with her grandson, the Duke of Cambridge, of whom she is very fond, and his public, statesmanlike roles are increasing both in number and status, such as his historic visit to Israel and the West Bank in June 2018.

What is, however, not so well known is that the Queen and her son and heir, Charles, for some time regularly meet in private. The public impression is they come together rarely, at family events such as Christmas at Windsor or the odd palace balcony appearance. But nothing could be further from the truth as, with no private secretaries of royal aides of any description present, the two – mother and son, monarch and heir, the two most senior figures in the monarchal system – meet and discuss matters of state. The conversations are apparently focused on business and sometimes over dinner or tea. Her Majesty and Charles see these meetings as crucial for the smooth running of the country and succession.

Some years ago the Queen, known around Whitehall as 'Reader No. 1', had Charles added to the distribution of the dispatch boxes so that he is seeing everything she is. This was done to ensure Charles is up to speed in the event that something should happen to her such as incapacitation or death. She has likely sought to avoid his being unprepared for the role he is stepping into, much as she was when her father, King George VI, died. Considering her age, this is an altogether smart and sensible idea and in complete contrast to the other great regal matriarch, Queen Victoria, who infuriated her eldest son and heir, Bertie, Prince of Wales, with her inconsistencies.

Queen/Empress Victoria applied rules to other people, her own family included, which she flagrantly broke herself without the bat of an eyelid. This behaviour frequently made her infuriating to her loved ones, her government ministers and her servants. She herself apparently never understood the cause of their irritation or certainly never showed it. She criticised her son Bertie roundly for his bad behaviour after he embarked on a series of adulterous affairs, which she blamed on his laziness and idle mind, yet she was determined to exclude him from royal work or, more importantly, matters of state. She refused to allow him to see state papers and denied him a key to the red boxes, thus forcing upon him a life of aimlessness. Thus, the heir to the throne felt he had been reduced to the role of glorified ribbon cutter, unveiling buildings and statues and having very little influence where he felt it mattered.

In stark contrast to her great-great-grandmother, Elizabeth II recognises a simple, and for Charles painful, fact that the role for which her eldest son was born has all but already passed him by, however much public opinion may have softened towards him. History, fate and his own nature have conspired to place Charles in an unenviable position. For years, his own parents seriously doubted his suitability for the throne. Both Elizabeth and Philip, according to sources close to them, regarded their eldest son as something of a 'loose cannon': too quick to anger, given to tantrums and driven by an almost revolutionary zeal to 'make his mark' on the country and world with his various initiatives, causes and beliefs that they and many believed teetered dangerously on the brink of quackery.

Charles's apparent need to be viewed as a shaper of ideas, a pioneer, and to enjoy growing political influence was a serious source of concern to advisers both past and present. Some of these advisers have told me that the prince actively seeks out controversy, because that way he can raise the debate, a debate or subject that would otherwise go unnoticed or be swept under the carpet. His former deputy private secretary, Mark Bolland, has admitted that during his time in Charles's service he 'tried to dampen down the prince's behaviour in making public his thoughts and views on a whole range of issues'.

Mark wrote in a statement that was released to the media as the prince began a High Court case against the *Mail on Sunday* [for publishing comments allegedly made in his journal about China's regime] 'The Prince's expressions of his views have often been regarded with concern by politicians because we would be contacted by them – and on their behalf. Private Secretaries to government ministers would often let us know their views and, typically, how concerned they were.' Mark's views may be tainted by his abrupt departure from Charles's household with little credit, particularly after important work such as his successful running of 'Operation Mrs PB', his carefully managed PR campaign that secured enough public acceptance of Camilla that eventually the royal marriage was possible. He used all the dark arts and even used the young princes, William and Harry, to get public acceptance for Camilla, even claiming they had met and got on when actually they had not and did not.

Mark Bolland's assessment of the prince should not be taken too lightly. He, after all, did have the prince's ear at a crucial time and his ability to help shape the news agenda with his close relationships with newspaper editors during his tenure should not be disregarded.

For, in truth, there is little doubt that the prince has achieved much in his self-defined role as the Prince of Wales and raised the debate on compelling global issues such as genetically modified crops, religious tolerance, saving the rainforests and eliminating the use of single-use plastics.

The prince is fully aware that he will have to control his passion on many of these issues, and also ensure, when a constitutional clash may occur when he is monarch, he keeps his controversial views to himself. A campaigning king, after all, no matter how worthy, would leave him and the institution he serves open to damaging accusations of his being an unconstitutional monarch.

'To suggest that the prince would do anything to undermine the position of constitutional monarch is to totally misjudge and misinterpret the nature and intentions of the Prince of Wales,' said one senior member of the Royal Household. 'He is fully aware, more than anyone, of his responsibilities of his future role and the importance of those responsibilities.'

That said, I have little doubt that when his time comes he will use his even greater convening power to take a lead in areas to which he has devoted so much of his life. He will not just abandon causes he has championed. Why should he? Much as his mother has done with the Queen's Commonwealth Canopy initiative, begun in 2015 as a network of forest conservation programmes throughout the fifty-three countries of the Commonwealth of Nations, he will be able to bring people with influence together to try to make a real difference. If anything, that ability to assemble leaders in particular areas inspired by harmony and sustainability will increase when he is elevated to the role of monarch. He certainly won't lose that burning desire just because his will be the head wearing the crown. If anything, that head will be even more uneasy unless he is doing his best to make a difference. His determination to save the planet for future generations won't just fade because he is sitting on the throne. 'I don't want to be confronted by my future grandchildren and them say, "Why didn't you do something?"' It is a question that will always drive him to do more.

Many close to him believe that, as King Charles III, he will not only wish to convoke the important meetings, but wish to have a seat at the table, too, where he can make a meaningful contribution. Again, there is nothing wrong or unconstitutional with that. I have witnessed first-hand on my travels with the prince that very often at such meetings he will listen and mentally take note, not in any way to try to cajole the group to his way of thinking. The fact that the meeting is taking place and the subject of choice is being debated at a high level, where change can be effected, is a form of success. The prince more than anyone is well aware that sailing the monarchy into dangerous, potentially unconstitutional, waters would be both irresponsible and self-defeating.

There was a time, after all, in the aftermath of Diana's death – and even more recently than that, when many long-serving staff at Buckingham Palace were quite convinced that they were serving the penultimate monarch – when Charles wouldn't have had a crown left to hand down to William. But the temperature has undoubtedly changed. Through hard work and consistency, and perhaps the popularity of his sons and their wives, the goodwill they have generated, such fears have all but subsided. The prospect of Charles the silver-haired king' seems at last to have been embraced by the wider public.

Mindful of her lengthening reign, the Queen was prompted

to urge a resolution to the 'Camilla problem' through marriage. Mindful of his duty, Charles complied. This was a smoothing of the way forward to the next generation, not simply the glorious resolution of Charles and Camilla's enduring grand romance. It was made clear to Charles that he had to fit in with the bigger picture and accept the shifting shape of the monarchy as envisaged by the Queen. It was a calculated risk and it appears to have paid off. The warm receptions given to Charles and Camilla when on tour, and the more positive press coverage of Camilla, is increasingly gentle but never effusive.

There is no escaping the lingering feeling that, while Charles may have many supporters, his greatest asset is also his greatest weakness. Camilla, as consort and Duchess of Cornwall, is a constant reminder of his personal failings of the past. However, more than a decade of marriage, and the fact that his second wife undoubtedly gives strength from their mutual and obvious love, should be taken only as a positive.

But, no matter how optimistic the palace try to be, the reality is that Charles and Camilla have both brought far too much baggage to the relationship, particularly that they committed adultery, which at the very least contributed to the breakdown of his marriage to Diana, for it to be presented as anything approaching love's young dream. For years the prince bemoaned what he felt was an unfair portrayal of the woman he loved. He reportedly said to respected journalist Gavin Hewitt in a 1998 interview discussing his relationship with Camilla Parker Bowles (according to Hewitt's book *A Soul on Ice: A Life in News*), 'I thought the British people were supposed to be compassionate. I don't see much of it.' Over time the general public has grown to accept Camilla. She may not be universally popular but she is at last now getting credit for the public work she does and her role supporting the heir to the throne, For the general feeling is that, with Camilla at his side, Charles is a less abrasive, even spoilt, figure, and behind the scenes the groundwork has undoubtedly been laid for the shift in responsibility from the Queen to Charles.

Just as it seemed accepted that Her Majesty was slowing down, following the retirement of her consort, the Duke of Edinburgh, and with her celebration of her ninety-second birthday in April 2018, the figures didn't match the newspaper stories. Despite claims to the contrary, her workload had increased by 25 per cent, according to a new study. It was no surprise, however, that Charles clocked up the highest number of engagements in 2018 so far. Research conducted by *Write Royalty* showed the Queen had carried out 125 engagements at that point since January. Prince Harry did not even make the top ten, as he had been busy planning his May wedding to Meghan Markle, and neither did the Duchess of Cambridge, who welcomed her third child, Prince Louis, into the world in April. Charles was thrilled, and with the name, too, a nod to his beloved great-uncle.

'A Royal Family sweetens politics by the seasonable addition of nice and pretty events,' the great constitutional theorist Walter Bight wrote. This world had stood the test of time, for the world delighted in one of those 'pretty events': Louis's birth on St George's Day 2018 (23 April). Once, again the world's media had gathered in their hundreds behind steel pens outside the Lindo Wing in Paddington, London, excitedly reporting the birth of the new fifth in line to the throne, the Queen's sixth great-grandchild.

'He is the first baby to be impacted by the change in the ancient law of the feudal system of primogeniture,' an American anchor said, struggling to pronounce that word, trying to explain how boys no longer automatically leapfrog girls. Louis had replaced his uncle Harry as fifth in line to the throne, but, due to the new rules, he was still ranked lower than his sister, Charlotte. A republican self-publicist, shouting at the top of his voice on a megaphone, was loudly booed and drowned out by royal fans' cheers as Prince William and Kate emerged on the steps of the maternity wing with their baby, wrapped in a G. H. Hurt & Son shawl.

The following day the prince issued a charming statement about the birth of his third grandchild, saying it was a 'great joy'. 'The only trouble,' he added affectionately, 'is I don't know how I am going to keep up with them.'

The reality was that the Queen's increased workload was down to the debilitating cold that had forced her to cancel a series of engagements over the same period the previous year, not that she had decided to go on some manic work drive. She hasn't changed her schedule much for years. Her routine is well ordered, too. After breakfast, she scans some of the newspapers before reading her correspondence. She receives 200–300 letters from the public each day. She chooses a selection of letters to read herself and tells her staff how to respond to them accordingly.

She will then meet with her private secretaries and examine official papers. Policy papers, Cabinet documents and State papers are sent to her in 'red boxes' and, where necessary, she signs and approves them. Then there will be a series of official meetings followed by the likes of ambassadors and high commissioners.

*Above left*: Born to be king. Baby Prince Charles in his christening robes, 9 April 1949
*PA Archive/PA Images*

*Above right*: Prince Charles and Princess Anne with Nurse Lightbody leave Buckingham Palace for Euston Station to catch the night train to Scotland, May 1953
*PA Archive/PA Images*

*Below left*: Charles with his great-uncle and 'honorary grandfather', Earl Mountbatten of Burma, being escorted ashore at Malta from the Royal Yacht Britannia, April 1954
*Tophams Picturepoint/PA Images*

*Below right*: The seven-year-old prince in the grounds of Balmoral Castle, November 1955, wearing a kilt of the Balmoral tartan (restricted to members of the Royal Family). He has always loved Scotland and is proud of his Scottish ancestry *PA Archive/PA Images*

*Top left*: Queen Elizabeth II with the Duke of Edinburgh and their children, Princess Anne and Prince Charles, at Balmoral Castle, Scotland, April 1953 *PA Archive/PA Images*

*Top right*: Making a happy group on the lawns at Balmoral: the Queen, the Duke of Edinburgh and children Princess Anne, Prince Charles and baby Prince Andrew on his father's knees, September 1960 *PA Archive/PA Images*

*Below*: Charles with his sister Anne and his beloved grandmother, Her Majesty Queen Elizabeth, the Queen Mother, and one of her corgis in the garden of Clarence House, August 1960 *PA Archive/PA Images*

*Left*: An apprehensive Charles, accompanied by his father, Prince Philip, arrives for his first day at Gordonstoun, May 1962 *PA Archive/PA Images*

*Right*: Charles as Head Boy at Gordonstoun, July 1967, with his mother, The Queen

*PA Archive/PA Images*

*Left*: Cambridge University undergraduate Charles takes a bike ride through the city, 1969

*PA Archive/PA Images*

*Left*: In an interview with David Frost for *A Prince For Wales* – a documentary commemorating his investiture at Caernavon Castle

*Fox Photos/Getty Images*

*Below*: Wearing the silk and ermine regalia of his investiture. The coronet was presented by the Goldsmiths' Company of the City of London *Central Press/Getty Images*

*Above*: The Queen placing the coronet of the Prince of Wales on Charles's head during his investiture ceremony, 1 July 1969, whilst an official holds the Seal of Letters Patent *Central Press/Getty Images*

*Right*: Riding in a carriage with his mother, Queen Elizabeth II, after the ceremony *Keystone France/Getty Images*

*Left*: Celebrating his thirtieth birthday during a visit to Balmoral Castle, November 1978   *Ron Bell/PA Images*

*Below*: With Lord Mountbatten in conversation about their common passion for polo, January 1979

*Tophams Picturepoint/PA Images*

*bove*: Windsurfing, 1979

*lton Archive/Getty Images*

*ight*: Visiting the Cheshire Regiment as
*lonel-in-chief, November 1979*

*n Graham/Getty Images*

*Above left*: Queen Elizabeth II with the Prince of Wales and his fiancée Lady Diana Spencer at Buckingham Palace after a Privy Council Meeting, March 1981

*PA Archive/PA Images*

*Above Right*: Just married *PA Archive/PA Images*

*Below left*: Prince Charles and Diana ride in an open coach through cheering crowds after their wedding, 29 July 1981 *Tophams Picturepoint/PA Images*

*Below right*: The couple pose for the press during their honeymoon at Balmoral, August 1981 *Anwar Hussein/EMPICS Entertainment/PA Images*

*Left*: With baby Prince William in Kensington Palace, January 1983

*Anwar Hussein/EMPICS Entertainment*

*Right*: On the Royal Yacht *Britannia*, May 1985, in Venice, Italy

*Anwar Hussein/EMPICS Entertainment*

*Below left*: Family holiday on Tresco, Scilly Isles, June 1989 *PA Archive/PA Images*

*Below right*: At the Falls of Muick during the traditional Balmoral summer holiday, August 1997 *Fiona Hanson/ PA Archive/PA Images*

*Right*: (From left–right) The Duke of Edinburgh, Prince William, Earl Spencer, Prince Harry and Prince Charles walk behind Diana's funeral cortège

Adam Butler/PA Archive/PA Images

*Below left*: The Prince (far left), alongside Prince Harry, Earl Spencer, Prince William and the Duke of Edinburgh watch Diana's coffin leave Westminster Abbey following her funeral service, 6 September 1997

Fiona Hanson/PA Archive/PA Images

*Above right*: The mourners wait as the hearse prepares to leave Westminster Abbey

Fiona Hanson/PA Archive/PA Images

*Left*: The Prince of Wales flanked by his sons during a photocall at Highgrove Estate, Gloucestershire, at the beginning of the two young princes' summer holidays, July 1999

Toby Melville/PA Archive/PA Image

The Queen and each visitor meet alone, usually for no more than twenty minutes. If there is an investiture, the ceremony begins at 11 a.m. and lasts just over an hour. If the Queen is on engagements, she usually has three visitors per morning. Then she will have a private lunch.

Afternoons are usually spent on public engagements, but these are carefully selected from hundreds of invitations sent to her each year, often by lord lieutenants, the Queen's representatives in the county, and her team ensure her programme is shaped appropriately so it is not 'overly taxing'. Queen Elizabeth's evenings include a weekly audience alone with the prime minister when they are both in London, usually at Buckingham Palace at 6.30 p.m. on a Wednesday. As with her private meetings with Charles, no written record is made of these meetings and tradition dictates that communications between the Queen and prime minister remain totally confidential.

She once helped bring Tony Blair back down to earth the morning he became prime minister by reminding him of his relative youth and inexperience of government.

Recalling the meeting on 2 May 1997, at which she formally invited him, he was reminded of the prime ministers she had dealt with before he was born. 'I got a sense of my, er, my relative seniority, or lack of it,' said Mr Blair, who was forty-three at the time and had never held a government office

At about 7.30 p.m. on weekday evenings, a report on the day's parliamentary proceedings, written by one of the government whips, arrives. The Queen insists on reading these the same evening. She sometimes attends film premieres, charity concerts or a reception for a charity of which she is patron, but more and more the younger members of her family are representing her at such events. She also hosts official receptions at Buckingham Palace, Windsor Castle and the Palace of Holyroodhouse. Other receptions or dinners may be linked to a state visit.

The Prince of Wales, like the Queen, is devoted to duty. His wife, Camilla, is convinced he is a 'workaholic'. She described life with her husband as 'exhausting' in an interview to mark his sixty-fifth birthday. She joked about his reaching retirement age. 'Luckily, he has caught up with me now. We are both pensioners and he can join in with me collecting the bus pass.'

She went on, 'I am hopping up and down and saying, "Darling, do you think we could have a bit of, you know, peace and quiet, enjoy ourselves together?" But he always has to finish something.' She says Charles is always 'working, working, working' and is 'not going to stop'. 'My husband is not one for chilling,' she added. The duchess also disclosed that her idea of 'bliss' would be to sit in the sunshine with her husband enjoying some peace and quiet, but that she rarely got the chance.

Others close to the prince say, however, that time is catching up with him. The fact that he eats so little, too, means he sometimes finds himself exhausted by early evening. 'Yes, his workload sometimes does take its toll on him. He admits it himself, but he is a driven man and wants to do as much with the time he is allotted to make a real difference,' the source said. 'Sometimes he is so tired he almost falls asleep over his papers. But nobody can tell him to slow down, not even the duchess, who leaves him to do his thing,' said the source.

The prince regularly carries out around twenty-five royal engagements a week. Like his mother, he is up early, usually before 7 a.m. His 'calling tray' consists of the days' newspapers and Radio 4's *Today* programme in the background. From 8 a.m. onwards, if he hasn't got early engagements, he spends the next two hours poring over paperwork and making handwritten notes in black ink. Over the phone he also chases up projects ranging from the environment to organic farming, architecture and the improvement of interfaith relations.

If he is on an engagement, he likes to use the Royal Train, as it gives him the security and privacy to work. Most engagements start at around 10 a.m. He is often met by the local lord lieutenant or his or her deputy. Flanked by a royal-protection Range Rover, a police Range Rover and six bikes, Charles's dark blue Jaguar pulls up at the entrance of the said engagement. He will meet local dignitaries and perhaps unveil a foundation stone to commemorate a new building. He may be called upon to deliver a speech or off-the-cuff address. If it is a keynote speech, he will have worked on it for hours; if it is just a few remarks, he will manage that with a few tried and tested quips.

There are many similarities between mother and son, and while there was undoubtedly some tension after the publication of Jonathan Dimbleby's brilliant biography – when the author revealed Charles felt his parents lacked affection towards him as a child – this has subsided. It led to a period of tension between parents and son, particularly with his father.

Even before the Dimbleby book, Charles had voiced his concerns of his relations with the Duke of Edinburgh. He wrote in a private letter, with a strong nod to his own paternal misgivings, on 27 September 1987, 'Relationships with fathers can be such complex ones. . .So often, I suppose one must long to have got on better or to have been able to talk freely about the things that matter deeply, but one was too inhibited to discuss.'

They have grown closer in recent years, but the duke and prince will still loudly disagree, so much so that, if a stranger walked into a room during one of their debates, one would have thought a serious fight was about to take place.

When he is called upon to take the lead at milestone moments for his mother – and in recent years there have been many – the prince has always delivered them graciously. On the Queen's ninetieth birthday, with a few heartfelt and carefully chosen words, Charles spoke for the nation as he paid a touching tribute to her. Her actual birthday, 21 April, is usually an entirely private affair, but on this special occasion the Queen – accompanied by the Duke of Edinburgh, the Prince of Wales and the Duchess of Cornwall – was joined by crowds of well-wishers in the shadow of Windsor Castle to light the first of a thousand beacons in her honour. Charles wished his mother, our first-ever nonagenarian monarch, the 'most special and happiest of birthdays'.

He spoke too of the love and affection for her throughout the country and the Commonwealth. He could not have put it better. Then, after drawing a laugh from the crowd by calling her 'Mummy' – his affectionate introduction for the sovereign during the royal celebrations – Prince Charles added significantly, 'And long may she reign over us.' It was a sentiment shared by all those who heard it there and live on television.

He then called for three cheers and the enthusiastic crowd duly obliged. With that, the prince handed the torch to the Queen and invited her to light the principal beacon on a six-metre pole at the start of the Long Walk. After the lighting was over, the Queen,

Prince Charles, Prince Philip and the Duchess of Cornwall were driven back to the castle for her birthday party of sixty special guests, including twenty-eight members of the Royal Family.

It had been a long and joyous day for the Queen. Earlier, she had driven through the streets of Windsor with the Duke of Edinburgh at her side, waving and smiling to thousands who had turned out to cheer her. Holding onto the roof of the specially adapted open-top Range Rover, the Queen, resplendent in a lime-green coat and matching flower-adorned hat, stood upright and proud. The crowds, who stood a dozen deep, sang 'Happy Birthday' and handed her flowers and presents as the Queen and the Duke of Edinburgh walked from her castle to the Guildhall. It was only a short distance. But it took her half an hour to complete, as she diligently thanked them all for their gifts. At one stage, Prince Philip lifted Ethan Lynch, aged four, who had been waiting with his mother in the crowd for four hours with a bunch of flowers, over a barrier so that he could personally hand the bouquet to the Queen. It was a lovely touch.

In May 2016, in what many saw as a deliberate attempt to show the public warmth between mother and son in archive newsreels and never-before-seen home movies and photographs, the prince reflected on his mother's sixty-year reign – both as Great Britain's queen and as his own mother. Previously unseen photographs and cine films from the Queen's private collection – many of them shot by the Queen herself – capture family life. The prince also shares footage from various family holidays, including one sequence, filmed by the Queen, in which we see a young Prince Charles and Princess Anne playing in the sand at Holkham beach in Norfolk.

Highlights include private cine-camera footage, taken on Coronation Day behind the scenes at Buckingham Palace, which shows Elizabeth juggling the dual role of mother and Queen as she walks along the corridor of Buckingham Palace and poses for official photographs.

There are also cine-film sequences on board *Britannia*, at Windsor and at Balmoral, all of which give the viewer a fascinating insight into the life of the Royal Family in the 1940s and 1950s. It worked to a degree. But, while there is little doubt that over time mother and son have grown much closer, Charles's relationship with Philip has occasionally been so egregious that at times they have communicated only in writing.

'Of course they love each other,' said one source close to the prince. 'They always kiss each other when they meet, but on occasion they fundamentally disagree about big issues. 'These discussions may have looked quite heated if you were an outsider looking in for the first time, but actually they are just passionate people, passionate about what they believe in. That doesn't make them enemies, it just means they disagree,' the senior figure pointed out.

In truth, Charles's unique and at times isolated childhood did leave him lacking in the parental love he craved. In turn, it had an impact on Charles the man and his complex character. Perhaps this has driven Charles to prove himself. He is restless, with an endless desire to prove himself – to whom, God alone knows. 'The trouble is I always feel that unless I rush about doing things and trying to help furiously I will not [and the monarchy will not] be seen to be relevant and I will be considered a mere playboy,' he wrote in a private letter of 31 March 1987.

Nothing much has changed. In reality, a workaholic himself, he now appreciates that neither his mother nor his father should be blamed and over time the prince has grown to understand their position and their position on the issue. After all, the Queen, then Princess Elizabeth, was just twenty-two when her eldest son and the heir to the throne was born on 14 November 1948, almost exactly a year after her wedding. Even then her father, the king, was in frail health and she was preparing quietly for her role as Queen Elizabeth.

When Charles was born a forty-one-gun salute was fired by the King's Troop, Royal Artillery, and in Trafalgar Square the fountains were floodlit blue; outside Buckingham Palace almost four thousand gathered to watch the comings and goings of the medical team. Such was the prudery of the time that even the princess's friends weren't told that the birth had not been easy and she had had to undergo a caesarean section. Like most husbands of his era, Philip was not at his wife's bedside. Instead, he got so restless pacing up and down an equerry's room waiting for news that his private secretary, Mike Parker, took him off for a game of squash on the palace court.

When the king's private secretary, Tommy Lascelles, brought the good news, Philip bounded upstairs into the Buhl Room, which had been converted into an operating theatre. He then held his firstborn, still wearing his sporting flannels and open-neck shirt. Always matter-of-fact to the point of seeming indifference, he declared that Charles looked like a plum pudding. As soon as his wife came round from the anaesthetic, Philip presented her with a bouquet of red roses and carnations – thoughtfully provided for the occasion by Parker. For the first month of his life, the baby slept in a round wicker basket in the dressing room adjoining the princess's bedroom, and she happily breastfed him. It was only when she contracted measles that she heeded the advice of doctors and handed him over to the nursery staff.

According to Philip's cousin Marina, the Duchess of Kent, he was similarly entranced by the new arrival. 'I am so happy for Philip, for he adores children and also small babies,' she wrote in a letter to her mother. 'He carries it [the baby] about himself quite professionally, to the nurse's amusement.' Nevertheless, Philip showed no inclination for being a nappy-changing, hands-on kind of father. At the time, he not only had his career in the Navy to consider, but he was also fitting in royal duties and trying to maintain a remnant of his former bachelor lifestyle by going out regularly on the town with Parker.

Philip certainly saw nothing wrong in handing the baby over to nursery staff. In his own early years, he had effectively been brought up by a nanny himself. So, each morning at 9 o'clock, little Charles would be taken to see his mother. And, in the evenings, engagements permitting, the Queen would join him in the nursery. But that was about the extent of it. They lived largely separate lives. 'To my knowledge, she never bathed the children,' recalled Mrs Parker. 'Nanny did all that.' It was therefore to his nannies that Charles, a shy and sensitive child, turned to for affection. The most important source of love was Nanny Helen Lightbody – he called her Nana – who got him up in the morning, dressed him, slept in the same room as he did and comforted him when he awoke during the night.

He worshipped Mummy – but from afar. She was, Charles admitted in Jonathan Dimbleby's biography, 'a remote and glamorous figure who came to kiss you goodnight, smelling of lavender and dressed for dinner'. Aside from this nightly ritual, the Queen always found it difficult to hug or kiss her son, preferring to leave such tactile displays of emotion to the nannies. Like her husband, she is by nature physically undemonstrative.

After King George VI died in 1952, their mother became even more distant when she assumed the role of monarch. Godfrey Talbot, the BBC's court correspondent at the time, recalled, 'She had been trained since the cradle by her father that duty came before everything, including her family. She reluctantly had to abandon her family and they virtually didn't see their parents for months on end. It was very upsetting and bewildering for [them].'

In 1953, the new Queen and the Duke of Edinburgh left on a long-delayed tour of the Commonwealth, knowing they wouldn't see their children for six long months. Elizabeth cried as she said goodbye to them. Her long absence exacted its inevitable toll. When they were at last reunited, the Queen recalled later, the children 'were terribly polite. I don't think they really knew who we were.' It was a heartbreaking admission. Most of her 1950s female contemporaries were stay-at-home mums – admittedly with nannies – but the Queen had just inherited the ultimate juggling act.

Philip had little understanding of his son's fears and inhibitions and was inclined to laugh at them. Of course, he made fun of Anne, too. But she could deal with that, cheerfully braving his ridicule, saying anything she wanted and even laughing with him. This contrast was reflected in the children's relationships with their parents. Charles, who sometimes gave the impression of being terrified of his father, gravitated to his mother, who provided him with a sympathetic ear. Anne was close to Philip.

Whether the Queen ever made much effort to temper her husband's behaviour with Charles is doubtful: she is a woman who believes firmly in letting a man be head of the family.

In 1994, Charles revealed to his official biographer, Jonathan Dimbleby, that he felt 'emotionally estranged' from his parents and all his life had yearned for a different kind of affection that they'd been 'unable or unwilling to offer'. They were hurt by these very public revelations, but all that Philip would say on the record was that they did their best. However, according to the opinion of Lady Kennard, also recorded in Dimbleby's biography, their best wasn't so bad. Philip, she insisted, was a 'wonderful parent. He played with his children, he read them stories, he took them fishing, he was very involved.'

During holidays – Christmas and the New Year at Sandringham, Easter at Windsor and most of the summer holidays at Balmoral – the whole family would play football, with the diminutive Queen acting as goalkeeper. 'Nothing has the same meaning and soul-refreshing quality that Balmoral can provide,' Charles noted after returning to Cambridge University for his final year in 1969. He wasn't always a devoted student. He preferred the outdoors to musty old libraries. 'Any excuse to escape from Cambridge and plod across ploughed fields instead of stagnating in lecture rooms is enormously welcome,' he noted after he went shooting while at university in January 1969.

There would also be endless picnics. 'We grew up singing on the way to and from barbecues,' recalled Anne in Ingrid Seward's book *My Husband and I: The Inside Story of 70 Years of the Royal*

*Marriage.* 'Mostly First World War songs – we have quite a repertoire of those.' The Queen was always a very competent singer. 'I think we were very lucky as a family to be able to do so much together. We all appreciated that time.'

Charles clearly had a different perception, allowing the negative to outweigh the positive. For all his faults, the Duke of Edinburgh would later put a great deal of effort into trying to help mend his eldest son's disastrous marriage. He would also help to provide much-needed stability for his traumatised grandsons after the death of their mother.

The Queen Mother, who viewed Charles as her favourite grandchild, returned his affection, so much, it now emerges, that she tried to sway his parents' choice of schooling because she rightly predicted it would bring him misery. Previously unpublished letters written to her daughter, the Queen, revealed that she pleaded for the sensitive Charles not to be sent to Gordonstoun, the remote Scottish boarding school he hated and later described as 'Colditz in kilts'.

She argued instead for Eton College, Windsor would have been far more suitable for the sensitive prince. 'I have been thinking such a lot about Charles,' she wrote in a missive dated 23 May 1961 and addressed to 'My Darling Lillibet'. 'I suppose that he will be taking his entrance exam for Eton soon. I do hope he passes because it might be the ideal school for one of his character and temperament. However good Gordonstoun is, it is miles and miles away and he might as well be at school abroad.'

She added, 'All your friends' sons are at Eton and it is so important to be able to grow up with people you will be with later in life. And so nice and so important when boys are growing up that you and Philip can see him during school days and keep in touch with what is happening. He would be terribly cut off and lonely in the far north. I do hope you don't mind my writing my thoughts on this subject, but I have been thinking and worrying about it all (possibly without cause).'

She had cause, but Prince Philip was adamant that his firstborn would attend his own alma mater, a place Charles described as 'hell'. Author William Shawcross, who reproduces the correspondence in his book *Counting One's Blessings*, details how the Duke of Edinburgh argued Eton College was far too close to Windsor and the prince would be 'harassed by the media' there.

Queen Elizabeth and Prince Philip saw their children only after breakfast and after teatime. This certainly doesn't sound good, but it doesn't mean the Queen and Philip were dreadful people. 'She had been brought up in that style herself,' author Robert Lacey, the historical adviser for Netflix's *The Crown*, and author of *The Crown: The Official Companion*, explained to *Town & Country*. He further added that the Queen thought it best to have nannies raise her children while she was travelling, rather than bring them along.

In contrast, the Queen Mother knew how to nurture him. I think the key to their relationship is that she saw in him the same sort of insecurity she saw in her husband George VI. In other words, she knew Charles needed to be given a lot of support and to be bolstered emotionally, which is what she did very well, rather better than his parents.

In his book *Charles: A Biography*, royal author Anthony Holden says Charles took every opportunity to escape Gordonstoun and visit the Queen Mother at her Scottish home, Birkhall.

There, says Holden, 'The Queen Mother listened to Charles's plaintive outpourings about his loneliness, his homesickness, the impossibility of blending into school like other boys.'

'She provided a much-needed shoulder to cry on,' respected royal writer and the Queen Mother's biographer Hugo Vickers wrote in his excellent biography *Elizabeth: The Queen Mother* 'You must remember that, when the Queen was away on her tour of the Commonwealth from November 1953 until May 1954, the Queen Mother was really Prince Charles and Princess Anne's guardian. They were very young then and they would share weekends at Royal Lodge in Windsor Great Park, and they spent a long Christmas holiday together at Sandringham. I think it was then that Charles in particular bonded with his grandmother.'

They had a completely mutual adoration. Their sense of humour was the same, they enjoyed the same activities and the Queen Mother instilled a love of culture in him, taking him to the ballet when he was very young and walking him through the corridors of Windsor Castle explaining all the paintings.

Until her death she kept a boyhood photo of Charles on her desk and her letters about him radiate affection. 'Charles is a great love of mine. He is such a darling,' she says in one, later telling the Queen, 'He is intensely affectionate. I'm sure that he will always be a very loving and enjoyable child.'

Her personal letters to the prince are perhaps the most doting. She is thrilled when he sends her flowers after an appendix operation in 1964, saying, 'My darling Charles, I can't tell you how touched and delighted I was.' He in return tried to make light of his misery. Even when down he would joke about the masters and teachers and his own inadequacies. On his attempt to learn the trumpet he recalled, 'I can hear the music teacher now . . . She would put down her violin and we would all stop and she would shout – she had a heavy German accent and somehow that made her more agonised – "Ach! Zoze trumpets! Ach! Zoze trumpets! Stawp zoze trumpets!" So I gave up my trumpet.'

But mostly his memories of the place filled him with dread. 'I hate coming back here and leaving everyone at home. . . I hardly get any sleep at the House because I snore and get hit on the head the whole time. It is absolute hell,' he noted about boarding at Gordonstoun, in a private letter of 9 February 1963.

One incident to this day irritates him, by the severity and unfairness of its consequences. It is the so-called 'Cherry Brandy incident'. When Charles arrived, his housemaster warned the other boys that to be caught bullying the heir to the throne would risk expulsion. This had, unsurprisingly, the opposite effect. Charles was picked on at once, 'maliciously, cruelly and without respite'. A prince – let alone an insecure prince – would have found it hard enough to befriend his peers. 'Even to open a conversation with the heir to the throne was to court humiliation, to face the charge of "sucking up" and to hear the collective "slurping" noises that denoted a toady and a sycophant,' Dimbleby observed in his book *The Prince of Wales*.

The prince took this thuggery on the chin, without complaint. He was far too proud to let it show. But privately he was miserable, and hated returning. He described it as 'absolute hell'. Charles wrote in a letter home in 1963, describing the tough time he was having, 'The people in my dormitory are foul. Goodness, they are horrid. I don't know how anybody could be so foul.'

As Charles grew older, and his peers became more mature,

so things began to improve. His school life was still not to his liking, but nor was it all misery. There was an unusually wide range of extracurricular activities to choose from. This allowed him to spend many happy hours in the art room painting, or at the potter's wheel, or swimming. He also became so proficient in a canoe that he could paddle from Hopeman Beach to Findhorn Bay – a distance of twelve miles, but about double that when allowing for wind and tide.

In his second year, he joined the crew of *Pinta*, one of two ketches owned by the school. On his first trip in the summer of 1963, he sailed into Stornoway Harbour on the Isle of Lewis. He and four other boys were given shore leave to have dinner and then see a film. Naturally, the four were accompanied by the Prince's detective, Donald Green. As they walked towards the Crown Hotel they began to attract a small crowd. By the time they were in the lounge, a larger crowd had gathered outside the main window and flash bulbs were going off as folk jostled to get a photograph.

Charles retreated from the room and, followed by his police protection officer, found himself in the public bar. Everybody was looking at him and he thought he should order a drink. He explained, 'I went and sat down at the bar and the barman said, "What do you want to drink?"

'I said the first drink that came into my head, which happened to be cherry brandy, because I'd drunk it before when it was cold out shooting. Hardly had I taken a sip when the whole world exploded round my ears.' At that very moment a female journalist walked into the bar and the 'incident' was destined to make headlines around the world.

At first, the palace denied the story. But two days later the palace was forced to withdraw its denial with press secretary Commander Richard Colville claiming that he had been misled by the prince's protection officer. Once back at school, Charles was sent for by the headmaster and was demoted a rank in the school system. His Scotland Yard PPO Green fared worse and was removed from royal duties. Charles still smarts about it to this day. He said, 'I have never been able to forgive them for doing that because he defended me in the most marvellous way and he was the most wonderful, loyal splendid man. . .I thought it was atrocious what they did.'

*Chapter Five*

# A SUMMER OF DISCONTENT

———~———

'She [Diana, Princess of Wales] understood that there
was a real life outside of palace walls.'

PRINCE WILLIAM, DUKE OF CAMBRIDGE

Casually dressed with a shirt and no tie and nervously ringing
his hands, Prince William, the Duke of Cambridge,
looked uptight. As he walked into a room to address a select
group of journalists to introduce a film about his mother, the
late Diana, Princess of Wales, he admitted that the prospect of
speaking candidly about her so publicly had been a daunting
experience. 'At least at first,' he added. In time, however, he said
the ordeal for both himself and his younger brother, Prince Harry,
had developed into a sort of healing process too.

In his introduction, which lasted just a few minutes, William
also admitted that he didn't know if cooperating so publicly
with such a personal documentary film had been a wise move
and even told us, half jokingly, that he hoped he and his brother

would not live to regret it. 'Not only is this the first time we've spoken so openly and at length about our mother, it is also the last time.' As far as both brothers were concerned, this was a one-off.

I was one of the chosen few invited to watch the exclusive preview of *Diana, Our Mother: Her Life and Legacy*, which was to be screened on ITV on Monday, 24 July 2017, at 9 p.m. to widespread acclaim. William and Harry, had not simply endorsed the film, made by Oxford Film and Television, producers of ITV's *Our Queen at 90*, they had starred in it. Indeed, the film was built around contributions from both princes, who talked candidly about Diana and paid tribute to the many ways she had shaped their lives. It was intended as a documentary, they said, that in years to come the princes could show their children.

It was certainly a watershed moment for William, Harry and the royals. Watching Diana's sons open up so candidly about their iconic mother was, undoubtedly, compelling television viewing. They both gave revealing raw testimony, after both being interviewed for approximately forty minutes at Kensington Palace. At times it was clearly challenging for both William and Harry to deliver and perform on camera. On occasion they looked close to tears.

Their courage to do so is commendable and the film they have backed and starred in is, undeniably, a touching tribute. Personally, as a Fleet Street reporter who has covered the royal story since 1990, I found it a moving and, yes, emotional too, journey down memory lane as I was there reporting on Diana's public work and private life as she travelled the world. It was a significant watershed moment for the monarchy. For by backing and starring in the film, the princes had established a very different template for our new constitutional monarchy going forward. It hints at a more 'touchy-feely' style of monarchy – with a sovereign (ultimately Prince William) determined to do things his way: a 'Diana-style' monarchy.

Throughout, William seemed happy to abandon the stiff-upper-lip style – 'never complain, never explain' – of his cherished and revered grandmother, Elizabeth II, despite her undoubted success in her role. A bastion of consistency, the Queen still hasn't given a full and frank personal interview and I doubt she ever will. For, when it comes to one's personal life and media, her view is clear: 'keep schtum'. It is a policy that has served the older generation well, but it is advice both princes have flagrantly chosen to ignore. By making the film, William and his brother were effectively telling the older generation of royals, 'That was then, this is now.'

It was clear that bearing one's soul didn't come as naturally to William as it does to Harry – wearing his heart on his sleeve, like his mother. This film brought back memories to those who knew and loved Diana, and introduced this iconic figure to a new, wider audience. It certainly brought a tear to the eye.

I was astonished by some omissions in the cast list, not least, apart from still photos and television footage, that there was no mention of the father, Prince Charles, who after all had to raise them after Diana's death. He was kept informed, but he was not asked or needed for the film as it was clearly about his sons' mother. But, if he had taken part and paid tribute to his ex- and late wife of fifteen years, it would, perhaps, have been a positive, even cathartic, act for the prince.

One source close to Charles said, 'I suppose it is about their mother. But, even if the prince were not actually in it, it would have been nice if they had acknowledged his contribution to their upbringing. He was and tries to be a jolly good father after all.'

There is no doubt Diana was a remarkable woman. Like her sons, she was never afraid of the controversial. She would roll up her sleeves and get involved. Her sons have followed her lead in their public duties. For that, and keeping her legacy and memory alive, they should be commended.

The film promo boasted, 'Through the personal and intimate reflections of her two sons and of her friends and family, many of whom have never spoken before, the film will offer fresh and revealing insights into Princess Diana, an iconic figure who touched the lives of millions.' There were onscreen cameos by Diana's brother, Earl Spencer, and other members of the princess's circle, including William van Straubenzee, Lady Carolyn Warren and Anne Beckwith-Smith. None of them had spoken publicly about Diana since her death but agreed to appear in the film, speaking sincerely about her life and loss.

Those who had spent the most time with Diana and undoubtedly knew her best as an adult and during her time as a princess – her Scotland Yard PPO, Inspector Ken Wharfe MVO, her only private secretary, Patrick Jephson, and her butler, Paul Burrell RVM, who had all penned bestselling memoirs about the princess – were notably excluded. So too, however, as we've seen, was their father, the Prince of Wales.

Yes, Charles had been consulted about the film in as much as they had told him they were doing it. Other than that, he was in the dark. He was not mentioned once for his contribution to raising his sons as a single parent, be that in the chat ahead of the film, in it or after it. Yes, it may have been a film about their mother, but a mention of how their father had done his best to support them in its aftermath and in the years that followed might have been nice. The lack of acknowledgement from his sons for his efforts undoubtedly saddened Charles. 'It was as if he had never existed,' one of his friends said. Clearly, this film diminished, even dismissed, his role in their young life.

The princes had gambled. They had focused understandably on their late mother; after all, it was the twentieth anniversary of her death. They hoped it would remind the public, especially the generation too young to remember her, of their mother's warmth and humour and also her achievements. It was, by the very nature of what it set out to achieve, a sugar-coated portrayal of Diana – their bold bid to take charge of the narrative about her.

The resultant documentary was a commendable piece of work. It chronicled Diana's personal journey, her campaigns supporting the homeless, people living with AIDS and to ban landmines. She was seen as a pioneer and yet still a victim. Despite the prince's calls for openness about mental health in the months that preceded it, it did not tackle her mental frailties or her clandestine affairs. It was a candy-coated portrayal of somebody who, in person and in reality, was far more complex.

'We won't be doing this again,' William said. 'We won't speak as openly or publicly about her again, because we feel hopefully this film will provide the other side from close family friends you might not have heard before, from those who knew her best and from those who want to protect her memory, and want to remind people of the person that she was. Twenty years on, Harry and I felt that it was an appropriate time to open up a bit more about our mother.'

Initially, Diana's sons, who had been children at the time of her death, found they could remember very few specifics about their mother when they began the film-making process. They even felt the need to caution their collaborators, film-makers Ashley Getting and Nick Kent, not to expect too much from them. 'They prefaced their interviews by saying, "We don't actually have that many memories of our mum",' Getting and Kent recalled.

In truth, their grief and bereavement had suppressed or in some cases wiped out many memories. Perhaps they were too raw. But, relatively quickly, when the producers started the interview process on camera, somehow those memories, stored deep inside them, returned to the surface. There was one photograph of Princess Diana hugging Prince Harry that featured in the film. Without words it told anyone who saw it everything about that wonderfully playful relationship.

'She would just engulf you and squeeze you as tight as possible,' Harry remembered, 'and, being as short as I was then, there was no escape; you were there and you were there for as long as she wanted to hold you. Even talking about it now, I can feel the hugs that she used to give us and, you know, I miss that, I miss that feeling, I miss that part of a family, I miss having that mother. . . to be able to give you those hugs and give you that compassion that I think everybody needs.'

In addition to sharing fond memories of their mother, William and Harry also open up about their final phone call with Diana, and about the trauma of having a loved one ripped from their lives so suddenly. Another heart-wrenching moment involves William revealing how he keeps his mother's memory alive for his young children, Prince George and Princess Charlotte.

The age-old narrative of Diana, the saintly, wronged young wife and, by default, Charles (by the very fact that he wasn't mentioned once) the calculated, sinful older husband, had returned ahead of what would be a pretty tough month in public-relations terms for Charles. If that wasn't bad enough, what followed was more bruising.

Never-before-seen videotaped confessions made by Princess Diana herself were aired on UK television as part of the anniversary coverage. The tapes, captured by her speech coach Peter Settelen, show Diana reflecting on her early life, her relationship with Prince Charles and her time in the public eye.

This footage, aired in the documentary *Diana: In Her Own Words* on Channel 4, was recorded at Kensington Palace in the early 1990s and the tapes were never intended for public viewing, but part of coaching to prepare Diana to present her account of her life and marriage to Prince Charles.

It was also part of preparation for her famous 1995 *Panorama* interview with journalist Martin Bashir, in which she blamed Charles and his mistress Camilla Parker Bowles for the breakdown of her marriage with her infamous comment, 'Well, there were three of us in this marriage, so it was a bit crowded.'

Ralph Lee, Channel 4's deputy chief creative officer and head of factual, who commissioned the film, somewhat disingenuously, tried to justify using the material, saying, 'The tapes, which show a relaxed and off-duty Diana, are hugely illuminating about her personality, humour and charm. Combined with historical context and interviews with her closest confidants, this film provides a nuanced, multilayered portrait of the most famous woman in the world and a mother who has shaped the future line of the royal family.'

The Spencer family, led by Diana's brother, Earl Spencer, vehemently disagreed and insisted that it was they who owned the footage, despite the fact that Scotland Yard eventually returned the tapes to voice coach Peter Settelen in 2004 after a lengthy dispute between both parties.

Seven of a total of twelve tapes were found by police in a 2001 raid on the home of Diana's butler, Paul Burrell. Settelen launched legal action to have them returned to him and then sold them to US network NBC, which broadcast some of the material in 2004. In 2007 the BBC paid £30,000 to use excerpts in a documentary, but it shelved the project after pressure from the palace. The other five tapes are said still to be missing.

This time, much to Charles's chagrin, the film was cut and it aired, anyway, with record viewing figures for Channel 4, who were thrilled by their commercial decision. Charles had always been consistent. As he had admitted to Jonathan Dimbleby, he had tried to be faithful in his marriage until 1986, when, 'It became clear that the marriage had irretrievably broken down.' Once again, however, he was cast as the villain of this narrative. It was as if time had stood still. Diana ripped into him from beyond the grave, even mocking his wooing techniques, saying he was all over her 'like a bad rash' at the start of their courtship.

In the footage – fifty hours filmed over eighteen months in 1992 and 1993 and never intended for public consumption – Diana makes several startling revelations. She admits she and her husband did not have sex for seven years before their acrimonious split in 1992. She also claimed Prince Philip had encouraged Charles to cheat on her, telling him he could always go back to Camilla after a suitable time lapse and she recounted how she once went sobbing to the Queen for help saving her marriage. She says the monarch simply replied, 'I don't know what you should do. Charles is hopeless.'

In another section Diana reveals how she 'got burned' after she fell 'deeply in love' with one of her bodyguards, Barry Mannakee, a married man who was sacked amid rumours that they had become too intimate and who was killed in a freak motorbike crash weeks after his sudden exit. She talked too about how she was driven to bulimia because she did not feel she was good enough for the Royal Family. Some of the footage shows genuine voice-coaching exercises and a young Prince William heard walking into one recording session.

William explained, 'Part of the reason why Harry and I want to do this is because we feel we owe it to her. I think an element of it is feeling like we let her down when we were younger. We couldn't protect her.' He went on, 'We feel we at least owe her twenty years on to stand up for her name and remind everybody of the character and person that she was. Do our duty as sons in protecting her.'

So-called 'anniversary journalism' is by its nature benign. Even so, William and Harry knew going ahead with their documentary was a risk. It was touching and made compulsive viewing and the way they spoke of her, with a modern openness, was a natural resistance to pain. It was a programme about the love of a mother for her two sons, and, in crass terms, the scoop on their last conversations with her previously unshared reflections and private photos. It was also, by virtue of the fact that it avoided the subject, a reminder of the nation's extraordinary reaction at the time, not the public grief, but the public anger towards Charles and the Queen over their perceived coldness towards the princess.

The entire period was excruciating for Charles, like a *Groundhog Day* nightmare. In the last of the documentaries aired in the UK – BBC film focusing on the days around the time of Diana's death – at least Charles was awarded some praise. William and Harry made a final contribution. They did it, they said, because they wanted to 'stand up for her name', saying they felt they had let her down in the past by not protecting her. By this time Charles had decamped, tail between his legs, to his beloved Birkhall to escape the furore.

Diana, after all, was not always what she appeared to be. A mistress of manipulation, some of her security detail found her level of hypocrisy too much to take. One PPO, who left her service many years earlier, was so frustrated towards the end of his tenure that one morning he discharged all his bullets into a tree in a garden of a landed family where the royals were staying. 'That should wake them up,' he said to a shocked colleague. The SO14 colleague with him urged him to reload quickly to avoid a backlash and say nothing about the incident. Before leaving, the same PPO, whom I've chosen not to identify, remarked to his replacement, 'Good luck, you're going to need it. If these kids [Princes William and Harry] were brought up on a council estate somewhere in south London they'd have been taken into care by now.' He was deadly serious. Diana let the pair run free and wild as young children. Harry's nanny, Jessie Webb, frequently sandwiched the little prince up against the wall with her frame, saying it was the only way she could catch him and 'gain control'.

William and Harry would roam around Highgrove, relieving themselves from the top of the giant haystack in the garden when they were so inclined, much to the annoyance of their 'papa', who caught them in the act on occasion. He was not necessarily the most active father, but on weekends off he would often go looking for his sons to keep an eye on them and he was always aware of their antics, whether it had been go-karting around his garden and tearing it up in the process, or smashing cricket balls through the ancient glass of his woodshed. On another occasion Harry burrowed himself in a huge haystack and was struggling for breath before eventually being found in some distress just in time by his policeman. On another occasion he caused a major ruckus when he disappeared again on a hot summer's day. He had crawled into one of the prince's giant urns as it was cooler inside and could not hear the increasingly desperate staff and parents calling his name.

There was an unspoken 'understanding' between Charles and Diana during this time which meant that during the week the prince rarely went to Kensington Palace and they, effectively, used Highgrove at weekends on a rota basis, neither being there when the other was. James Hewitt, Diana's lover, became a frequent visitor to both residences at this time, and of course would stay the night with the princess, although he took care that his arrivals and departures were screened from prying eyes and, even more important, prying cameras.

James would even join in the play fights the protection officers would have with William and Harry around the garden pool at Highgrove. Such was her state of domestic bliss at times that Diana would roar with laughter when she was thrown into the pool fully clothed, making an almighty splash. Of course, her sons did not know the sleeping arrangements of their mother and the dashing Guards officer. He was just another avuncular figure in their lives.

That is not to say he stood in for Charles, but was just a fun figure to William and Harry. The prince was not a rough-and-tumble-style father. He would leave that side of their childhood often to their bodyguards, such as stalwarts Inspector Ken Wharfe, Sergeant Reg Spinney, Sergeant Dave Sharpe and Inspector Trevor Bettles. Wharfe recalled that they would often turn up at his bedroom at Kensington Palace (used by the Scotland Yard officer on duty). As regular as clockwork the princes would knock at the door. 'Ken, do you want to fight?' It was not really a request or even a question: it was a statement of intent.

The two princes would pile in and made a perfect royal tag team. 'One would go for my head and the other attack my more sensitive parts, landing punches towards my groin, which, if they connected, would make me keel over in agony,' he recalled in his best-selling memoir *Diana: Closely Guarded Secret*, which I co-wrote with him. Their parents seemed to appreciate that their sons could let off steam in this way. Charles would pop his head around the door and, with a slightly quizzical look on his furrowed face, would ask, 'They're not being too much bother, are they, Ken?'

'No, sir, not at all,' he would gasp as he recovered from another fierce royal punch.

Charles adored his sons but he rarely actually joined in such horseplay. It was not his style and, more often than not, he was not around or was away on business. One such occasion was when Diana urged her bodyguard to help set up a go-kart race at Highgrove, around Charles's beloved garden without the prince's prior knowledge. Despite their high birth and high-ranking position, William and Harry as boys were at heart just brothers in search of adventure, both thrill-seekers who loved speed.

Wharfe telephoned Martin Howell, boss of Playscape Racing, where Diana herself had become a regular racer at its Buckmoor Park, Kent, circuit and at another venue in Streatham since the mid-eighties. She was a very keen and competitive racer and had introduced her sons to the junior karting experience at these venues privately on a regular basis. One weekend at Highgrove the boys kept pestering Diana to take them go-karting and so she begged Ken to call Martin and arrange for him to bring down two of the go-karts.

The karts, capable of speeds of up to forty miles an hour, arrived and Wharfe and Howell set up a course around the prince's grounds and within minutes the boy were racing at full tilt, tearing up Charles's beloved garden in the process. Diana, mischievous as ever, cheered on her sons as they skidded through her husband's secret garden, now a chicane as his sons battled for the lead. The prince was of course oblivious to it all. Weeks later, calmly, the prince spoke to Wharfe and half-jokingly teased him on whether he fancied becoming 'the next Bernie Ecclestone'.

If anyone overstepped the mark in correcting his sons, Charles in his idiosyncratic way would admonish the offender to let him know, albeit gently, who was the boss. On one occasion when it reached Charles's ears that Wharfe had been correcting William's pronunciation, the prince stepped in. As a youngster, William spoke with that slightly clipped upper-class English accent. He persisted in pronouncing 'out' like 'ite' (as in 'kite'), and Wharfe corrected him, but the prince insisted he was right because his father always said it that way.

'Ken, I understand you have been giving William elocution lessons,' he said, his tone a little but not overtly critical. The policeman had clearly overstepped his remit, and this was the prince's gentlemanly way of telling him to keep his nose out of family business. He sheepishly made his excuses and left. 'When Diana found out about my telling-off she thought it was hilarious,' he said, and urged the policeman, an excellent mimic, to retell the story acting out all the voices.

In the middle of a marital nightmare, the prince could be remarkably good humoured, side-splittingly funny without even realising it. Prince Charles's comedic timing is sublime. Sometimes I am sure he doesn't know he is being funny. Even during the height of the tension during the Wales's marriage those closest to the couple, such as their PPOs found themselves chuckling at some of his remarks, much to the annoyance of the princess.

One memorable occasion summed up the distance between Charles and Diana, as well as Diana's absolute lack of appreciation of her husband as well as his sense of humour. It came on the evening of the state banquet held in honour of King Olav V of Norway in London. The prince's policeman, Superintendent Colin Trimming, was off duty, and Inspector Ken Wharfe had to take the lead in organising and overseeing security for both principals. That night, in April 1988, Diana was in a particularly impatient mood, he recalled. Wharfe told me, 'The princess was not above showing her frustrations physically, on this occasion tutting loudly and tapping her feet. The tension was always heightened when she had to attend state dinners at her husband's side and having to dress to the nines.'

Charles was extremely relaxed. He knew the form on state occasions like this, when all the senior, and many of the so-called 'minor', members of the Royal Family were on parade. Everything had to be done in almost military fashion. Royalty would arrive according to ascending order of rank, with the most senior, the Queen herself, arriving last at exactly the time listed in the programme. 'It may sound a little absurd, but this is how the business of monarchy works and state banquets, when the principals turn out in all their finery, tiaras, dress uniforms, evening dress, decorations and all, is when the business of royalty becomes very serious indeed. Diana did not quite see it like that. As far as she was concerned, a state banquet was just an irritation, something she had to do,' Ken said.

She asked if she could head off early and she didn't want to hang around waiting at the palace any longer. The Scotland Yard officer explained that they couldn't go because they had to stick to the order, and Princess Anne had been delayed in traffic. 'Ma'am, it's really not as simple as that, there is an order. . .' But, before Wharf could finish, she snapped back, 'Ken, I know all about their bloody orders. All about them. I want to go now. Simon [her chauffeur] is ready, and I want to go now.'

Fortunately, Charles, also in evening dress, appeared in the hall right on cue, tugging on his shirt cuffs as is his wont in his slightly nervous manner, like an actor in a West End comedy. He clearly sensed an impending tantrum from his volatile wife.

'Are we ready to go, Ken?' he asked. There was a stony silence from both of them as the policeman again pointed out that it was not their slot yet.

'Have I got time for another martini, then?' the prince asked politely. Wharfe, finding the situation and the prince amusing did his best not to laugh. It struck him as all rather absurd. The frost emanating from Diana became icier towards her policeman.

'Is anything the matter?' the prince asked, not directing his question to anyone in particular. Diana was spoiling for a fight and he sensed it.

'Well, Charles, there is, actually. I want to go now. I don't want to hang around here. Why can't we go now?'

'Diana,' Charles replied reasonably, 'you know the system. We have to go at the set time, so that we arrive just before Her Majesty.' He took a measured step back as though preparing himself for an onslaught. Diana, drawing herself up in her high heels (or 'tart's trotters' as she called them), turned on him.

'But Charles, why can't you go on your own? I can get there earlier. Nobody will worry about me,' she said.

Of course, she knew that if she turned up without her husband the waiting media would plaster it all over the front pages, speculating, quite rightly, that the Prince and Princess of Wales had had yet another row. When Charles pointed this out to her, however, she became even more frustrated.

The prince retreated to his study, asking butler Harold Brown for yet another martini. As his wife paced up and down like a caged animal, she shouted, 'Charles, I have really had enough of this. I'm off.'

'No, Diana, we really have to wait,' he insisted. Whereupon he ordered another martini from Harold and departed again. At this point, Wharfe let out a little chortle.

'Do you find my husband funny, Ken?' Diana snapped. 'Well, do you?'

Wharfe replied, 'Well, actually, I do, ma'am. I think he has a great sense of humour. It's not too far removed from my own.'

Diana was clearly exasperated. 'So, what kind of humour is that?' she retorted curtly. Ken was destined for the doghouse for days after that. For the rest of that night she said not one word to him.

It was an amusing incident but also a telling one. It demonstrated the extent to which the relationship between Charles and Diana had soured and how difficult it could be for anyone caught in the crossfire.

Charles rarely realises when he is being amusing, which makes him even funnier. I remember reporting on an engagement the prince was undertaking in the Iwokrama Rainforest in Guyana in February 2000 during his first official visit to the Caribbean, a nine-day tour that covered Trinidad and Tobago, Guyana and Jamaica. In the welcoming ceremony the prince happily donned a crown of eagle feathers as he was made honorary chief of Surama village, home to Amerindians deep in Guyana's Amazon Basin rainforest. He then took part in a traditional welcome 'dance and lovers' jig, joking, 'I think given half a chance. . .the old one-two and the two-step can come in handy.' Once again, he was hysterical without even knowing it.

About two hundred Amerindian villagers had waited to catch a glimpse of the royal visitor. Some of them had walked up to sixty miles across difficult terrain for the prestigious event. I was standing behind a group of indigenous dignitaries lined up to meet him in their traditional dress as the prince cheerily shook hands while sporting the Indian headdress that had been given to him, much to the delight of the travelling photographers.

'That'll get in the linen [newspaper],' one of the snappers said rather too loudly, and drew a frown from the prince. I was not bothered about the niceties of the latest tabloid snap but in what the prince said as he engaged with them through an interpreter. One unfortunate Amazonian Indian chief seemed particularly interested in the prince and looked a little stressed. He was with his wife and baby and she appeared animated and upset. Instinctively and sympathetically, the prince asked, 'Is everything all right?'

It clearly wasn't. With a hangdog expression, the chief, in his local dialect, explained that he had been travelling with his wife and children for two days to get to meet him. The prince, who had flown in on a light aircraft, pondered the problem for a few seconds and responded, 'The trouble is you've got to go all the way back.' He clearly had no idea how funny his remark was, made all the funnier by its timing, what the two of them were wearing – Charles in his beige safari suit and headdress and the chief with barely a stitch on – and the fact that there was delay as their chat was translated. I couldn't help chuckling to myself.

Diana's death, as the documentary film in 2017 showed, scarred William and Harry terribly. It was clear by the comments they made that it was still raw. Their film sidestepped sensitive issues such as both parents' infidelity. Inevitably, it was a stilted portrayal of the princess, perhaps an idealised version of her that lived in her sons' minds. I, however, found myself thinking more than once about Charles, and why he had just been airbrushed out in this way.

Charles had endured a miserable 'August horribilis' (summer 2017) but he weathered the perfect media storm. His mantra, to put up with it and shut up, worked. He was never going to win this PR fight against his now iconic, almost saintly, dead wife. The media made hay dragging up the so-called 'War of the Waleses', but the retelling of this sorry tale twenty years on felt tired even for the tabloids. It was, in the assessment of the prince and his team, a passing dark cloud. Yes, there would be rain, but it would pass. But what did upset him was his sons' decision to completely write him out of history.

Opinion polls showed his popularity had dipped. The prince and his staff noticed this, but said nothing. He retreated to Scotland with his wife and prepared for his busy schedule of events starting in September.

In the last of the Diana documentaries to be aired in the UK in August 2017, *Diana: 7 Days*, the BBC focused on the days between her death and funeral. During the documentary, one of Charles's sons spoke up for him publicly. Harry praised his father for looking after him and Prince William in the aftermath of the tragedy.

'One of the hardest things for a parent to have to do is to tell your children that the other parent has died. But he was there for us, he was the one out of two left. And he tried to do his best to make sure that we were protected and looked after,' he said.

Many close to the prince said it felt like too little too late. But the prince was pacified.

## Chapter Six

# SOFT
# POWER

───~───

'Power is the ability to influence the behaviour of others
to get the outcomes one wants.'

JOSEPH S. NYE JR, *SOFT POWER: THE MEANS TO
SUCCESS IN WORLD POLITICS*

Although newspaper headlines in the UK screamed about
his troubled past, focusing on his failed relationships and
even his resulting mental-health issues, the Prince of Wales
seemed unconcerned. He cheerily got on with the job and let it
all go over his head. At this late stage in his life he had seen these
so-called media 'scandals' come and go before and learned to take
them in his stride. What was all the fuss about? he mused. 'It was
all such a long time ago,' the prince told an official.

'The prince has an important role to play today,' the official
told me as I accompanied the Royal party aboard the RAF
Voyager jet, the royal plane used on such official overseas visits,

on the spring tour of Europe in April 2017. The emphasis in this short comment was on the word 'today'.

Another senior member of the prince's household pointed out that the revelation, far from a negative, was in fact a positive. The aide said that, in his view, seeking professional psychiatric help through Dr Alan McGlashan – who was known to Charles's friend and mentor, the philosopher Laurens van der Post, not only for Charles's deeply troubled first wife Diana, but also for himself, to help him cope with the inward strain of an incompatible marriage – showed strength. It demonstrated that he had 'at least tried very hard to resolve their problems and even tried to save his marriage'. Surely in an epoch when his two sons and daughter-in-law, Kate, were rightly winning plaudits for their tireless work on their brilliant Heads Together initiative – a campaign to get more people talking openly about their mental health – this revelation should have produced positive coverage for Charles in the tabloids. 'Surely, this is something he should have been given some credit for,' one of his team said. I couldn't help but agree but for some reason, perhaps because it was about Charles and Diana, it was seen in a negative light.

The prince just brushed it all aside. In his view, it was all 'old hat' and not worth wasting time thinking about. In this uncertain post-Brexit-vote economic era, the heir to the throne was focused on the job in hand, doing his duty for Britain amid the 'soft power' battle to win hearts and minds abroad, at least among those close neighbours willing to listen. His position on Brexit is unknown. His position post-Brexit is, however, clear. We as a country, a great country, have to unite and work alongside the Commonwealth to make the best of our situation.

He and his family are determined to play their part as positively as possible.

Approaching his seventieth birthday after years representing the Queen and her government on diplomatic missions (to date, at the time of writing, he has visited forty-four of the fifty-three Commonwealth countries, many of them on several occasions), Charles has shown himself to be much more than some glorified travelling salesman, circumnavigating the globe with a fist full of trade deals like some faceless politician. Foreign and Commonwealth Office mandarins appreciate that Charles is a unique asset as Britain works to re-establish bilateral relations across Europe and the wide world after the triggering of Article 50 by the UK Prime Minister Theresa May in March 2017. Her signing and sending the letter to the EU's Donald Tusk, spelling out Britain's intention to leave the European Union, was just the starting gun being fired. A long and difficult drawn-out process of negotiation has to play out, with as much help as Britain can get.

When he travels in Europe he is often accompanied by a team of experts and politicians. On this visit he was joined by the brilliant and prepossessing Caroline Wilson, a Cambridge-educated barrister and former consul general of Hong Kong. She was appointed Europe director at the FCO in October 2016, where she leads our European network of embassies and consulates to promote our interests in Europe. Her mantra, much like the prince's, is 'trust your instincts, know what you want and believe in your ability to achieve it'. She acted as an adviser to the future king when he was on key visits around Europe such as the 2017 four-country tour to Romania, the Holy See, Italy and Austria until April 2017. She once described the Royal Family as a 'great national resource'. The Europe minister, Sir Alan Duncan, also accompanied the prince in Italy. When the Queen undertook state visits she used to be accompanied by the serving foreign secretary of the time, for these visits are much more than the series of photo opportunities and speeches at official black-tie dinners they can sometimes seem. Behind the scenes the diplomatic wheel is always turning on these royal tours.

As the Queen, ninety-two at the time of writing and the most travelled monarch in history, no longer makes these foreign forays, Charles is at the core at this subtle shift of emphasis in government strategy in using the royal brand. Personally, too, Charles is in a far better place these days. In public and in private, Charles and Camilla are an accomplished double act on the world stage. The duchess, in public personable and with a positive approach to the travelling media, came back to chat with the accredited group on the tours several times during our travels around Europe. Self-assured, she happily shared her thoughts about the visit. The prince, too, at the end of the tour, emerged, this time unusually without his jacket in a tailored, pink-striped Turnbull & Asser shirt and a handmade tie from the Italian firm E. Marinella. Laughing and joking, he was at one with himself.

It has not always been this way; his relations with the media chronicling his life's story have been at times tense. During the so-called 'War of the Waleses' between him and Diana, Charles was the victim of negative press. The media seemed determined to make him the villain of the narrative and Diana the victim. The truth of course lay somewhere in the middle, but Charles refused to enter the fray and urged his circle not to do so on his behalf. The result was that his popular ratings plummeted to an all-time low.

Now, his first wife tragically no longer around to set the media agenda, the narrative around Charles seems to be less about his private life – after all he is now content and happily married – and more about what the prince does, what he believes, what he says and what he can achieve.

This last decade has seen Charles taking an active lead in monarchal business as his ageing mother slips gracefully towards an unofficial retirement. There are those who insist Elizabeth II is still as spritely, fit and sharp as she was two decades ago. This is not true. She is still sharp on matters of state, but requires her schedule to reflect her age and capacity. Even she thinks those loyal subjects who believe nothing needs to change are deluding themselves.

The most significant step came when the Duke of Edinburgh publicly acknowledged he could no longer undertake the schedule expected of a consort and announced he wanted to step down and 'retire' before his 'sell-by date' in May 2017. His decision to step aside and quit public engagements came almost six years after he first hinted at his desire. 'I reckon I've done my bit,' he said on his ninetieth birthday in a television interview. His decision had the blessing of the Queen, who, aides stressed, would carry on. It would mean, Buckingham Palace explained, that she would carry out more solo engagements and attend more events with younger members of 'Team Windsor'.

Since then the Queen has stepped out with Prince William, Prince Harry, Prince Andrew and Prince Edward at her side. She also carried out the first joint engagement with the former Meghan

Markle, now Duchess of Sussex, in June 2018 on an 'away day' to Chester on the Royal Train, when she insisted Harry should not join them. She has undoubtedly missed Philip's presence keenly and the regular afternoon tea that they took together whenever possible. Those who questioned her willingness to continue have been proved wrong. How long she will actually continue as an active queen is unknown. But surely now it is only a matter of a year or two at most, from the time of writing, before she passes on the baton to her son and heir.

Charles and Camilla schmoozed their way across Europe in April 2017 on a nine-day overseas tour, meeting presidents and prime ministers and even enjoying a papal audience with Pope Francis in the Vatican City; he allowed them a tour inside the Vatican Secret Archive, where Charles was in his element. At one point, Charles beckoned over his quintessential principal private secretary, Clive Alderton LVO, to take a look at a particular document. Formally established in 1475, but actually much older, the archive now preserves more than 180,000 manuscripts, including 80,000 archival units, 1,600,000 printed books, more than 8,600 incunabula, printed documents dating from before 1501, more than 300,000 coins and medals, 150,000 prints, drawings and engravings and more than 150,000 photographs.

They were shown original documents relating to the Catholic Church and Britain. The rare manuscripts, not open to the public, are kept in the Sala Sistina of the Vatican Library. The royal couple were then shown a number of original rare letters, including the last letter ever written by condemned Mary Queen of Scots on 8 February 1587 before her execution for treason. They were shown a letter written in 1555 by England's Tudor

Queen Mary I and King Philip II of Spain, who set about the restoration of the Roman Catholic Church in England. There is a letter by Pope Paul IV condemning Thomas Cranmer, the leader of the English Reformation and Archbishop of Canterbury during the reigns of Henry VIII and Edward VIII and briefly under Mary I, who put him on trial for treason and heresy. He was eventually executed.

Later, during the traditional exchange of gifts that followed the private meeting, which lasted almost half an hour in a study within the Pope Paul VI Audience Hall in the Vatican – a modern structure used for papal meetings – the leader of the Roman Catholic Church urged Charles, 'Wherever you go, may you be a man of peace.' He said sincerely, 'I'll do my best.' He then gave the Pope a large hamper of produce from his Highgrove estate and framed photos of himself and his wife, while the pontiff presented him with a bronze olive branch, signifying peace, and copies of his writings on climate change bound in red leather, and other papal writings. 'I hope they're in English,' Charles said and was assured they were.

In Romania, where Charles had gone without his wife, he was on top form. It is a regular haunt for the prince, who is enchanted by the spirituality of the place and the unique history and traditional culture that live on in the countryside. He is a regular visitor to the country privately and even owns two homes in Transylvania, in central Romania, renowned for medieval towns, mountainous borders and castles, such as Bran Castle, a Gothic fortress associated with the legend of Dracula, which he lets out. He has long been fascinated by their ancient customs and he condemned the then ruling dictator Nicolae

Ceaușescu, the Romanian president, in a speech of 1 May 1989 for the 'wholesale destruction of the country's culture and human heritage'. He noted comedically later in a private letter, '[I] hope you receive this before some frightful undercover agent stabs me in the left buttock with a poisoned umbrella!'

Charles himself has appeared in a video being used to promote the country in which he claims distant kinship with Vlad Tepeş, the fifteenth-century Wallachian ruler on whom the Irish novelist Bram Stoker based his *Dracula*. 'Transylvania is in my blood,' he jokes in an interview. 'The genealogy shows I am descended from Vlad the Impaler, so I do have a bit of a stake in the country.'

He returned there in May 2018 for his annual visit, to recharge his batteries as well as using his time to promote skills and training in rural Transylvania. He met Romanian president Klaus Iohannis and later met Prime Minister Viorica Dăncilă in the capital, Bucharest, before travelling to the northwest for his retreat at one of his two properties in the deep, sparsely populated countryside, where bears and other wildlife roam freely. He established the Prince of Wales Foundation Romania in 2015, which supports the Eastern European nation's heritage and rural life, and sustainable development. He also attended the theatre festival in the central city of Sibiu.

Paul Brummell, British ambassador to Romania, said, 'The Prince's official visit in 2017 was a great success. He knows the country so well. That makes a real difference, fostering bilateral relations.' Within days the then UK foreign secretary Boris Johnson followed up on the prince's visit with a meeting with Romania's foreign minister and former director of foreign intelligence, Teodor Meleşcanu, when they discussed bilateral relations and regional security. There is a sense that after the tabloid headlines of the nineties, focusing on his dysfunctional marriage to Princess Diana, Charles is now being recognised for what he does, not what he did.

'Soft power' diplomacy is of course nothing new, but Charles does bring his diplomatic touch. Coined by Joseph S. Nye Jr, a Harvard University academic, it describes the ability to attract and co-opt rather than coerce, which is seen as 'hard power'. There is little doubt that Charles – while representing his mother on such tours – carries the clout of a king. Covering this tour at close quarters, one could see that the beguiling allure of the monarchy was indisputable. The brand clearly serves as a key soft-power tool for attracting others to the values and culture of Britain.

The prince is increasingly seen as pivotal in its use going forward and clearly has increasing authority. When he talks to presidents and prime ministers, they listen. With the Queen no longer expected to go abroad, the status of Charles's foreign forays has been upgraded, too. They are state visits in all but name. Using the soft power of 'brand royal' is what senior sources say is part of a long-term plan.

In recent years all things royal have helped bolster brand Britain. The 2011 wedding of William and Kate and the 2012 Diamond Jubilee celebrations were huge global media events that drew viewers and crowds in their millions. Public support and media attention were repeated in 2013 with the birth of the Duke and Duchess of Cambridge's first child, Prince George. The Diamond Jubilee celebrations generated £10 billion in tourist revenue for the British economy. Global viewing figures for the 2012 Olympic opening ceremony were at 900 million, peaking at the Queen's James Bond cameo. The wedding of the Duke and Duchess of Cambridge brought an estimated £2 billion to the UK economy. The balance between politics and a love for country can be neatly solved by a constitutional monarchy. It is a symbol of cooperation among nations, a byword for duty and peace. This whistle-stop royal tour has confirmed Charles as emblematic of Britain. Crucially, for when he becomes king, he has shown on his travels that he has the natural abilities to transcend the grind of political demands and to stand as an active symbol of what is good about our country.

Importantly, the question of his being an 'interfering' king after the so-called black-spider memos to ministers has been resolved too. The term, which he dislikes, refers to the private letters and memos written by the prince to British government ministers and politicians over many years. They are controversial due to the Prince of Wales's position as the heir to a monarch, who by convention remains politically neutral. These letters were written by hand before being sent to be typed, but after the letters were returned for the prince to sign, often, in flowing black or red ink, he underlined text and added exclamation marks. It was these additions and his distinctive spirally handwriting that gave his letters their nickname. Despite the 'black spider' revelations, insiders say the prince knows all the parameters of the top job and will not upset the constitutional apple cart for his own agenda. Like the Queen, he is kept up to date with all government plans. He meets regularly with ministers, which is, of course, within his remit as heir to the throne. He was confused by newspaper reports ahead of US president Donald Trump's visit to Britain in July 2018 that Charles would 'rant' at him, metaphorically thrust a copy of his book on climate change into his hand and demand he act on it. If there is one thing that infuriates the prince it is people who try to double-guess him. He cannot understand why people do that.

Another of his pet hates, although he has mellowed over years, is the media's insatiable desire for a photo-op. 'I'm not very good at being a performing monkey. . .I'm not prepared to perform whenever they want me to perform,' he said as far back as 1994. The passage of time and perhaps familiarity with the press corps who loyally cover his engagements has made him less fractious. More often than not these days, with a little shove from Camilla, he obliges lensmen such as the urbane Chris Jackson from Getty Images, ever present and diligent Tim Rooke from Shutterstock and of course the legendary *Sun* chief photographer Arthur Edwards MBE, almost a decade his senior, who has captured the prince's image around the world for more than forty years.

That said, he is not naïve and knows the top job will bring with it unwanted restrictions. Those who know him and have been alongside with him for years know that. Clarence House went as far as officially to deny reports that Charles believes becoming king will be a form of 'prison'. Claims by the respected writer and author Catherine Mayer quoted an unnamed official saying how Prince Charles is worried that he will not achieve ambitions linked to his interests before 'the prison shades' close. *Time* spoke to fifty of the prince's friends and associates for the article. I am aware that who said it still believes, despite the denial, that it reflects at least in part how the prince feels.

A Clarence House spokesman said, 'This is not the Prince of Wales's view and should not be attributed to him as he did not say these words. The prince has dutifully supported the Queen all his life and his official duties and charitable work have always run in parallel.' Mayer told BBC Radio 4's *Today* programme that the 'prison shutters' quote is 'part of a longer quote' and had been 'taken out of context' by other news organisations. She said the term 'prison shades' referred to concern among those close to the prince that, now he was taking on more of the Queen's duties, 'there's a big impact on what the Prince of Wales actually does already, in terms of time, so the reference was to his dwindling lack of time'. She added, 'He is absolutely not saying he doesn't want to be king and nobody in his household is saying that.'

To suggest such action is to misunderstand the complexity of a man driven by duty with a relentless personal motivation. Up early, he begins each day by doing a series of exercises, originally designed for Royal Canadian Air Force pilots, to keep his bad back mobile. Once galvanised, it is straight down to work.

His diary is always packed with scheduled meetings or engagements. When he does have a moment to himself, he fills it with painting watercolours or reading. Indeed, in purely commercial terms, he is lauded as one of Britain's most successful living artists, selling millions of pounds' worth of signed lithographs of his paintings, earning £2 million from his artistic output, since 1997. He doesn't pocket the cash. All of the money he makes from his paintings goes towards his charitable foundation.

He paints only with watercolours, always in the open air, often on holiday or during a break in his schedule during overseas visits, and usually in one sitting. He does not sell the originals – although he has occasionally given them away as gifts such as to the Sultan of Oman, Qaboos bin Said al Said, in 1995, who joked that he didn't know where he would put it amid his collection of 'Asprey perfection'.

In a 2013 documentary, Charles discussed why his hobby is important to him. 'We walk away and shuffle off our mortal coil, but these things live on' (the 'these things' referring to his paintings). He lives the fullest of lives. This is not a man waiting around to be given his next job, whether that job be becoming monarch or not. So, whenever he is asked about becoming king, he has a stock answer: 'It is in the lap of the gods.' Becoming king will have its personal sadness too: the passing of his beloved 'mama'. It is something he has said he prefers not to talk about, and he is certainly in no hurry.

'If it comes, then you have to deal with it,' he says.

Asked about his role in public life, the prince has said he has always tried to find his own path: 'The trouble is, there isn't a job description, so you have to rather make it up as you go along, which doesn't always appeal to everybody else.'

## Chapter Seven

# 'PERNICIOUS LIES'

---∿---

'By all means, marry. If you get a good wife, you'll become happy. If you get a bad one you'll become a philosopher.'

SOCRATES, CLASSICAL ATHENIAN PHILOSOPHER CREDITED AS ONE OF THE FOUNDERS OF WESTERN PHILOSOPHY

After months of speculation the beautiful biracial bride stepped out of the Rolls-Royce on the stroke of noon revealing a stunning pure white gown – with open bateau/boat neckline – designed by the British designer Clare Waight Keller, the artistic director of the French fashion house Givenchy. For this American actress it was the perfect part and the perfect stage. She knew how to hold herself; she knew how to perform.

The lines of the dress extended towards the back, where the train flowed in soft round folds cushioned by an underskirt in triple silk organza. Keller also designed a veil representing the distinctive flora of each Commonwealth country united in one spectacular floral composition, five metres long, made from silk tulle with a trim of hand-embroidered flowers in silk threads and organza. Perhaps the most striking part was a diamond bandeau tiara, but that was only on loan from the Queen. The devil was in the detail and the new bride had left nothing to chance.

The bridegroom, Prince Harry, had handpicked several flowers the day before from the couple's private garden at Kensington Palace to add to the bespoke bridal bouquet designed by florist Philippa Craddock. The spring blooms included forget-me-nots, which were Princess Diana's favourite flowers and were a nod to his beloved departed mother. The couple specifically chose them to be included in Meghan Markle's bouquet to honour Diana's memory.

The bride's bouquet was a petite design, pulled together in a gentle, ethereal, relaxed style with delicate blooms including scented sweet peas, lily of the valley, *Astilbe*, jasmine and *Astrantia*, and sprigs of myrtle all bound with a naturally dyed, raw silk ribbon. The myrtle sprigs were from stems planted at Osborne House on the Isle of Wight, by Queen Victoria in 1845 and from a plant grown from the myrtle used in the Queen's wedding bouquet of 1947.

The tradition of carrying myrtle started after Queen Victoria was given a nosegay containing myrtle by Prince Albert's grandmother during a visit to Gotha in Germany. In the same year, Victoria and Prince Albert purchased Osborne House as their family retreat, and a sprig from the posy was planted against the terrace walls, where it continues to thrive.

Their ten young bridesmaids and pageboys, including Prince George and Princess Charlotte, played their roles to perfection. The excitement of the day became too much for one of the younger ones in the party, who started to wail just before Meghan entered St George's chapel.

Harry, like the best man, his older brother, William, was immaculate in the blue doeskin frock-coat uniform of the Blues and Royals, both with the military rank of major (retired). Touchingly, as she approached him, he told Meghan, 'You look amazing.'

It had all the hallmarks of the grand finale of a Hollywood love story, only this romantic tale starred a real-life prince with the historic Windsor Castle as its backdrop. The event attracted a television audience of 1.2 billion around the world, too. Imbued with centuries-old tradition, it featured British pomp and pageantry at its finest.

The service combined tradition with a fresh modernity as well as the bride's African-American heritage. One of the highlights was Karen Gibson and the Kingdom Choir performance of Ben E. King's soul classic 'Stand By Me'. The gospel choir also performed Etta James's uplifting version of 'Amen/This Little Light of Mine' as the newlyweds left the chapel.

An American bishop, Most Rev. Michael Bruce Curry, aged sixty-five, who presides over the Episcopalian Church, passionately addressed attendees, secretly knowing he was sick with prostate cancer when he travelled to the UK. 'There's power. . .power in love,' said the Bishop, who was invited to speak by Meghan on the advice of the Archbishop of Canterbury, Most Rev. Justin Welby. 'If you don't believe me, think about a time when you first fell in love. The whole world seemed to centre around you and your beloved.' He concluded the passionate address saying he had better wrap up as, 'We gotta get y'all married.'

The couple then exchanged vows and rings made by Cleave and Company. In her vows, Meghan, a feminist, noticeably deleted the promise to 'obey' her husband, while the prince broke with royal tradition by choosing to wear a wedding ring. His brother, Prince William, chose not to wear a ring, and this has been true of most royal men. Prince Charles, however, wore his wedding ring from his marriage to Diana on the same finger as his signet ring. Meghan's ring was fashioned from a piece of Welsh gold, gifted by the Queen; Harry's ring was a platinum band with a textured finish.

When the Archbishop of Canterbury declared that the couple were married a huge cheer run around the Berkshire town, where an estimated 100,000 people stood beyond the castle walls watching the ceremony unfold on big screens amid a carnival atmosphere.

The bride's mother, Doria Ragland – oddly, Meghan's only invited relative, who had stayed with her daughter overnight before accompanying her to the chapel – looked an isolated, solitary figure. Dressed in a pale-green Oscar de La Renta dress, with a neat hat, an emotional-looking Doria Ragland sat silent and alone on the bride's side of the chapel for some time. Sensing her awkwardness, the Prince of Wales graciously took her hand as they left to sign the register for the royal wedding of their two children.

As the register was being signed, nineteen-year-old cellist Sheku Kanneh-Mason – who won the 2016 BBC's Young Musician of the Year award – performed three pieces by Fauré, Schubert and Maria Theresia von Paradis. He was accompanied by musicians from the BBC National Orchestra of Wales, the English Chamber Orchestra and the Philharmonia.

After the service, the couple – who had been given the title Their Royal Highnesses the Duke and Duchess of Sussex, conferred on them by the Queen – kissed in front of cheering well-wishers on the steps of the chapel. A confident, beaming Meghan made the first move. 'Shall we kiss?' she asked. 'Yes,' her prince and now husband replied.

Walter Bagehot had written that 'A princely marriage is the brilliant edition of a universal fact, and, as such, it rivets mankind' when describing a previous royal wedding in the same chapel, that of the future King Edward VII to Princess Alexandra of Denmark. This amazing spectacle was not only Harry and Meghan's wedding: it was embraced by a nation; it was a modern, inclusive, uplighting wedding; it was about hope, love and the future.

There were so many touching moments that day. One stood out and changed stilted perceptions. When Charles, immaculate in his grey Anderson & Sheppard morning suit and buttonhole from the garden of his Highgrove estate, smiled at Meghan and gently placed her arm under his as she approached the quire in St George's Chapel. He was delighted to be able to welcome her into his family after she'd asked him to stand in for her father, Thomas Markle, whose ill health prevented his attendance. Those watching couldn't help but be enchanted by Charles's poise at a moment that could have been awkward.

Then, in an equally heartwarming moment, Harry whispered words that seemed scarcely to register. Almost shaking with tension, Prince Harry turned to his father, who had accompanied his glamorous bride down the aisle, and said, 'Thanks, Pa.' It was a sign of love between father and son.

It had not all been plain sailing in the tense weeks leading up to the wedding. In fact the stress had, on occasions, got to both bride and groom, so much so that both Harry and Meghan had had regular appointments with the acupuncturist to the stars, the 'divertingly handsome' Ross Barr, in the lead-up to the wedding. Barr, whose treatments deal with anything from infertility to hair loss and relationship problems, has been regularly treating the couple since Meghan moved to London.

If the treatments were meant to have reduced stress, they failed to have a lasting impact on Harry, who in the build-up to the wedding was, according to an inside source, 'petulant and short-tempered' with members of staff. He insisted, on occasions, raising his voice: 'What Meghan wants, she gets.' At times sources close to the Queen said he was 'downright rude'. Once his tiresome behaviour reached the Queen's ears, she asked to see him privately and put him firmly in his place.

William has total respect for the Queen. When she talks, he listens. She is the one person, perhaps with the exception of his wife Catherine, who is able pull him in line with a quiet word. Indeed, it was she who made it clear to both him and his brother that their noble Heads Together mental-health campaign appeared too separate from the rest of the royal family and the traditional type of engagements expected of the family.

Given his seniority in the royal pecking order, William expects deference from his younger brother and the other royals. However, he does not always show his father the same level of courtesy he demands. William was, for example, happy enough for Harry to pursue his passion for the Invictus Games. The Games have been a major success and this still slightly peeves William. He makes sure his younger brother is aware he is No. 1 in the hierarchy of status. All the staff, even the palace switchboard, know William can be 'difficult' or 'a little grand'. He hates 'sucking up to' people and lobbying for the country. This was evidenced by his dislike of lobbying FIFA delegates for England's 2018 World Cup football bid. When it all fell by the wayside, William looked for others to blame for putting himself in that position.

Less than a month later, all eyes were on a slightly edgy Meghan, the newly ennobled Duchess of Sussex, as she walked a few paces behind the Queen for a series of engagements in the walled city of Chester in Cheshire, England, on the River Dee, close to the border with Wales. Without the reassuring presence of her husband, Harry, who had been constantly at her side on every public occasion up until this moment, this was quite a test. It involved unveiling the Mersey Gateway Bridge at Catalyst Science Discovery Centre in Widnes, Cheshire, and also opening Storyhouse Theatre together. They then had lunch in Chester's Town Hall with, of course, the Queen taking the leading role.

Meghan passed this nerve-shredding introduction into royal life with flying colours and the laughter and whispered asides between Queen and granddaughter-in-law were both spontaneous and entirely natural. Not even a mix-up over who should be first into the royal limousine spoiled the rapport between the two women. Some were surprised at the speed of this first joint engagement of the Queen and Meghan. The decision was taken because it was felt the Duchess of Sussex might need extra help to adjust to life inside the Royal Family.

What commentators were unaware of was that, behind the

smiles for the cameras, the two women had disagreed over the younger woman's choice of headgear. The Queen's aides had, on instruction, advised the duchess that the Queen would be wearing a green hat to match her green outfit (a nod to those who had died in the Grenfell Tower fire disaster a year earlier). The message from the Queen was effectively an advisory notice to Meghan that she would be expected to comply. The Queen, however, was a little baffled to learn that the duchess had decided she would not be wearing a hat.

'I don't think the duchess fully understood,' one senior figure close to the Queen said. 'This was not a request. They are for others to make, not the Queen.' In the end the duchess, showing the stubborn streak her father had claimed in one of his many newspaper rants that she had inherited from her mother, ran the gauntlet and went without a hat. After being dubbed 'inappropriately dressed' for having bare shoulders at the Queen's birthday parade a few days earlier, she stepped off the Royal Train looking demure in a cream-coloured, very much over-the-shoulder Givenchy sheath designed by the brand's British stylist and artistic director Clare Waight Keller. Clearly, she didn't want to be criticised again. Her stubborn streak and lack of deference, even respect, had been duly noted, particularly by the Queen's senior staff.

The Prince of Wales is a stickler for showing deference to the Queen and her office. His two sons aren't quite the same, however, at acquiescing to *him* and *his* office. In the build-up to the royal wedding and beyond Harry, had begun to show his father, who was, after all, bankrolling the entire event, much more respect. Charles, after all, did everything he could to ensure his youngest son had the wedding he wanted. To this day, however, Charles admits he often finds it difficult to gauge either of his sons' occasionally unpredictable moods. 'In that aspect of their nature, both princes are very much like their mother,' one close source confirmed. 'They both have quite extreme mood swings, just as Diana did,' said a former courtier. 'She could be your best friend one minute and the next your worst enemy.'

Inevitably, much of the source of any tension between father and sons came down to Diana and their perception of the way he treated her. Somewhat in the mix, too, is their confused relationship with Camilla. Charles, who detests direct confrontation, often did not quite know how to react when such refractory situations exploded before him.

The previous summer, twenty years on from Diana's death in that car crash in a Paris tunnel, relations between the prince and his sons may not have been glacial but they were certainly frosty. The prince had to remain tight-lipped as the ghost of his late wife came back, once again, to haunt him, as the world relived her tragic story – the story of his betrayal that, according to a Diana-obsessed press, resulted in her becoming the ultimate victim. He was never going to win this one, and he knew it.

Again, just as his acceptance ratings had been on the rise, the woman who infamously publicly questioned her husband's suitability to be king in her 1995 BBC *Panorama* interview with Martin Bashir was again uppermost in the nation's mind. Once again, from beyond the grave, footage of her resurfaced and showed her mocking the prince with yet another rapier thrust.

Back at the height of their marriage crisis on 20 November 1995, a huge 22.8 million people tuned in to watch Diana's jaw-dropping, heavily rehearsed performance. That programme damaged Charles's reputation so much that it led to serious calls from senior establishment figures for the crown to skip a generation to Prince William after the Queen's death. Diana's actions, they said, had been an affront to the monarchical institution and forced the Queen to decide 'enough is enough' and instruct her son to divorce. One ICM poll for *Prospect* magazine backed her decision.

Afterwards a bruised Charles confided that interest in his fractured marriage had wounded him: 'I feel so unsuited to the ghastly business of human intrigue and general nastiness. . .I don't know what will happen from now on but I dread it.'

Ultimately, Charles agreed with the Queen that there was nothing else left but divorce, but the prince was deeply concerned by what came next. 'God knows what the future will hold,' he had written in a private letter after the announcement of his separation from Diana on 11 December 1992. What came next, Diana's death in a tragic car accident in Paris on 31 August 1997, almost shattered Charles's chance of becoming king and rocked the institution of monarchy to its foundations.

Diana's death had led to a mass outpouring of national grief the like of which had never before been seen. There was an intense opprobrium towards Charles, Camilla and the Queen over their perceived coldness and aloof, haughty response. They were the villains, she the saintly victim. The facts didn't seem to matter.

I attended Diana's funeral as a journalist. Twenty years on, it was still fresh to me. A great calm fell over central London that morning, 6 September 1997, as millions took to the streets to pay their respects, lining the route along which the princess's coffin would be borne on a gun carriage, from Kensington Palace to the

Abbey. Roads closed. Everywhere her famous face peered out from the thousands of newspaper and magazine special editions being sold on the streets. It seemed the nation had come to a complete halt. More than two billion people sat and watched the sombre event. Bathed in warm sunshine, thousands upon thousands packed the funeral procession route as the muffled sound of the bells of Westminster Abbey tolled. That day the Prince of Wales, his two sons, the Duke of Edinburgh and Diana's brother, Earl Spencer, heads bowed, walked with the coffin.

Inside there were 1,900 invited guests within the spectacular Gothic interior of the Abbey. Then, as the bells of Big Ben tolled eleven, the procession reached the west door. Eight Welsh Guardsmen, bare-headed, their faces taut with strain, carried the quarter-ton coffin on their shoulders as they slow-marched the length of the nave and a hush fell over the Abbey. Prince Harry broke down when the coffin passed. As the tears flowed down his small face, his father pulled him closer and his brother William laid a comforting hand on his shoulder. As the 'Libera Me' pierced the air and our souls, I felt the emotion of that magnificent piece fill the Abbey, moving every one of the throng of mourners. Prince Charles looked as though he was being torn apart as the music played. Then he had to endure the rapier-thrust eulogy of Diana's brother Charles Spencer.

What I remember most as part of the congregation was the extraordinary sound that, like a distant shower of rain, swept into the Abbey, through the walls, rolling on and on to the alter. It was a wave of noise that eventually reached its crescendo. It took me a couple of seconds to realise that it was the sound of people clapping outside after hearing Spencer's address on loudspeakers. The earl had spoken the plain truth as he saw it, and the people respected him for his courage as well as for the tribute he had paid his sister. William and Harry joined in the applause; so too, generously, did Prince Charles. The Queen, the Duke of Edinburgh and the Queen Mother sat unmoved in stony-faced silence.

England's rose may be dead, I thought, as I walked back along the Victoria embankment towards my office at the *Daily Express*, but she had certainly made the world sit up and take notice while she was here. She was a magical person, a woman of great character, strength, humour, generosity and determination, but also one prone to deep depression. It is a truism to say that someone's death tends to make us view that person through rose-tinted glasses.

The twentieth anniversary of Diana's death exposed an unhealthy breach between father and sons. In Channel 4's anniversary offering, *Diana: In Her Own Words*, endless footage of the late princess conveyed how Charles had always treated their marriage as a sham, and reported that, when she went to see 'the top lady', she was told there was nothing to be done because her son and heir was 'hopeless'. Worse, in ITV's *Diana, Our Mother: Her Life and Legacy*, her sons William and Harry paid heartfelt tributes, but in doing so – whether consciously or not – they wrote their father out of the script.

When Prince William said that his mother gave him 'the right tools' for life, some heard a hint that his style of monarchy will perhaps be different from his father's and his grandmother's. Her sons also organised a rededication of their mother's grave this year. Instead of using the twentieth anniversary of her death on 31 August, they chose her birthday, 1 July. This date came during

Charles and Camilla's planned tour of Canada. The Archbishop of Canterbury was there, as was the then-three year old Prince George. But the Prince of Wales wasn't, and it seems likely his sons had planned it that way.

It is difficult to know whether the prince's reputation, so often damaged by Diana, will ever be rehabilitated enough for him to be as cherished a monarch as he would like to be. In some ways, however, Diana's untimely and tragic death was a liberation: it meant that Charles could marry Camilla and ensured too that the House of Windsor wasn't eclipsed by a superstar freewheeling in their world. She remains an ever-present threat, certainly as far as certain media organisations are concerned. If everything is going well, then the late princess isn't mentioned. If there is a blunder, Diana's name is cited to suggest how out of touch Charles is.

The bottom line is that Charles and Diana were not compatible, and their 'fairytale' marriage, unlike the marriages of his sons, was doomed from the start and the prince knew it. The couple shared that infamous and deeply awkward engagement interview when asked about love. 'I had a long time to think about it, because I knew the pressure was on both of us. And, um. . .it wasn't a difficult decision in the end. It was what was wanted,' Diana said, adding quickly, 'It's what I want.' Asked if they were in love, Charles followed up Diana's quick 'of course' with that infamous and damning line, 'Whatever "in love" means.' They were words that would be repeated on air, in books and in newspapers time and again and established the *parti pris* narrative of an uncaring older husband who wilfully wrecked the life of the pure young woman who was devoted to him.

On 29 July 1981, the world watched the wedding of the Prince of Wales and Lady Diana Spencer in awe. A 600,000-strong crowd packed the streets of London in the hope of catching a glimpse of the couple as they made their way to St Paul's Cathedral.

Around 750 million more people viewed it on television all over the world, making it then the most watched programme ever broadcast. Britons enjoyed a national holiday to mark the occasion and watched as Lady Diana, dressed in an ivory silk, taffeta and antique-lace gown designed by Elizabeth and David Emanuel, made the three-and-a-half-minute walk up the red-carpeted aisle, her twenty-five-foot train following behind her. Unlike his sons William and Harry, however, over their own marriages, Charles knew that his to Lady Diana was a mistake long before he made his wedding vows. It is something he deeply regrets to this day.

The fact that good people do wrong doesn't make them less good. Equally, however, it doesn't make the wrongs committed less wrong. Worse, perhaps, is when somebody knowingly makes a dreadful decision, a life-changing one, and doesn't have the strength to reverse that decision before it is too late. Very often that person has to live with it or the consequences of that moment of indecision for a lifetime. For Charles, his big 'wrong', or certainly that big 'wrong decision', was marrying a totally incompatible twenty-year-old woman when he knew in his heart it was not right. It led to deep unhappiness for him and Diana, to their both committing adultery and the pain that causes, and also both being forced to admit it publicly in excruciating television interviews.

The holier-than-thou brigade persist in lambasting the prince over his treatment of Diana and choose to ignore the obvious good in the man and his lifetime of service, his vision and his passion for the world and humanity. They're fixated on his apparent neglect of his young bride and his subsequent adultery (seemingly ignoring her adultery with at least three other men), which in their blinkered view marks him out as deeply flawed, some kind of pariah and unsuitable for kingship.

The prince has accepted there is no point in fighting against this bigoted and distorted portrayal of his character, particularly in the aftermath of Diana's death. For some, as far as he is concerned, the mud has stuck and no amount of hard work by the prince will remove the stains. The prince also knows that the failings of his first marriage and the tragic circumstances of Diana's death continue to severely dent his popularity. The truth is he has agonised over his mistake for years. He believes he let down not only the monarchy but himself and Diana, too, through his inability to call off the wedding.

What frustrates him to this day is that one version of history, Diana's version, is so ingrained in the popular psyche that it has gone down as 'historic fact' when, in his view, it is a tissue of lies peddled by a Machiavellian princess at the time to a sympathetic press. What's more, after years of soul searching, the prince, his circle say, wants what he has described as 'unbelievable and pernicious lies' reproduced in the tabloids corrected.

The truth is that Charles was deeply unsure of Diana's suitability as his wife at the time and after a few meetings believed they were totally incompatible. Long after Diana's death and after he had wed Camilla, his frustration over the matter boiled over into a sense of profound injustice over what he believes are 'lies' that are both deeply malevolent and harmful to his reputation.

He has candidly told his close circle of friends, 'I desperately wanted to get out of the wedding in 1981 when during the engagement I discovered just how awful the prospects were, having had no chance whatsoever to get to know Diana beforehand.' The prince was, of course, when referring to the 'awful' prospects, speaking of Diana's bulimia and her alarming and irrational mood swings and temper, which he found impossible to deal with.

He had started dating the beautiful Lady Diana Spencer, third daughter of Earl Spencer, by 1980, at a time when the pressure for him to marry was beginning to gain momentum. He soon realised just how ill-matched they were. In the middle of one conversation in the weeks leading up to the wedding, Charles was talking to Diana about his day and his work commitments, when she would stare back at him blankly. She seemed incapable of grasping any of the intellectual thread of what he was saying. Then she would, he recalled to friends, for no apparent reason, well up and burst into tears. A sympathetic man, Charles was at a total loss as to what to do. He did seek professional help. But as the media frenzy unfolded, despite his sense that there was something very wrong, he felt it was impossible for him to back out of the wedding.

'Things were very different in those days,' Charles explained [to close friends], 'the power and influence of the media driving matters towards an engagement and wedding were unstoppable.' Charles was right of course. The so-called 'Fourth Estate' was all powerful and the ruthless tabloids were driving the story at relentless speed. It was a fraught atmosphere for all the characters involved. Photographers and tabloid reporters were hounding Diana in a way that would be totally unacceptable today. Grown men would surround her car, thrusting their camera lenses towards this teenager like a swarm of locusts. They were completely out of control. Diana felt under siege and said so. This frenzied situation was becoming dangerous.

Diana was just nineteen years old when she first started dating the prince. She was chased by the media in their cars countless times and was frequently forced to race through traffic lights after they had turned red. She was risking her life. 'They chased me everywhere,' she said. 'We are talking thirty of them.' She never complained about the press to Charles – she didn't feel confident enough to – and she got zero practical support from Buckingham Palace. She was on her own. So she had no choice but to put her head down out of fright and smile her way through the ordeal.

The prince, of course, was well aware of the intrusive and unwelcome attention she was getting from the media and he did feel responsible. He felt it was his duty to do something to protect her, but he was powerless to do so. It didn't seem right to him that he had a team of armed Scotland Yard PPOs looking after him and she, a defenceless young woman, had nobody. He didn't need a letter from his father, the Duke of Edinburgh, to remind him of that. Inevitably, his curt missive came anyway. Philip wrote Charles a letter – because that is the 'regrettable' way they communicated, the author Sally Bedell Smith writes – telling him it was unfair to Diana's reputation to dawdle. Either propose or release her, he advised. 'It was measured and sensitive,' said Charles's cousin, Lady Pamela Hicks, who told Smith, author of *Prince Charles: The Passions and Paradoxes of an Improbable Life*, that she had read the letter. Some, including Bedell Smith, say Charles felt he was 'bullied into marriage'. That is not the case.

His parents were obviously keen for their son and heir to throne to marry and produce an heir himself, but to this day, despite forthright claims to the contrary, he absolutely does not blame his father or mother for the ill-conceived marriage with Diana and his inability to back out. He knew, however, once the press machine gathered momentum, that he had no way out. The prince explained to a close friend years later, 'To have withdrawn [from the marriage], as you can no doubt imagine, would have been cataclysmic. Hence I was permanently between the devil and the deep blue sea.'

For Charles and Diana, despite the glaring problem that they barely knew each other, the die was cast. A date was set for the marriage and nothing would be able to change it. Diana, too, we now know from her own lips and from Andrew Morton's brilliant *Diana: Her True Story*, was having second thoughts. She told her sisters just days before the wedding that she didn't think she could marry Charles because he was still carrying a torch for Camilla Parker Bowles. '. . .I went upstairs, had lunch with my sisters who were there and said, "I can't marry him, I can't do this, this is absolutely unbelievable." They were wonderful and said, "Well, bad luck, Duch [their nickname for her], your face is on the tea towels so you're too late to chicken out." So we made light of it.' She later also revealed that the couple had met just twelve times before she walked down the aisle. It would have been unthinkable today.

Diana also recalled on the Settelen tapes that she had felt sorry for him at Earl Mountbatten's funeral, which she said led to the clumsiest of sexual advances by Charles. 'I said "My heart bled for you as I watched,"' she said. 'I thought, "This is wrong you are lonely, you should be with somebody to look after you."' She went on, 'And the next minute he leapt on me, practically. It was strange. I thought, "This isn't very cool". . .but I had nothing to go by because I'd never had a boyfriend.'

Despite all their misgivings, Charles proposed to Lady Diana Spencer on 3 February 1981. 'It was like a call to duty, really,' Diana revealed in audio recordings used in the documentary *Diana: In Her Own Words*. 'He sat me down and said, "Will you marry me?" I thought the whole thing was hysterical, getting married. It was so grown up. And I laughed. I remember thinking, "This is a joke." And he was deadly serious,' Diana reflected afterwards.

In reality, neither Charles nor Diana was actually in love with the other, although both may well have been enamoured with the idea of being in love, he with a much younger, beautiful woman and she, as somebody who loved the romantic fiction of Barbara Cartland, being swept off her feet by a charming prince. The result was the last of the great arranged royal marriages in an epoch when such arrangements were doomed to failure and acrimony.

Charles obviously loves his sons – the result of this marital union – and there were periods in the marriage when they, like any couple, felt closer after the birth of a child. He respects, too, the profound love they share for their late mother and the way they have cherished her memory. But he is, according to an impeccable inside source, equally irritated by some of the 'unbelievable and pernicious lies' promulgated long ago by the media – 'aided and abetted by somebody rather close to me [Diana]' – who he believes, 'lived hand to mouth with the press'. He abhors such malevolence. Those close to him say he would like the stories spread about him by Diana and the media corrected because he feels they are in danger of wrongly becoming 'historical fact' and totally distorting what really happened.

One of the falsehoods disseminated by the princess is the 'news' that he and Diana had spent two nights together, one on board the Royal Train (which Diana and her family denied at the time). The Duke of Edinburgh was reportedly furious about this and is said to have sent his eldest son a strongly worded letter – although nobody other than the sender or recipient has ever seen it – warning Charles that his reputation as a gentleman and her honour would be under threat if he didn't propose to Lady Diana.

That tryst-on-the train story was a well-publicised and often-recited one that heaped pressure on Charles unfairly because the incident never actually happened. The timing of the *Sunday Mirror* story was certainly sensitive, as was the subject matter. The editor, Bob Edwards, insisted he had an impeccable source (as it turned out, one of the local policemen assigned to watch the train overnight in the sidings). The Queen's press secretary, Michael Shea, was robust in his response and made it clear the palace took 'grave exception' to the report. After making further checks, Edwards refused to print an apology and said he would print their correspondence, thus giving himself another splash story – under the banner headline 'PRINCE CHARLES AND LADY DIANA' – agreed by the palace.

Diana herself was deeply shocked and upset by the story. After all, she knew that she had not secretly visited the royal train. She was devastated, too, by the implication that her boyfriend had been two-timing her while she was tucked up in bed miles away. By December 1980, Diana's infuriated mother, Frances Shand Kydd, was growing tired of the slights against her daughter's good character and wrote an uninhibited letter to the editor of *The*

*Times* for publication, protesting in the strongest terms about the 'lies and harassment' that Diana had been forced to endure since the romance with Charles had been made public. 'She [her daughter] had denied with justifiable indignation, her reported presence on the Royal Train.'

It is an 'extraordinary' fabrication that has haunted Charles ever since it was first circulated. It irritates him to this day, quite possibly because it is the one story that, more than any other, set him on a course to the altar out of protecting his own and Lady Diana's honour, despite the fact that there was not a shred of truth in the story.

He explained to a close friend, 'The most extraordinary and pernicious of these is that first of all I secreted Diana on board the royal train on the eve of our wedding. This was endlessly denied at the time. The truth is the *Daily Mirror* [it was actually the *Sunday Mirror*] had mistaken a private secretary's blonde secretary for Diana. The press obstinately stuck to this story. Then, years later, they pushed the invention even further, claiming it was the Duchess of Cornwall [I had secreted aboard the royal train] after all.'

Charles reportedly 'wept' his heart out on the night before his 1981 wedding to Lady Diana Spencer as he felt torn between his feelings for former girlfriend Camilla and his new partner Diana. It is also claimed, once again totally falsely, that he smuggled his then married mistress into his suite of rooms at Buckingham Palace for a secret tryst on the same night, just hours before marrying Diana. Charles regards this as 'monstrous'.

He told a friend, 'One of the worst lies of all is that the duchess was smuggled into Buckingham Palace the night before our wedding in 1981. The idea that this could even have happened and that I could have done any such thing is beyond belief, and yet this monstrous nonsense has persisted.' He went on, 'There are doubtless endless other lies and inventions that I have no idea about including – may I add? – the duchess being with me in Switzerland while I was skiing. I dare say there is nothing that can be done about all of this.'

Even the BBC compounded a myth involving the duchess that riles the prince even now. In 2001 it wrote, 'But, for the woman who has in the past suffered such indignities as being labelled the "Rottweiler" and having bread rolls thrown at her by Diana fans, to have come this far down the Highgrove path without facing further hostility must in itself count as a significant achievement.' The *Daily Telegraph*, too, in 2007 wrote, 'Her unpopularity was such that an irate shopper was reported to have thrown a bread roll at her in a supermarket in Wiltshire.'

Charles went on, to friends, 'Another persistent lie is that the duchess had bread rolls thrown at her by angry shoppers in a store in Chippenham. This was in fact a totally fabricated media exercise stunt which involved actresses throwing bread rolls at one another. A lookalike actress was employed and placed in the store in Chippenham.'

Many will still cling to what they have been told. I have no doubt that the prince is sincere in what he has told his close circle and that the truth has come to light now.

## Chapter Eight

# FATHER AND SONS

———∽———

'It is your selfless drive to effect change, whether that is to improve the lives of those who are on the wrong path, to save an important piece of our national heritage or to protect a particular species under threat, which William and I draw inspiration from every day.'

PRINCE HARRY, DUKE OF SUSSEX, IN A SPEECH AT A BUCKINGHAM PALACE GARDEN PARTY IN HONOUR OF THE PRINCE OF WALES'S SEVENTIETH BIRTHDAY

The whirs and clicks of the photographers' cameras went into overdrive as the royal party, led by the Prince of Wales, stepped onto the back steps of Buckingham Palace. But he knew they weren't really trained on him. The four royals – Charles, Camilla, Harry and Meghan – stood underneath a specially erected awning with the words 'THE PRINCE OF WALES'S 70TH BIRTHDAY PATRONAGE CELEBRATION', topped off with his heraldic badge of three white ostrich feathers emerging from a

159

gold coronet. A ribbon below the coronet bore the motto *Ich Dien* – 'I Serve'.

After the last blast of 'God Save the Queen', all four duly descended the steps and began working the crowd, meeting a number of the 6,000 people who were invited from 386 of Charles patronages and 20 of his military associations. A number of guests from the police, fire and ambulance services, mountain rescue and the RNLI also attended.

Inevitably, though, the photographers' lenses focused on the newly ennobled royal, the Duchess of Sussex, immaculate in a silk-crepe pencil dress from the British brand Goat and a Philip Treacy dome hat, as this was her first official engagement since marrying Prince Harry.

Harry, the newly created Duke of Sussex, then marked the occasion with a speech of self-deprecation and rare warmth towards his father. 'Pa,' he said, using the term of endearment again, 'while I know that you've asked that today not be about you, you must forgive me if I don't listen to you. Much like when I was younger. Instead, I ask everyone here to say a huge thank-you to you, for your incredible work over nearly fifty years.'

He praised Charles's 'selfless drive to effect change' in a heartfelt speech. 'We are here today to reflect on and to celebrate my father's dedicated support to all of you and the work that you do.'

He went on, 'As I was preparing for this afternoon, I looked through the long list of those who had been invited. Pa, I was again struck by the range and diversity of the work which you are involved with. It is your selfless drive to effect change, whether that is to improve the lives of those who are on the wrong path, to save an important piece of our national heritage or to protect a particular species under threat, which William and I draw inspiration from every day.'

Occasionally, however, the level of belligerence has shocked the prince, as both boys have, on occasion, challenged him. William has even been known to speak firmly in his father's face. It is reminiscent of his mother's hot temper, which Charles had to deal with on a frequent basis during their marriage.

In private, William sometimes defies his calm, family-guy demeanour. It is this chameleon-like characteristic that makes his father go, on occasion, on to the *qui vive* when dealing with him. 'William has quite a temper, and can fly off the handle at the slightest thing. He demands deference from those ranked below him, but in truth when looking upwards he rarely gives it,' said one former member of the Royal Household. 'The prince is wary of his mood swings,' the source said. 'We all were.'

The grandfather of three is particularly conscious of avoiding confrontation with his eldest son when it comes to his dealing with Prince George, Princess Charlotte and newborn Prince Louis, whom he adores. After newspaper talk that he felt edged out by the Middletons, the Duchess of Cambridge's parents, Michael and Carole, over the time he spent with them, matters improved. He has revealed that he now shares precious moments with his grandson, Prince George, messing around in the garden. 'The most important thing is I got him planting a tree or two,' he said.

For a time there was some friction between father and son, particularly when William felt his father was 'using' his popular son in what could be perceived as PR opportunities. During a media day, the prince's PR team revealed how a 'doting' Prince Charles had turned his garden at Highgrove into what was described as a 'toddler's paradise'. It was reported in 2015 that the heir to the throne, whose gardens at his private Gloucestershire home are his life's work, had recently refurbished the tree house once played in by Prince George's father, Prince William, and uncle, Prince Harry, for the little prince to inherit. To cap that he has also installed a £20,000 hand-made artisan shepherd's hut, complete with a little bed, wood-burner and French oak wooden floors, in his wildflower meadow for George, then two, to enjoy. William was furious at his father that the revelations had been planted in the tabloids.

William is also easily irritated if photographs of his children appear in the background of official photographs of his father without being cleared by him first. 'He can be a bit of a control freak when it comes to things like that,' one former member of the household said. So it was a little surprising that, for his seventieth-birthday exhibition at the palace – entitled Prince & Patron, for which the prince loaned out his favourite artwork, trinkets, and family photos to help present a glimpse of his home life – among them was a never-before-seen photograph of him cradling his firstborn grandson, George, with his elder son, the Duke of Cambridge, by his side.

The three future kings, rarely captured together in a photograph released to the public, look relaxed, with the then baby George fast asleep in his grandfather's arms. Charles and William both have open-necked shirts, in a casual family photograph likely taken at Clarence House or Kensington Palace in 2013. George is pictured leaning into the prince's elbow, as the duke, who would have been settling into life as a new father, sits protectively behind them both.

It was the first time such a candid family photograph of the three heirs together had been shown to the public and obviously would have had to be cleared by the censor – William – in order to be allowed to be shown. 'Ha, perhaps William is mellowing. The Prince of Wales would have to have got sign-off on that before allowing it in the exhibition,' an inside source told me.

Another senior figure said of William, 'All this Mr Nice guy to media is an act, a public face. He can be vindictive. He does not have the intellectual capability or the patience of his father.' That in itself can make William short-tempered when dealing with Charles. 'He lacks his father's charm too,' said another. Another well-placed source remarked, 'The Boss has a temper, too, but it does not go on and on. He flares up and then it is forgotten about. With the Duke of Cambridge it is rarely forgotten.' He will never say resolving a situation, such as posing for a family portrait for his father's seventieth birthday, is easy. His default position is always, 'It's difficult. . .'

William is extremely competitive, too, even when it comes to media coverage, although he gives the impression it does not concern him. In reality it does. As Meghan and Harry again hogged the headlines while appearing in Cardiff on 18 January 2018, he had an engagement, too, and chose to debut his new and dramatic buzz cut as he cheered up patients at a London hospital that afternoon, knowing the papers would feature him, too.

In truth, fathers and sons rarely see eye to eye when the children have become young men. By the time one is old enough to realise that maybe his father is right, the son usually has children of his own, who think he is wrong too. The Royal Family are no different. The Prince of Wales, as a single father, has done his best to avoid confrontation with his boys during their development. But he and William did clash over the son's comment about destroying the palace's priceless ivory collection. Charles told William he was being 'naïve' during a 'frank exchange of views' five years ago according to an informed source. He rebuked William for telling zoologist and chimpanzee expert Dr Jane Goodall he would 'like to see all the ivory owned by Buckingham Palace destroyed'. William was left in no doubt after the conversation with his father that he should have chosen his words more carefully.

Charles, while appreciating his son's sentiment, believes there is a vast difference between calling for action against illegal traders now and ordering Buckingham Palace to rid itself of an enormously important and historical collection of artefacts that form part of the Royal Collection Trust. Items include an Indian throne and footstool (1840–50), carved from ivory and the centrepiece of the Indian section in the Great Exhibition of 1851, and a pair of late-eighteenth-century, seven-storey ivory pagodas acquired by George IV. The idea of such historic items, and others such as Henry VIII's quill pen, being broken up filled Charles with dread. That said, there are many who know William and his stubborn streak, and believe he will take some form of action when he is king, despite his father's heartfelt protestations.

Harry, while prone to volatility, too, is a much warmer man, far more prone to emotional outbursts, but perhaps not as calculating as his older brother. Charles, by giving them so much freedom and independence he himself was not afforded as a young man, has in effect allowed them to develop their own ideas and interests, but also that streak of defiance. 'HRH has changed things unbelievably for his sons and to their advantage,' one former courtier said. 'A decade or so ago, before he married the duchess, the prince gave them their own court that he personally funds. He did this in spite of the fact that for his own staff it proved more difficult because they, effectively, lost control of the boys. But the Boss wanted his sons to have their own staff so that they would not be puppets run and controlled by his office, the mother ship, if you like,' the informed source said.

It was no surprise, then, that it was Harry, not his older brother William – who was on official duties with the Prime Minister marking the anniversary of the Manchester Arena terror bombings – who was on hand to speak up for his father on his big day. His delivery of his heartwarming speech about his father to mark Charles's seventieth birthday (albeit six months early) at a special garden party was both funny and sincere. Those gathered at Buckingham Palace that day to celebrate the work of the prince's charities and military associations three days after the royal wedding hung on his every word before loudly cheering the older prince for his lifetime of public service. That said, William subsequently approached Charles's top aide, Clive Alderton, and made it clear that he would like to do more joint engagements with his father in his seventieth-birthday year, otherwise, he felt, he would be unfavourably compared to his younger brother and not be seen to be supportive of his father.

More than four hundred charities and organisations that Charles supports were represented at the palace event. In his speech to his father, Prince Harry also said, 'Currently there are your two major charities, the Prince's Trust and the newly formed Prince's Foundation, which has brought together your work supporting vulnerable young people in society, the environment, culture, heritage and education.'

He went on, 'These sit alongside your eighteen military associations and more than four hundred and twenty patronages, ranging from music and the arts to rare breeds and plant life. Although the subjects vary enormously, I know that the way in which you work with each of them does not,' Harry said. 'His [Charles's] enthusiasm and energy are truly infectious; it has certainly inspired William and I to get involved in issues we care passionately about and to do whatever we can to make a difference.'

He added, 'In fact, many of the issues William and I now work on are subjects we were introduced to by our father growing up. His passion and dedication are remarkable and, seeing so many of you here today, I cannot fail but to be in awe of the drive he has had for so many years to contribute to the enrichment of society both in this country and around the world.'

Behind Harry, Meghan carried herself perfectly. She shared a joke with a humble Prince Charles and Camilla about a bumblebee that attacked Harry at the podium. Indeed, many believe Harry's newfound warmth towards his father is due to the Prince's new bride. William, too, has been known to be far from deferential towards Charles. More than that, it is her newfound relationship with Charles that is proving to be key. 'When Meghan met the Prince of Wales she was bowled over by his gentlemanly charm,' said an inside source. 'She told Prince Harry he was wonderful; welcoming, warm, hardworking, kind and stable. She made it clear that he should appreciate him and bond more.' It led to a softening of relations between the prince and his second son. He now had somebody other than his older brother to discuss family matters with and Meghan's opinion really mattered to Harry.

In turn, Charles, charmed by the beautiful actress, has been completely taken with her, telling friends, 'She is so intelligent and so nice. She makes Harry happy. We could not like her more.' Harry was delighted. She has made a few slipups, however. When the prince invited the Duchess of Sussex to join him and Camilla on a private tour of his Prince & Patron exhibition in the state rooms of Buckingham Palace to mark his seventieth-birthday year, she enthusiastically accepted. She was keen to see a special display of more than a hundred works of art personally selected by the prince. But, when her advisers were told they would be joined by John Bridcut and his documentary crew, she belatedly pulled out. Cancelling on the prince after one has accepted is not the done thing.

Meghan, meanwhile, has actively charmed her new father-in-law. She consulted Charles about the music for the wedding, while the prince has taken time to discuss the complexities of life in the 'Firm'. It helps that Meghan is fascinated by British history, and royal history in particular, more so than her husband, who is not a star pupil when it comes to history, and sources say she is poring over lever-arch files of notes as she studies the Commonwealth. She always turns to the prince for help if she is confused and he takes time to explain the complexities.

Charles sees his work ethic and his passion for philanthropy reflected in his new daughter-in-law, who has campaigned to raise awareness of women's issues. It will not have escaped his notice that she shares his belief in organic food. Camilla, too, has played her part as a sort of 'super-granny' dispensing humorous, down-to-earth advice to Meghan. It is understood that the two 'outsiders' have become close in a short space of time and they were seen clasping hands as they greeted one another at the palace.

And the result of Meghan's magic is a resumption of a much closer relationship between Harry and Charles. There has certainly been plenty to work on for the newly ennobled Duchess of Sussex. It is hardly a secret that William and Harry endured a difficult adolescence after the death of their mother Diana in 1997, when they were just fifteen and twelve respectively. Their father, whom they blame for being absent during much of their childhood, has often been the target of their unhappiness. In the days before his work as a full-time royal, William notably preferred to focus on his young family rather than spend time with his father in the West Country or London. Since then, there has been a *froideur* between William's court and that of Charles.

The Queen, too, has been taking a keen interest in the Duchess of Sussex, thanks not least to their shared love of dogs. The day before the wedding, the Queen, who weeks earlier had lost her last corgi, appeared to share a car with Meghan's beagle, a rescue dog called Guy. Harry declared that even the Queen's corgis loved Meghan when she took tea with the sovereign. During his engagement interview, Harry said that when Meghan Markle had tea with Queen Elizabeth the corgis took to her right away, even going so far as to lie on her feet. It raised a few insiders' eyebrows. 'It was very sweet,' said one. 'Harry didn't quite share his fiancée's enthusiasm.' The insider added, 'For the last thirty-three years, I've been barked at. This one walks in, and absolutely nothing. . .just wagging tails.' The reality is that the Queen hates anyone trying to pet her dogs. They respond to her and only her. Visitors who try to get into her good books by patting the dogs are sharply told, 'Don't do that, they don't like it.' The insider said, 'What she really means is she doesn't like it.'

More significant still is that the transfer of the Queen's trusted aide, Samantha Cohen, from Buckingham Palace to Kensington Palace is seen as a sensible way of trying to maintain order. Samantha, a no-nonsense, straight-talking, middle-aged Australian, has considerable diplomatic expertise after seventeen years with the Royal Family, and will help guide the young couple in their new Commonwealth roles.

The William and Harry courts have until now been dominated by military aides and mentors such as former SAS troop commander Major Jamie Lowther-Pinkerton and former Household Cavalry Captain Ed Lane Fox. Even Miguel Head, William's long-serving private secretary and before that press secretary, was recruited from the Ministry of Defence. His replacement shows a different type of courtier and shows William, perhaps with the Queen's advice too, planning for his future roles as the next Prince of Wales and then king. For his new top aide, Simon Case, doesn't have a military pedigree but instead is a well-respected civil servant working in the Department for Exiting the European Union (Brexit). His job there was Director General for Northern Ireland and Ireland, which means he has been responsible for one of the most difficult areas of the Brexit negotiations. Prior to that, he held a number of senior positions within the civil service, including serving as principal private secretary to the Prime Minister.

It is clear that the Queen sees the younger royals as having the star quality to take the 'Firm' forward and safeguard its future in a changing world. The spiritual, yoga-loving HRH the Duchess of Sussex, the first American to get that royal prefix to her title, is in no small way part of that. The Duchess of Cornwall, standing alongside Meghan, beamed with pride at the garden party in her husband's honour. Charles, who doesn't take praise well, looked a little awkward as Harry heaped admiration on him. Eventually, when his son had finished, he raised his arm and waved his black top hat in the air in acknowledgement, and at the same time acknowledged the part played by those gathered before him.

On the immaculate lawn, an eclectic mix of people mingled, young and old, all with different stories on how the prince had changed their lives. As they tucked into the neatly cut sandwiches, iced coffee, juices and teacakes, they were in buoyant mood. Many were happy to chat, everyday people, whose lives had been touched in some way by the generosity and enterprises of the prince. David Bellamy from the British Red Cross was a first responder at Grenfell Tower fire in west London in June 2017 and at the Manchester Arena terror atrocity that happened a month earlier. 'Grenfell was heartrending' he said. 'When you turn up and witness, it is mind-numbing. Obviously, you click into gear to support people but afterwards you have to remember to support yourself.'

Speaking about the prince, who is president of the British Red Cross Society, Mr Bellamy said 'He is a great example, a very enthusiastic person to have as a figurehead for any charitable organisation, inspirational to ourselves and in his leadership of our charity.' Tom Rebair, from Newcastle, who won the Prince's Trust

Young Ambassador of the Year Award, said, 'The Trust has done a lot for me. Coming to events such as this is just phenomenal. I had a breakdown when I was fourteen. I blamed myself for being bullied at school and felt worthless. So I self-harmed and attempted suicide. I then developed OCD [obsessive-compulsive disorder] and later developed anorexia. I ended up in hospital twice; at one point my heartbeat had dropped to eighteen beats per minute. My body was shutting down.'

He went on, 'Life is hard enough, but add stigma into the mix and it can feel unbearable. I became a Young Ambassador because I wanted to spread the word about the Trust's work and help break down the stigma surrounding eating disorders, particularly in young men like me.' He said being a Young Ambassador had made him a more complete person: confident, employed and 'proud of what I have achieved'. 'I now promote getting mental-health issues for men out in the open. I have had an eating disorder, which in men is not something that is very well spoken about,' he said. 'I met the prince. He's a brilliant and inspirational man.'

Sporting bright pink hair, social worker Lois, another young ambassador for the Prince's Trust, aged twenty-two at the time, said, 'I was on the programme four years ago and now I am a Young Ambassador. My key role is to do a lot of speeches hoping to inspire others and combine that with my social work. He has never treated the Prince's Trust as a project: he is treating it as his passion to actually make an impact on young people's lives.'

The prince felt the approach of his seventieth birthday provided a sensible opportunity to review his charities to ensure that they continued to deliver the maximum benefit for those people they were set up to help. Although his office denied the change, announced in March 2018, was anything to do with his preparations to be king, it was of course part of the reason for the decision. The seamless transition of the throne has meant that Charles needed to appear in public more frequently during 2017 and 2018 in support of his mother. As a direct consequence, it meant some of his foundation's major beneficiaries saw an inevitable decline in monetary support from Charles.

The Queen has been slowly scaling back her duties over the past few years, and has cut the number of official events she attends by 11 per cent, down from 332 to 296. Inevitably, as Charles's official outings in her place were stepped up, his charitable donations decreased, with the total grants handed out to good causes backed by the heir to the throne having more than halved in a year, from £7.7 million in March 2016 to £3.1 million in the twelve months to March 2017. There is nothing sinister in that. It is a consequence of his change in status and direction. Business in the Community had a cut in funding from £1.6 million in 2016 to £545,000, according to Companies House. And the Royal Drawing School's grant also took a cut, dropping from £439,000 to £93,000.

The prince turned to his most trusted aide to implement the changes to his charity empire. This was Michael Fawcett, nicknamed 'Fawcett the Fence' by the media, who have painted the prince's powerful former valet as a pantomime villain after he was accused in the Peat Report of selling official gifts. Fawcett, who resigned twice from Charles's employment and was once paid a £500,000 severance package, has bounced back each time, and was appointed chief executive of the newly created Prince's Foundation.

A controversial figure at court of whom the prince once said, 'I can manage without just about anyone except Michael' had been chief executive of Dumfries House, the country house in Ayrshire that, since being bought by a consortium headed by the prince in 2007, has been turned into a hub for the local community. The Foundation is now responsible for the work of four current charities: the Prince's Regeneration Trust, the Prince's Foundation for Building Communities, the Prince's School of Traditional Arts and the Dumfries House Trust.

Streamlining twenty-one various charities and trusts into four areas enabled the prince to cut running costs by close to £1 million. It was essential, he felt, if they were to be sustained going forward. The party at the palace was as much a celebration of those who had worked so hard for his causes as it was for him. Charles stressed he was not 'stepping back from my charitable work or downsizing in any way'. He said, 'Now, as I approach something of a milestone in my own life [seventieth birthday] I have had a chance to reflect on how best to ensure my charities can continue to help those people and causes they were initially set up to serve, both now and for many years to come.' An independent review, he said, was appointed to examine what changes were needed to let his organisations work 'as efficiently as possible', while also allowing him 'to use my own time with them to greatest effect'.

The seventieth-birthday party for Charles at the palace came, as we've seen, six months ahead of his real birthday in November. Prince Harry, in a nod to the fact that his grandmother, as monarch, celebrated two birthdays a year, a real one and an official one, drew a loud laugh when he joked, 'How very royal!'

## Chapter Nine

# THE CAMILLA QUESTION

—~—

'If you are a positive person, you can do so much more.
People are either glass half empty or glass half full. You just
have to get on with it, being British!'

HRH THE DUCHESS OF CORNWALL

The well-preserved fourteenth-century stone-presses in the
fields around the sun-soaked winery confirmed the area's
long history of grape-growing and winemaking. Bathed in
sunshine and embraced by the stunning Lassithi mountains, the
Duchess of Cornwall, in a flowing, loose-fitting outfit selected by
her long-term loyal dresser Jackie Meakin, stepped out of her car
onto a dusty road in the idyllic setting of the commune of Alagni,
south of the city of Heraklion.

Standing in a long line, it seemed the entire Lyrarakis family,
old and young, had turned out to greet the dignitary who had
come all the way from England to visit them in Crete and shine a
light on their winery and their work. Domaine Lyrarakis, a small

family-run winery that exports its wine to many foreign markets, including the UK, was established in 1966.

She may not have known a lot about Cretan wine, but actually Camilla is something of a vino expert. It is in the blood. Her grandfather, Philip Morton Shand (known as P. Morton Shand) was an acclaimed English journalist, architecture critic and wine-and-food writer and her father, Major Bruce Shand (MC and Bar), also worked in the wine industry after doing military service. With a friend, he first took over Block, Grey and Block in South Audley Street, a firm of old-fashioned wine merchants that supplied Oxford and Cambridge colleges. The firm eventually ran into difficulties, and he joined Ellis, Son and Vidler, of Hastings and London, with which he remained until his retirement. So his daughter knows a thing or two about wine.

On this beautiful May Day, Camilla worked the line, watched at a relaxed distance by her ever-present PPO, Inspector Mark Andrews. She has become something of an expert in small talk. Direct and warm, she thrusts out her hand and with her rich and mellow voice she says, 'Hello,' always looking the person she is greeting directly in the eye. At five foot eight, she is not an imposing woman, but she carries herself well. Thanks to her blonde locks, immaculately coiffured, beautiful blue eyes and winning smile, people warm to her natural, no-nonsense approach.

She was then given a brief tour before being ushered inside the cool, atmospheric wine cellar surrounded by wooden barrels. The duchess sat down ahead of being served a selection of premium and the rarest Cretan wine, along with cheese and other delicacies.

'Rob, won't you join me in the wine-tasting?' the duchess asked me with a warm smile. I didn't need to be asked twice and happily joined in. They first served white, which, despite its pedigree, was a little sharp for my taste, but the Mandilari rosé of 2015 certainly hit the spot. The extensive portfolio consists of a range of monovarietal wines – Vidiano, Plyto, Mandilari, Assyrtiko, Vilana, Thrapsathiri, Kotsifali – some from single, 'premium' vineyard plots, as well as blends of indigenous with international varieties: Syrah, Cabernet, Merlot. All top-quality. The fruit precision, purity and supple texture was top-drawer, as was the final glass of red and local cheese.

It was a welcome break from covering the prince, whose relentless schedule without a break in the searing heat can take its toll on everyone except, it seems, the prince himself. When planning the schedule, the prince and duchess's private office takes the stamina of the principals into consideration. The duchess often has a break, for food or simply a change of clothes, in her schedule, whereas the prince goes from one engagement to the next unabated.

He had clearly been excited by the prospect of this official visit to Greece. His senior communications officer, Constantine Innemee, a Greek national, had taken the lead on arranging the media opportunities on the visit. To the less adventurous linguist it may have seemed all Greek, but, given his father's Greek origins, Charles made sure his pronunciation of the language was correct too, occasionally checking with his press man whether he had got it right, before making a speech.

In his keynote address of such a tour, Charles is never one to shirk a challenge – especially when Greek is in his 'blood'. At the president's dinner at the presidential mansion in Athens on 9 May 2018, Charles tackled his father's native tongue and was greeted with rapturous applause for his efforts. In Greek, which he had been practising ahead of the trip to Athens and Crete, Charles said, 'We want to thank you for your warm welcome and heartfelt hospitality.' He went on, 'Our countries lie at opposite ends of the continent that we share. Our languages resemble each other only a little; our climates, I need hardly say, even less so! Yet there is, and has long been, an essential bond between us and between our people.

'In Britain, as across the Western World, the profound influence of Greece has, since ancient times, shaped the way we think, the way we build, the way we learn and the way we govern.' Quoting poet Percy Bysshe Shelley, he went on, 'We are all Greeks. Our laws, our literature, our religion, our arts have their root in Greece.' And, speaking of his family ties, he added, 'For my part, my own connections to Greece have particular meaning – after all, it is the land of my grandfather.'

He said, 'We are both, of course, seafaring peoples; nations which have long looked beyond our borders for opportunity and discovery. We are both *exostrefis* [outward-facing] – facing outward, not inward; looking to the world around us not just for strength and prosperity, but to understand our place within it. We share a spirit of openness with which, through history, we have welcomed new ideas and new people.' Time and again the 'tides of history' had brought us together, he said. He said both countries stood for 'freedom, democracy and tolerance'.

He continued, 'In the Second World War, Greece bravely endured such terrible suffering and privation, as so many of your own parents and grandparents will have known at first hand. My own grandmother, Princess Alice, remained in Athens during those dark years and did whatever she could to help some of those most in need.' It was typical of the personal and political the prince always cleverly manages to weave into such important addresses. He concluded, 'I thank you once again for your heartfelt and warm reception to your country, which is always so hospitable. I raise my glass to everyone's health, and to the welfare and friendship of our two peoples. Long live Greece! Long live the United Kingdom!' he said with gusto.

A few days later, now on a solo mission, Camilla, happy in the cool of the wine cellar, raised her glass and toasted the Greeks and the Cretans, saying, 'I never had Greek wine before, but it is delicious. I will certainly have it again.' The small group raised their glasses, too. Her role is not always front-of-house like that of Charles, but, in her own quiet way, she is just as effective.

Afterwards, outside, she happily posed for photographs, relaxed and amiable. Indeed, the wine stood her in good stead, for in half an hour she would be linking arms and performing traditional Greek dancing with her husband and villagers after touring crafts and produce stalls in Archanes. It was a perfect end to what had been another hectic two-country tour of France and Greece.

On board the RAF Voyager, the duchess came to the back of the plane to chat to the handful of media, including me, who were left on the trip, some having returned home early from France ahead of the royal wedding. She smiled as she handed me a box of chocolates, one of the many presents she had been given.

'You might like to share these around,' she said. It was typical of a thoughtfulness that has made her a favourite with the travelling press. It seems strange that people still judge her so harshly. Yes, she was at the centre of the break-up of Charles and Diana's marriage, but people don't seem to appreciate that the marriage was so dysfunctional it would have ended anyway. They seem, too, to ignore Diana's own adulterous affairs and focus only on Charles and Camilla, believing the perverse narrative that Diana alone was the wronged party in that situation.

Camilla seemed relieved to have completed another royal tour and supported her husband on his travels, which is no mean feat. She came to this job late in life and, make no mistake, their tours are gruelling affairs for all involved: hundreds of engagements need to be carried out, thousands of people met, all the time your own duty in front of the press being judged by the way you look and perform. The duchess is also a nervous flyer and finds long-haul visits particularly testing. When flying with the military all the announcements made by the cabin crew are not played in the section of the plane she is in with the prince. It apparently adds to her anxiety.

The duchess has, after all, come to all this VIP international diplomacy late in life. The prince is different. Military-trained, he had been doing it all his life. He is like a machine. He never eats lunch whilst carrying out royal engagements, partly so he can pack as much into the day as possible. He starts his day with a bowl of seed with a tiny amount of yoghurt to mix in. If anyone is asked for a breakfast meeting they are reminded, politely, not to order any. He may stop for a slice of fruit cake or a crumpet, just the one, and tea. Dinner, however, he never misses, and eats and drinks well, often with a strong mixed martini or two beforehand.

Charles will also have had enough water to keep him hydrated during the day, but not so much that he will need frequent loo stops. Years of experience have taught him exactly how to hydrate his body to just the right degree. Some of his staff, who do not necessarily share his lunch-less habits, carry their own food to keep them going during the day or, now wise to this, make sure they eat a big breakfast and snack on the road when the opportunity arises, such as on a visit to a vineyard or market stalls. That said, his staff and those who work in his slipstream say he is very generous. 'He always remembers Napoleon Bonaparte's old saying that an army marches on its stomach,' said one former member of his kitchen staff. 'To be effective, an army relies on good and plentiful food. He would always make sure his staff were well fed and watered, even if he stuck to a pretty rigid diet.'

Camilla is a dedicated and dutiful wife and travel companion for the prince. She has no desire to be the star of these well-planned roadshows. She is the support act as he delivers his powerful addresses and soft-power diplomacy. He is more relaxed when she is around and those lengthy state dinners must seem less tiresome with his wife at his side. They share a similar sense of humour; it connects them. She will also actively do her best to make a photo opportunity work for the travelling photographers, who are all supremely loyal to her for it.

She has the knack of reading media situations well, particularly photo opportunities such as in Australia on the Gold Coast beach as the couple visited the Commonwealth Games in April 2018. 'Don't go in, darling,' warned Charles in vain as the duchess slipped off her shoes, showing off her rose-pink-painted toenails, and dipped her toes into the gently lapping waves at Broadbeach. Camilla instructed her assistant to hold her wedge shoes as she enjoyed her time in the waves. She knew it would make a good newspaper photograph and a headline, even a small one, and it did.

Just ahead of the long-haul visit to Australia, which the duchess had originally decided not to attend, the issue was fudged. Ahead of the important Commonwealth summit, which would see the heads of government grant the Queen's wish that Charles would be the organisation's next head, it just looked wrong. Eventually, after her husband arranged for them to arrive privately and enjoy a few days of downtime, they stayed privately with Sir Michael Hintze at Deltroit Station near Tumblong, New South Wales, ahead of the official tour of Australia.

Charles, a proud supporter of the Commonwealth for decades, is dedicated to maintaining the Royal Family's strong connections with the organisation through official visits, military links and charitable activities. It was his sixteenth visit to the realm of Australia and he has (so far, at the time of writing) visited forty-four of fifty-three Commonwealth countries, many of them on several occasions.

The image of the future King of Australia being welcomed by Queensland Governor Paul de Jersey and Queensland Premier Annastacia Palaszczuk with the same level of ceremony as if it were the monarch herself – including a twenty-one-gun salute and an inspection of the Royal Guard of Honour from the Australian Army, Royal Australian Navy and Royal Australian Air Force – was important and not lost on Charles and his aides. Her aides persuaded Camilla of the importance of her going and, at a pre-tour press conference, her private secretary Amanda McManus said the duchess would just have to 'get on with it'.

It didn't start well for the duchess. Perhaps the local media wanted to make mischief about the leak that she hadn't been that keen to go. The Commonwealth Games' opening ceremony at the Carrara Stadium featured spectacular celebrations of the laid-back beach lifestyle and Australian indigenous culture. Prince Charles officially opened the games on behalf of his mother following the celebrations, reading her message to the enthusiastic crowds, and the Parade of Nations drew thunderous applause, particularly when Australia emerged onto the track. But onlookers took to social media unfairly to criticise the duchess for looking 'bored' and 'miserable' and 'uninterested' as she watched on from the VIP box.

Everywhere the couple went, however, they got a warm reception and, although a largely antimonarchy press tried to stir up trouble about her leaving early ahead of her husband, it didn't detract from what had been one of Charles's best-received visits in years. The crowds on this visit – which took him from Brisbane and the Gold Coast onto the Great Barrier Reef and up north to Cairns, Gove and Darwin, the farthest north he had been in Australia as well as the Pacific islands of Vanuatu – were enthusiastic, very large and welcoming. Camilla, too, proved popular for the short time she was there. The media later seemed to warm to her and liked her attitude, as they did when Charles, for once, took off his tie to watch the Commonwealth Games basketball in Cairns.

Before Charles set foot in Australia, former prime minister Paul Keating ambushed the visit by telling the press that the prince 'would be happy' if the country became a republic. Keating, an old political campaigner with his own agenda, was of course twisting the facts to suit his own agenda. It was hardly likely the constitutional heir to the throne would say anything unconstitutional. Charles's position on the matter, like that of the Queen, has always been consistent. The palace line has always been that it will be for the Australian people to decide, as both Charles and the Queen have made clear in public speeches.

The prince has always been passionate about Australia and its people. Before leaving he declared, 'I love Australia and Australians and I love coming here. I was really touched by the welcome from the crowds both here and in Vanuatu.' The prospect of his taking over as monarch delivered only a minor boost for the republican movement. If Charles ascends to the throne, 55 per cent of Australians said they would support a republic. A hard-core 35 per cent would want him as king with 10 per cent uncommitted. He used the visit to strengthen his charitable associations, donating thousands of pounds of his own cash to buy several defibrillators for use by the Royal Flying Doctor Service. He is patron of an association in the UK that raises cash for this vital service.

He cares deeply about the indigenous people, too, and their traditions and customs. He believes allowing them to die out – and along with them their profound knowledge learned over many centuries – would be an act of partial self-destruction on the part of humanity. On this visit he made a special visit to the 'farthest north he has ever been' to meet aboriginal clans. Wherever he is in the world, the preservation of remote tribes and peoples is always on his agenda, and has been for some time.

As far back as 1988, he was urging people of the importance of preserving such culture. 'It would seem to me that there is still a prejudiced misconception in certain circles that people concerned with the environment, and what happens to this Earth, are bearded, be-sandalled, shaven-headed mystics who retreat every now and then to the Hebrides or the Kalahari Desert to examine their navels and commune with the natives,' he said in a speech at European Year of the Environment Eye-catcher Awards.

And when he'd met a tribe in Papua New Guinea in 1966 singing the national anthem, he was moved to tears. 'It was the most moving, touching thing I have ever experienced, I think, to see these people, miles from Britain, singing the national anthem. And the tears practically rolled down my cheeks.'

For Charles, preservation of such cultures is vital on so many levels. His concern from the very start was that Western culture was accelerating away from values and perspective that had up until then been embedded in its traditional roots. 'The industrialisation of life was becoming comprehensive and nature had become secularised. I could see very clearly we were growing numb to the sacred presence that all traditional societies feel very deeply,' he writes in *Harmony*.

On his last visit to Australia in April 2018, I flew in a military helicopter behind him as we ventured deep into the Australian Daintree Rainforest near Mossman Gorge, thirty minutes by helicopter from Cairns. First he took part in a traditional smoking ceremony, said to help ward off evil spirits. He did so with sombre respect. I watched at close quarters as Charles waved an aboriginal hunting boomerang for the cameras. But this was not just for show. He was there for a reason: to show the world what we must preserve.

'I suppose this one doesn't come back?' he said. Aboriginal elder Roy Gibson, a quietly spoken, dignified man, said, 'No it just hits the animal on the neck.' He was also shown a hundred-year-old wooden sword used in previous fights between indigenous communities. He was there to meet an indigenous people, to discover the traditions of its 50,000-year-old history. He marvelled at how the Kuku Yalanji aboriginals made use of the forest as a rich resource and was awestruck when he was shown how leaves from a certain tree could provide relief for mosquito bites.

The following day the prince received a blessing as he met aboriginal leaders in a traditional welcome ceremony in Nhulunbuy in the Northern Territory. And he was given a spiritual blessing by the world didgeridoo master in a yidaki healing ceremony during a tour of the Buku-Larrnggay Mulka Art Centre in Gove, which showcased the work of the area's indigenous people. The didgeridoo was blown close to his chest during the thirty-second blessing, after which Charles smiled and said, 'I feel better already!'

Stepping off the plane, he was handed a woomera – a traditional spear-throwing device – as he was greeted by aboriginal leader Galarrwuy Yunupingu. He went on to take part in a colourful welcome ceremony, where he was presented with a feather-stringed headdress called a malka string, and a string basket known as a bathi. Charles remarked how it was the farthest north he had travelled in Australia before joining a procession and watching the singing and dancing of the Rirratjingu people atop sacred Nhulun Hill. Nobody, I believe, participates with more sincerity and respect than the Prince of Wales. He hears their complaints, too, and passes them on to those who need to know.

Charles's role in enlightening the world and people who are ignorant of traditional and indigenous methods is paramount.

He has expended vast energy helping to save what remains of those traditional approaches. 'I knew they would be needed for a rainy day,' he says. His big hope is finding a path to reintegrate traditional wisdom with the here and now.

Attitudes to the monarchy in Australia are, on the whole, becoming more considered. After all, the real power still lies with an elected government and a prime minister and his or her cabinet. Even former prime minister Malcolm Turnbull, an ex-chairman of the Australian Republican Movement, declared himself an 'Elizabethan', saying there was no urgency for a referendum while the Queen reigns. In 1999, the same Mr Turnbull declared that the monarchist prime minister of the time, John Howard, 'broke this nation's heart' by sticking with the Windsors during a referendum on whether to keep the monarchy. As we saw earlier, Scott Morrison took over as Australian PM in August 2018, after Mr Turnbull was ousted by party rivals in a leadership contest.

Poll after poll, since the marriage of William to Kate and the arrival of their photogenic progeny, have reinforced a near-two-decade nadir in republican sentiment in Australia. It remains to be seen if Charles, as Australia's king-in-waiting, can cultivate this country's sentiment in a way that the younger royals seemed to have done. But his passion for Australia is genuine, as is his determination to serve. One question I am always asked when on tours of the Commonwealth is the 'Camilla question': will she be Charles's queen when he is king? Their story shows that love can conquer all.

Charles and Camilla's love affair came in three distinct stages; their friendship has been consistent. Among the young women with whom he became intimate at this time was Camilla Shand, a pretty country girl from the landed gentry who shared a love of the Goons. Cheeky and sharp-witted, she laughed with her eyes, which lit up with genuine warmth. Her father, World War II hero Major Bruce Shand, was a successful wine merchant and her mother, Rosalind, was a member of the Cubitt family. Her grandfather was Baron Ashcombe.

Charles's old university friend, Lucia Santa Cruz, who lived above the then Camilla Shand's apartment in London, had been keen to introduce her to Charles. He had been visiting Lucia in 1971 and she invited Camilla up for a drink, believing she and the prince would hit it off. It was there that Lucia made reference to the fact that Camilla's great-grandmother, Alice Keppel, had once been a mistress of his great-great-grandfather, Edward VII, which amused them both. She said, 'Now you two watch your genes,' because of their ancestors' adultery.

The prince had by then had several girlfriends, but his relationships with them were chaste, because of the need to leave women's virginity intact for their eventual husbands. Instead, his sexual experience was to be gained with experienced women, preferably married. Lady Tryon, an Australian married to an English peer and nicknamed 'Kanga' by the prince, is one such lover, according to reports.

Charles had been concerned for some time about how he would find the right woman with whom to share his life and responsibilities. Whoever he married, after all, would be as much married to the institution of monarchy as to him. He had even alluded to it in his first television interview. In Camilla he saw a woman with the strengths needed to handle the job. She was not fazed by him or monarchy; she had the right social credentials; she was Church of England; and he had fallen for her. By late autumn of 1972 they had become inseparable.

There was a catch, however, in that, at that time, she didn't feel the same as he did. While single and extremely fond of Charles, she had previously dated cavalry officer Andrew Parker Bowles, nine years her senior, since she was eighteen. She was, sadly for Charles, still captivated by the dashing officer. When Parker Bowles was posted to Germany in 1972, Camilla felt the relationship was over for good and was free to enjoy her liaison with Charles.

In the new year of 1973, Charles's next navy posting was to prove fatal for the romance. In early December he had joined his new ship, the frigate HMS *Minerva*, and was to sail on her to the Caribbean in January. He would be gone for eight months. Camilla joined him on a tour of the ship before it sailed and they had lunch on board. She returned the following weekend. He bemoaned the fact that it would be 'the last time I shall see her for eight months'. But it proved for him much worse than that. For Andrew Parker Bowles returned and the couple became engaged in March 1973. She jumped at the opportunity to wed the man she had been infatuated with for years.

Having changed ship to HMS *Fox*, Prince Charles moved on to Antigua where he was delighted by the English Harbour there, which had originally been Admiral Lord Nelson's dockyard during the eighteenth-century wars with the French. It was here that news reached him of Camilla's engagement to Andrew Parker Bowles. In May, he received a letter from his father informing him that his sister, Princess Anne, was to marry an army captain called Mark Phillips. It appeared to him that everything he held dear to him at home was being taken away.

Charles was devastated when he heard the news. He wrote to a friend that it seemed so cruel that fate should be this way. 'Such a blissful, peaceful and mutually happy relationship. . .I suppose the feelings of emptiness will pass eventually.' Charles and Camilla remained friends over the next seven years, and she became one of his most trusted confidantes.

When the Parker Bowleses' first child, Tom, was born in 1974, Camilla asked the prince to be a godfather and he happily accepted. The intimacy between Charles and Camilla returned after the birth of Camilla's daughter Laura, when her husband Andrew continued with his philandering ways. Camilla was drawn to the prince again and an adulterous affair ensued. She was not the first married woman to move in royal circles and have an affair, nor was she to be the last. Charles knew fully the dangers in conducting an affair with a married woman but was prepared to take the risk. He knew in time he must marry a woman who was suitable to be his queen consort. He was later to comment, 'I've fallen in love with all sorts of girls and I fully intend to go on doing so, but I've made sure that I haven't married the first person I've fallen in love with. I think one's got to be aware of the fact that falling madly in love with someone is not necessarily the starting point to getting married. Marriage is basically a strong friendship, so I'd want to marry someone whose interests I could share.'

The watershed moment came for Charles on the so-called 'Camilla question', when he decided and announced that his relationship with her was 'non-negotiable'. He laid down a marker in the late 1990s that sent a message not only to the general public but to the mandarins at the palace and to the Queen herself. He still felt aggrieved at the way his 'darling Camilla' was being treated but he made it abundantly clear he was not going to go along with it.

'All my life people have been telling me what to do,' he said when asked about his relationship with Camilla Parker Bowles in a 1998 interview with trusted journalist Gavin Hewitt. 'I'm tired of it. My private life has become an industry. People are making money out of it. I just want some peace.'

When I broke the world-exclusive story of the royal engagement of the Prince of Wales and Camilla in the *London Evening Standard* – and, according to the prince's biographer and friend Jonathan Dimbleby, 'bounced' Clarence House into issuing a formal announcement – the courtiers were ill-prepared. The wording of the statement that was released, long after the *Evening Standard* had broken the scoop, was simple enough. 'It is with great pleasure that the marriage of HRH the Prince of Wales and Camilla Parker Bowles is announced. It will take place on Friday 8 April,' the statement said.

My inside source had been right on the money and we were both elated and relieved. In the weeks that followed, the extent to which my scoop had caught Charles's team off guard was woefully apparent. My story marked the start of a torrid time for Clarence House officials, whose grasp on the finer and legal points of this royal wedding was exposed as being tenuous at best – if not altogether incompetent.

It started well enough. The ring, £100,000 worth of platinum and diamonds, had been a gift from the Queen. It was a thirties Art Deco design, a central square-cut diamond with three smaller ones on either side, which had belonged to the Queen Mother and was one of her favourites. When asked how she felt, Camilla said she was just coming down to Earth. The Prime Minister sent congratulations on behalf of the government. The Queen and the Duke of Edinburgh were 'very happy' and had given the couple their 'warmest wishes'. The Archbishop of Canterbury was pleased, too, that they had taken 'this important step'.

But soon critical newspaper headlines followed. The legality of the marriage was called into question; the impossibility of a church wedding turned Camilla into the House of Windsor's first 'town-hall bride'; and, for a while in the early spring of 2005, barely a day passed without the revelation of some apparent monumental oversight or error by Prince Charles's team. While they struggled to control the situation, they were also forced to address one key question they might rather have ignored: What did William and Harry think about their father marrying the woman who ostensibly helped break up their mother's marriage, a woman their mother loathed with a passion? William gave his blessing, saying that both he and Harry were 'delighted' at their father's happiness. Privately, their mood was more of acceptance than undiluted joy at the prospect of having Camilla as a stepmother.

Charles, William and Harry faced down the press when it was put to their father in public at a prearranged photocall just seven weeks out from the wedding, when the boys enjoyed a skiing holiday with him in his favoured resort of Klosters, Switzerland. 'How did he feel about the wedding?' a TV reporter asked. Charles knew the question was coming, as it had all been cleared with his communications team – but the impertinence!

'Your Royal Highnesses,' began the seasoned broadcaster

Nicholas Witchell, shouting from behind the barrier separating the royals from the media. 'It's eight days now to the wedding.'

'You've heard of it, have you?' Prince Charles interrupted, with a fake smile.

Caught a little off guard, Witchell, valiantly, continued, 'Can I ask how you are feeling and how, in particular, princes William and Harry are feeling at the prospect of the wedding?'

'Very happy,' replied Prince William immediately. 'It'll be a good day.'

'And Prince Charles, how are you feeling?' continued Witchell after a second or two of silence.

'It's a very nice thought, isn't it?' said Prince Charles, eventually, without a smile, then added a little sarcastically, 'I'm very glad you've heard of it, anyway.'

With that, he turned his head slightly away and, in a very quiet aside aimed solely at his sons, added, 'Bloody people. I can't bear that man. He's so awful. He really is.'

With most of the journalists unaware of what exactly had been said, the questioning continued in good humour, with William telling the press pack he was looking forward to his role as witness at the wedding; 'Very much so. As long as I don't lose the rings, it will be all right,' he joked.

Charles, who hadn't seen the microphones in the snow before he had spoken so loosely, had been unaware that his curmudgeonly remarks were being picked up. It was a gaffe more befitting of his father, Prince Philip, than the usually media-savvy and careful Prince Charles.

It proved another low point in Charles's relationship with the British tabloids and other media. During the collapse of his marriage to Diana he had grown to loathe the cynicism of the tabloids for the blatant commercialisation of his personal misery. 'We must realise that certain sections of the media have now proved to their own satisfaction that sensationalised royal stories are one of the best ways of selling newspapers in a recession,' he wrote in a memo to the Queen's private secretary on 23 October 1992, just weeks before his separation from Diana. In the intervening years nothing had happened for him to change his damning opinion.

Eventually, the location for the wedding had to be changed to Windsor Guildhall – which meant neither the Queen nor Philip attended. They did turn out for the Service of Prayer and Dedication at St George's Chapel, conducted by the Archbishop of Canterbury. Charles and Camilla used the wedding as an opportunity to earnestly repent the manifold sins and wickedness of their past deeds as each had been involved in the break-up of the other's marriage.

The couple chose the sternest possible prayer of penitence from the 1662 Book of Common Prayer to be read by themselves and their guests at the blessing of their marriage. The prayer read, 'We acknowledge and bewail our manifold sins and wickedness, which we, from time to time, most grievously have committed, by thought, word and deed, against thy Divine Majesty, provoking most justly thy wrath and indignation against us. We do earnestly repent, and are heartily sorry for these misdoings.' The ceremony date was also changed to 9 April to allow Charles to attend the funeral of Pope John Paul II, the third-longest-serving pontiff in history, who had died aged eighty-four in Rome.

However, as far as the palace were concerned – and Charles too – the marriage was a triumph. Camilla's deeply respected father, Major Bruce Shand, aged eighty-eight at this time and ailing, stalled going to the doctor until after the wedding. He knew something was very wrong but was desperate to see his daughter, so often maligned, remarried. It mattered a great deal to him that Charles should do the right thing by her. When he finally sought medical help, four days later, he was diagnosed with pancreatic cancer – and died fourteen months later.

Charles gave a touching speech at the reception, hosted by the Queen, in which he thanked 'my dear mama' for footing the bill and 'my darling Camilla, who has stood with me through thick and thin and whose precious optimism and humour have seen me through'. The duchess, looking serene, a vision, in an Anna Valentine dress with a golden headpiece by milliner Philip Treacy, emerged triumphant. It was the Queen, however, who had the last word.

Her Majesty compared the happy couple's relationship to the Grand National, which showed Camilla was accepted and she had finally got her man. She began by saying she had two important announcements to make. The first was that Hedgehunter had won the race at Aintree; the second was that, at Windsor, she was delighted to be welcoming her son and his bride to the 'winners' enclosure'. 'They have overcome Becher's Brook and the Chair and all kinds of other terrible obstacles. They have come through and I'm very proud and wish them well. My son is home and dry with the woman he loves.'

Many cheered, others were close to tears. For the prince, that day brought an end to his long life of loneliness. His soulmate was at long last at his side. They still had a long way to go to win over the people, but, as far as the palace and the prince were concerned, this marriage was the beginning of the end of the Camila question that had dogged the heir to the throne throughout his adult life.

When I revealed the couple's plans to marry, my inside source had been adamant that other key areas such as titles had been discussed well in advance of going public. The source said that Charles categorically intended his wife to be his queen consort when he became king: 'There was no doubt in his mind at the time about that and I honestly don't think anything has charged. In fact, I think he has hardened his resolve that this must be the case. For there to be any other outcome would, in his view, be to lessen his role as king. His marriage to Camilla is legal. She happens to be his second wife. That is it. Did any of Henry VIII's wives not get the title?'

Clarence House has inspired speculation about the duchess and her future role. Charles's office had always insisted that the duchess would be styled 'Princess Consort' when the time comes, indicating that she would eschew the title of 'Queen Consort' normally expected for the wife of a king. The decision, announced in 2005 before the wedding, has not officially changed since then, even as the public attitude to the marriage has softened. A redesign of the couple's official website has seen the explicit statement about this role quietly removed, leading to reports that she could be given the title of 'Queen' when the Prince of Wales accedes to the throne.

This book's exclusive insider source of the story had been spot on, too, that Camilla, when married, would not take the title HRH the Princess of Wales, even though it was her right to do so, as it would be insensitive and cause undue hostility with Diana, Princess of Wales, in mind. She uses the title HRH the Duchess of Cornwall instead, as the prince was Duke of Cornwall, which does not reduce her royal rank. It is a title of convenience.

When they wed, Clarence House issued what it described as a clarification of sorts with regard to the future title of Camilla. The official wedding announcement said, 'It is intended that Mrs Parker Bowles should use the title HRH the Princess Consort when the Prince of Wales accedes to the throne.' The big word in this statement was of course 'intended'. What Clarence House was in fact doing was buying time, time for a hostile public to warm to Camilla.

Since then Camilla, through hard work and the fact that time heals, has cemented her place in the Royal Family in recent years. The monarch marked her official ninetieth birthday by tidying up plans for her death and elevating the duchess to her most senior advisory body, the Privy Council. It was, as ever, all done very quietly. But it is unprecedented in modern times for a royal wife not in direct line to the throne to be a member of the Privy Council – the cornerstone of the constitutional monarchy, enacting Acts of Parliament and advising the sovereign on the use of powers that do not formally go through Parliament. It also showed the esteem in which the Queen holds Camilla, and reflects the Royal Household's efforts to prepare the public for succession.

The main reason the Queen wanted Camilla and William included was so they can be part of the Accession Council, which handles the succession to the throne after her death. The Queen wanted Camilla to be beside Charles when he formally succeeds her as monarch in a ceremony normally held at St James's Palace within twenty-four hours of the death of a sovereign.

Ever since the Prince of Wales married the Duchess of Cornwall in April 2005, the Royal Family have sought to avoid at great lengths any public uprising over the prospect of 'Queen Camilla'. Courtiers decided to play the long game. To a certain extent it has worked, but opinion polls still show the idea of a 'Queen Camilla' remains unpopular.

As he prepared to celebrate his seventieth birthday, I understand, Charles, like every Prince of Wales before him, was determined that his wife would also be his queen. Those private thoughts have only once been expressed publicly, when the prince indicated that the Duchess of Cornwall could become Queen Camilla when he ascends to the throne. Until then, the prince had always stuck to the line that his wife will be known as 'Princess Consort'. But, in an interview with NBC News in 2010, Charles had hinted that the duchess 'could be' given the title of 'Queen'.

I am told that Camilla will be named 'Queen Consort' on Charles's ascension. In reality, there would need to be an Act of Parliament to stop this from happening, not only in the UK but also in all the other realms in the Commonwealth. According to precedent, the wives of ruling kings become queen consorts but the husbands of sovereign queens do not have the right to a title.

The duchess, seventy-one at the time of writing, is said to have told friends previously that she would be 'happy' to use the lesser title when her husband ascends to the throne. The title issue will be decided in the court of public opinion and by the prime minister of the day. Clarence House has always fudged the issue and claimed that the constitutional issue surrounding the title would be 'a matter for the government of the day'. There was no such precedent for the title 'Princess Consort'.

All previous wives of British kings have been known as queens.

Women married to a monarch have historically been crowned as 'Queen Consort' except Queen Mary II, who, together with her husband King William III, reigned as joint sovereign from 1689 to 1694. Legislation might have to be amended if she insists on not being called 'Queen'. The new title could also have to be approved by the seventeen parliaments for which Charles will be head of state.

In 2002, on the death of Queen Elizabeth, the Queen Mother, at the age of 101, Charles was devastated. He said, 'She was quite simply the most magical grandmother you could possibly have, and I was utterly devoted to her.' But her passing came at a low point in the prince's life when he was beginning to feel that he might never be king. It is, some observers say, a fear that is highlighted with every passing birthday. If the Queen lives to the same age as her late mother, Charles will be almost eighty when he takes the throne, while Prince William will be forty-five. But as the prince told the NBC network interviewer Brian Williams when asked about the prospect of his becoming king, 'It's much better not to. . .You think about it a bit but it's much better not to. If it comes to it, regrettably it comes as a result of the death of your parent, which is not so nice to say the least.'

Camilla has assuaged Charles's loneliness, but knows when to leave him alone. When on the public stage, their togetherness makes them a redoubtable couple. He is the most prepared heir to the throne the country has ever had – wise, funny, intelligent and connected to his people in so many ways. All the talk that Camilla, should the situation arise, will not take the title 'Queen Consort' on her husband's ascension is wide of the mark. It is also totally self-defeating. Make no mistake, Camilla will be queen.

There would have to be a change in the law in Britain and several other realms before Charles becomes king for her not to be. There is little or no appetite for that.

To alter her status would be a PR own goal, like insisting a president's wife should not be allowed the role and title of 'First Lady' – especially when the government plans to use the royals to bolster our status on the world stage. She rarely puts a foot wrong on tour while representing the Queen or when supporting her husband. Camilla has earned her stripes – the Queen acknowledged this in 2012 when she awarded her daughter-in-law her highest personal honour, Dame Grand Cross of the Royal Victorian Order, to mark the seventh anniversary of her wedding to Prince Charles.

Camilla has earned her stripes through the love and loyalty she has shown to her husband and by devotion to duty to the Crown. She will, I am told, be deservedly given the correct rank when the time comes. Charles will rightly insist on it.

*Chapter Ten*

# HEIR MILES

———— ∼ ————

'I think it would be criminally negligent of me to go
around this country and not actually want to try and do
something about what I find there. I think that's my duty to do
so. If some people don't like it, that's too bad, isn't it, frankly,
because I think there are more important things to worry
about, which is this country.'

THE PRINCE OF WALES IN AN INTERVIEW WITH
SIR TREVOR MCDONALD IN MAY 2006

Half asleep, dazed by the dull hum of the auxiliary power unit
at the back of the plane and trying to ignore the myriad
clanking and whirring noises from the two Rolls-Royce Trent 772B
turbofan engines on the converted RAF Voyager Airbus A330, I
spotted the prince's new head of communications, Julian Payne. He
was at the back of the jet nicknamed 'Cam Force One' (a play on
America's presidential jet 'Air Force One' and the former UK prime
minister who had sanctioned the financing the plane for government

and royal use, David Cameron). We were heading back to Britain at a maximum speed, around 490 knots, after a demanding eleven-day Commonwealth royal tour to Singapore, Brunei, Malaysia and India with the Prince of Wales and Duchess of Cornwall, and Julian appeared, understandably, to be in good spirits.

A few hours earlier, just before take-off from Palam Air Force Station, New Delhi, the prince and the duchess had ventured to the back of the plane for an informal chat with the handful of photographers and writers who had accompanied them and reported on the visit. Charles was in ebullient mood and thanked us for our interest in the visit. The duchess seemed relieved that the testing schedule was at last complete. The choking smog that had descended on the city (the result of crop burning in the north of the country) had taken its toll on her, she admitted.

We chatted about a visit deep into the Borneo rainforest on which I had accompanied him, and where he came face to face with six of the great apes at a feeding spot at the Semenggoh Wildlife Rehabilitation Centre. The species has experienced a sharp population decline and this deeply concerned him. A century ago there were probably more than 230,000, but the Borneo orangutan is now estimated at about 104,700 and is classed as endangered. The prince recalled the moment he had been photographed offering a banana to an orangutan, against the better judgement of his Scotland Yard PPO, Inspector Jim Fishwick, who had quietly voiced his concern to his principal. Charles took the decision to go ahead, anyway, to the delight of the photographers as the orange-reddish brown ape, the size of a small man and around seven times stronger than a human, reached out to him.

For a split second they had touched hands in a Michelangelo *The Creation of Adam* moment. This comparison seemed to tickle the prince, although, in a chilled mood, this wild animal could easily kill a human with his bare hands in seconds. 'It was a truly remarkable experience,' the prince said, before joking that perhaps we would have had a much better story and photographic opportunity if the ape had grabbed him by the arm and swung him over his head and launched him into the jungle. The jovial ambience, which was genuine and warm, came to end when the prince was asked by a member of the RAF crew to return to his seat as the captain had made an announcement that he was ready for take-off.

The last stop on the so-called 'Commonwealth Tour' was to New Delhi, where the prince held talks with India's prime minister, Narendra Modi, at Hyderabad House. On the agenda were trade and bilateral talks and the upcoming Commonwealth Heads of Government Meeting (CHOGM) in London. In terms of wealth per head, or living standards, India remains far behind the developed world, but, in terms of global power and the Commonwealth, it is massive, set to overtake the UK to become the Commonwealth's largest economy as well as most populated one.

In his last public engagement on what had been dubbed 'The Commonwealth Tour', Charles delivered the third of his speeches underlining the importance of the Commonwealth and its diversity. Addressing guests at the British High Commission, the Prince hailed the bonds between Britain and India and urged the public to cherish their diversity. Using an Urdu word to refer to his wife as 'darling', he told an audience, 'I cannot tell you how delighted my *mehaboobaa* and I are to be back in India, a country that is so very special to us both.' Saying he had always believed the 'sheer diversity' of the Commonwealth is one of its greatest strengths, he warned, 'This diversity is to be celebrated and cherished, not only because it is so central to our identities and our sense of belonging, but also, if I may say so, because it offers us the best hope of addressing the most pressing challenges of our time.

'A one-size-fits-all approach to globalisation simply cannot be the answer and will, I am convinced, lead us into a sterile, monocultural homogeneity that creates ever greater problems whilst simultaneously robbing us of the solutions to address them.' Saying the world's challenges are 'already as urgent as they are profound', he pointed to climate change, food insecurity, overfishing and pollution as key concerns, and said he had great hopes for the combination of traditional knowledge and cutting-edge ingenuity within the Commonwealth's population. 'The challenges we face together and the aspirations we share make it as relevant and as necessary as it has ever been,' he said. 'It offers us all the hope that by working together, and drawing strength from our diversity, we might secure a safer, more prosperous and fairer future for our children and our grandchildren.' It was his third major speech about the Commonwealth during his trip, leading up to the CHOGM in London.

After a change in venue because of the thick smog engulfing New Delhi, the prince was quizzed by children from Lajpat Nagar-III School about his plans for when he is king. He took the grilling in good humour. One nine-year-old girl had a very specific query in mind: was he planning to build a fort when he was king? The pupil, named Pragya, was reassured as the prince agreed, 'I will!' to make the class laugh. He clarified afterwards that he did not, in fact, have specific plans for fort-building. It was a light moment in the final day of a long tour, which had seen the prince and duchess visit Singapore, Brunei, Malaysia and New Delhi.

Another asked for his favourite book. The prince took time to mull over the question carefully before responding. 'What do you think it might be?' he said. 'There are so many to choose from.' He then said, 'Have any of you read the *Harry Potter* books yet? They are very good books.' A second child then asked for his favourite actor, with the prince replying, 'Gracious me! When I think about it there are so many of them. There is a very good actor called Sir Antony Sher, who is a brilliant Shakespearean actor, and everything else. There are lots of others, though.'

The royal flight was about three hours into the return leg to RAF Brize Norton, Oxfordshire, and most of the passengers on the plane were by now lost in a deep sleep. A few of the small media contingent were laid out across four seats and snug under a duvet requisitioned from the business-class section by the RAF cabin crew, their heads resting on pillows. Julian Payne, who had worked tirelessly to help achieve maximum positive publicity for his boss on the visit, was a little demob-happy, clutching a piece of paper with handwritten scrawl in red ink all over it and on the back. Nobody could overhear us.

'What's that you're holding?' I asked, knowing full well it was a printout of a double-page-spread commentary I had written for the *Evening Standard* a few days earlier (headlined 'A CENOTAPH TRIBUTE OF UTMOST SIGNIFICANCE').

The article had given an essentially positive appraisal of the royal visit and had also looked forward to the symbolic moment when Prince Charles would lay the nation's wreath on Remembrance Sunday at his mother's behest. The prince had seen my article and it received an efficacious response. I recognised the prince's spidery handwriting in red ink scrawled all over the piece of paper his press adviser Julian Payne was holding. But that was as close as I was going to get to it. He had got my attention. I was fully awake now.

'But what does it say?' I pressed.

Public-relations babble followed, with him saying the fact that the prince had been reading my article mid-flight while others slept showed how engaged his boss was. I couldn't agree more, but all I really wanted to know was what the prince had written on the page? This, after all, was gold to a writer, a response from the horse's mouth to an article he had penned about the protagonist and the monarchy. The prince had opened by writing, 'How Kind' but I knew the devil was in the detail. I was indeed touched that the prince had taken time to read it and make detailed notes on it. As I audaciously held out my hand, he judiciously folded the piece of paper in two and placed it securely inside his pocket. But, before he returned to one of the fifty-eight business-class seats in the middle and upper sections of the RAF plane, he briefed me, leaving me with some salient points that his boss had covered in his notes.

My article had addressed how republicans presented a somewhat distorted view of the role of the constitutional monarchy, blinkered by their version of what form of democracy and head of state they want. I argued that republicans' core belief means that they often miss the point and the subtleties of our current system of parliamentary democracy and constitutional monarchy, with all its checks and balances, that have developed over a thousand years of history. Critics of the monarchy, I wrote, often site Charles's so-called 'black spider memos' that he writes to ministers on topics he cares about or feels as proof of what they say is the prince's 'unconstitutional' interfering in party politics.

Those with monarchy in their sights argue that Charles has and is repeatedly operating dangerously outside of his constitutional remit. The antimonarchists' view is that any king or queen regent (or heir apparent, for that matter) must not be in any way political or at least partisan as that would leave them and the system fatally exposed. It is true, I had written, that the overwhelming majority of prerogative powers are devolved to the sovereign's ministers, but the monarch can wield power in the event of what he or she perceives is 'a grave constitutional crisis'. Then, the sovereign can act 'contrary to or without ministerial advice'.

Charles has a very different take on it. 'I don't see why politicians and others should think they have the monopoly of wisdom,' he said during an interview with his biographer Jonathan Dimbleby in 1994 when asked about his involvement in politics. Indeed, ever since his youth Charles has built a reputation for his so-called 'interventions'. He has made thousands of public speeches, some controversially addressing areas of social policy. Every one has taken its toll. 'I find I have a terrible knotted feeling in the pit of my tummy as the courage is plucked from somewhere inside. . .Having made the speech I then usually have dreadful second thoughts and feel I shouldn't have done it and it would be so much easier to lead a quiet life,' he said on making speeches about politics, in a private letter, dated 1 May 1989.

Charles always agonises over his speeches. He chooses every word carefully. The prince knows, after more than half a century as a player on the world stage, that what he says and when he says it carries weight. At the World Jewish Relief Dinner in the Guildhall on 31 January 2017, for example, he felt it was an opportune time to express his views about the importance of reaching out beyond the boundaries of religion and community. He chose to praise the 'wisdom and dignity' of refugees, too. For Charles knew the timing of his words was significant given what is happening in the world in the President Trump era. It was not necessarily a veiled threat to the new US president – rather a clear message from an experienced statesman on the world stage on the importance of spreading a message of compassion and tolerance.

In my view, he deliberately spoke of the need to reach out beyond religious boundaries. It is something the prince believes in passionately and he has worked tirelessly for years to encourage dialogue among different faiths around the world in his public life. He went as far as he could to state his diametrically opposed view to Trump without actually saying the words 'Trump is wrong'. Charles's words came amid claims that, if a Trump state visit were to go ahead, the Queen and royals could be tarnished. He knew that if the elected government were to insist on such a visit, it must go ahead. We know, of course, that Trump's July 2018 visit to the UK was not a state visit as such. But Charles's position is unique. He is not, like the Queen, effectively constitutionally banned from appearing to be at odds with government policy. In fact, as heir to the throne he is perfectly entitled to have an opinion and also to make it public. So the prince's decision to speak so powerfully on the issues of the moment – while consistent with his view for years – is significant not only in this debate but for the future. When he feels these issues are too serious to ignore, such as human rights or religious affairs, he makes his stand.

A flaky report in the *Sunday Times* claiming that the prince and his son William deliberately snubbed President Trump when he made that July visit was wide of the mark. The newspaper reported that the pair were 'unwilling' to meet the president, leaving the Queen to greet him and First Lady Melania Trump at Windsor Castle alone. The story was a flyer. The Trumps' tour was not, as we've seen, a state visit and the only plan drawn up for him to meet members of the Royal Family involved the Queen in greeting the president and his wife Melania alone.

The prince has pontificated in books and articles on everything from the natural world to spirituality to the built environment. His private missives to ministers, some felt, were a different matter entirely, crossing over into party-political themes in what they say are specifically designed to try to achieve his 'political' aims and objectives. Vocal critics of the monarchal system that our unwritten constitution embraces believe such intervention is of real significance. In reality, he is just doing his job. He holds regular audiences for and corresponds with politicians, high commissioners and ambassadors as an integral part of his role. In doing so he is fulfilling his duty, supporting the Queen and indeed her government. It enables him to prepare for his future role and at the same time to be the most well-prepared and well-informed heir to the throne in our history.

Of course, he doesn't always see eye to eye with politicians in such meetings, sometimes finding them dreary or ill-informed. As for paying lip service to them, why would he? He once confided that he finds mixing with politicians 'excessively demoralising', which he fears gives him an increasingly jaundiced opinion of those politicians who, in his view, 'seem to lose touch with their souls'. The so-called 'black spider memos' I referred to in my article, which he had read, received plenty of the prince's red ink in his handwritten notes. First, the prince made it clear that he does not write and has never written what the press have dubbed 'black spider memos'. The phrase clearly irks him. This term, used as a handle for every missive the prince had written to government ministers, is an inaccurate media invention. It was first gifted to the headline writers by his former adviser, Dame Julia Cleverdon, a British charity worker who served for sixteen years as chief executive of Business in the Community. In a documentary she said on camera that Charles was always busy penning handwritten letters and referred to his chirography, usually in black ink, as 'spidery'. The press had their headline and a convenient handle to use every time Charles penned a note deemed 'inappropriate meddling and lobbying' of ministers.

The prince believes such a description is inaccurate. Any thoughts he has put to paper in private letters to ministers, he says, are for their eyes only. He knows it at the time of writing and the recipient knows it when reading them. What he writes is within any bounds of the unwritten constitutional. With this in mind, in Charles's view, it is his 'constitutional duty' as heir to the throne to act in this way. Drawing attention to key topics on which his unique position has enabled him to glean information, such as climate change, organic farming or youth empowerment, is demonstrating 'leadership'.

He minds deeply, he says, about the country and the people

he is born to serve and to do nothing, he believes, would be a dereliction of his constitutional duty. To leak details of such private meetings or correspondence, something he would never consciously do, would also be a breach of that unwritten code. Therefore, he is extremely conscious when preparing a speech or an article to ensure its contents come within the confines of his constitutional position.

The UK government's decision to defend the prince's position in court in what escalated into a hugely expensive ten-year legal battle with the *Guardian* newspaper does not show an obsession with secrecy, as some newspapers and commentators argued, but a robust interpretation of the complex position of the heir to the British throne and what is expected of the role and how it functions. In May 2015, this all came to a head over private letters sent by the prince to then Labour government ministers a decade previously. It was ruled in the Upper Tribunal of Britain's Administrative Appeals Chamber that twenty-seven of the letters could be released. The then government's veto on publication of the letters was declared unlawful by the Court of Appeal in 2014 – a decision that was upheld by the Supreme Court on appeal, which the sitting prime minister, David Cameron, called 'disappointing'. It was decided that the letters written in 2004 and 2005 would be published with 'provisional redactions' to protect personal data of people other than the prince.

The letters, which covered the period between September 2004 and April 2005 when Tony Blair was prime minister, reflected, according to the then attorney general Dominic Grieve, Charles's 'most deeply held personal views and beliefs'. During a visit to a Prince's Trust charitable project in London on the day of the ruling, the prince was ambushed by an overexcited TV reporter, Channel 4's Michael Crick, who started barking questions at him. Was he 'worried' about the release of the documents? Had he been 'behaving unconstitutionally' by writing letters like that? Not altering his stride, the prince gave a dismissive sideways glance at the persistent Crick, who rather self-importantly, and more for the camera than anything else, continued to shout questions one after the other without taking a breath or really waiting for a response. As the prince walked into the building, he could be heard saying disdainfully, 'Very predictable.'

For a journalist of Crick's wealth of political experience, they were naïve and heavily loaded questions, too, that the prince was hardly likely to address on a London pavement. Speaking for the prince afterwards, a Clarence House spokesman said Charles was 'disappointed the principle of privacy had not been upheld'.

At the heart of the matter is the potentially negative impact of the court's ruling on how the prince conducts his business. If he was so mindful, it could effectively stop the prince performing his duty freely and without fear or favour. It would mean that every time he put pen to paper and sent the letter to the government it could end up front-page news. That would serve nobody.

The court battle materialised after journalist Rob Evans from the *Guardian* newspaper applied in 2005 to see the prince's letters under the Freedom of Information Act (FOI) 2000, which was initially denied by the information commissioner. Several more contentious legal decisions followed. Evans wrote that his newspaper limited the request to cover just eight months because FOI rules allow applications to be refused if too much information is requested. In 2010, the FOI was tightened and now correspondence involving the monarch or heir to the throne cannot be made public for twenty years, or five years after the writer's death, whichever is longer.

Mr Grieve vetoed an original decision to order publication made by the Upper Tribunal in 2012, but it was eventually ruled that his actions were invalid, paving the way for the documents finally to be disclosed. The *Guardian*, the information commissioner and the Cabinet Office later published the documents to an underwhelming response. The released letters covered a whole range of areas. Frankly, apart from the principle of privacy being lost, the 'revelations' were hardly earth-shattering. Indeed, the prince had spoken out publicly on many of them before. The publication of the letters prompted Tory MP Zac Goldsmith to tweet, 'Prince Charles exposed for standing up for the environment, education, welfare of our soldiers, sustainable farming, etc. Outrageous.'

Writing to the then education secretary, Charles Clarke, in November 2004, the prince criticised what he described as modern teaching methods and said he favoured the creation of a teacher-training institute that would address a 'gap in the teaching of English and history' identified by his own Educational Summer Schools. He described himself as 'someone with such old-fashioned views'. Indeed, he once reportedly said when greeting Charles Clover, who was writing a book on Highgrove in 1993, 'Are you a graduate of English literature? They're the only people I have time for.'

The prince wrote to Clarke that his own summer schools were challenging the fashionable view that teachers should not impart bodies of knowledge, but instead act as 'facilitators' or 'coaches'; a notion Clarke said he found 'difficult to understand'. Asking for support for the initiative into 2005 and beyond, the prince added, 'Perhaps I am now too dangerous to associate with.' It's true he was never afraid to speak his mind. During a speech at a presentation of the Thomas Cranmer Schools Prize on 19 December 1989, he let rip. '[I and others] wonder what it is about our country and our society that our language has become so impoverished, so sloppy and so limited that we have arrived at a wasteland of banality, cliché and casual obscenity.'

To this day the prince champions the teaching of Shakespeare in schools. Perhaps he recalls how it fired his imagination when he was a teenage student. It was graduate Eric Anderson – who in later life would become headmaster of Eton College between 1980 and 1994, recruited to teach English at Gordonstoun – who first inspired Charles's passion for the work of the Bard of Avon. In 1964, Anderson put on a school production of *Henry V* and cast the talented Charles in the part of Exeter. The play was a success, but the audience of local people insisted that it was a pity that the best actor, Charles, was playing Exeter instead of Henry. He went on to play the lead role in *Macbeth*. Having discovered that he could lose himself as the character he was playing, the prince excelled on stage. Ever since, Charles has not only been a great supporter of the arts but of Shakespeare in particular. During the Shakespeare Birthday Lecture of 22 April 1991, he said, 'The marginalising of Shakespeare seems to be symptomatic of a general flight from our great literary heritage.'

In October 2004, the prince wrote to the environment minister Elliot Morley, wishing him 'well in your endeavours'

*op left*: Charles's beloved Highgrove
House, Gloucestershire
*ris Jackson/PA Archive/PA Images*

*op right*: Visiting Wiltshire Wildlife
Trust's Clattinger Farm, June 1999
*fan Rousseau/PA Archive/PA Images*

*Middle left*: On Mount Snowdon, Wales,
uly 2000   *PA Archive/PA Images*

*ight*: Accompanying the Queen Mother
uring the Braemar Gathering, Scotland,
eptember 2000. The event has been
ttended by the Royal Family for over
50 years
*vid Cheskin/PA Archive/PA Images*

*Left*: On a royal tour in 200●
the prince happily dons a
crown of eagle feathers as
he is made honorary chief
of Surama Village, home to
Amerindians in Guyana's
Amazon Basin rainforest

*Tim Graham/Getty Images*

*Right*: With President
Jagdeo of Guyana visiting
the Tagore Memorial
School on the Guysuco
Sugar Estate in Corriverton,
Guyana

*Tim Graham/Getty Images*

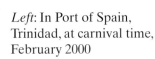

*Left*: In Port of Spain,
Trinidad, at carnival time,
February 2000

*Tim Graham/Getty Images*

*Right*: Visiting the Beetham
Child Development Centre
in Port of Spain, February
2000

*Tim Graham/Getty Images*

*Left*: The Prince and Camilla attend the Mey Games in Caithness, Scotland, August 2004

David Cheskin/PA Archive/PA Images

*Below*: Giving a speech at the Prince's Trust thirtieth birthday celebrations in May 2006

Pool/Anwar Hussein/EMPICS Entertainment

*Below left*: Prince Charles tours the Harapan Rainforest Project in Jambi, Indonesia, as part of a ten-day tour of East Asia in 2008  Chris Jackson/Getty Images

*Below right*: Presenting Prince Harry with his flying wings at Prince Harry's pilot course graduation at the Army Aviation Centre, Hampshire, 7 May, 2010

Anwar Hussein/EMPICS Entertainment

*Left*: Attending the wedding of his son Prince William to Catherine Middleton at Westminster Abbey on 29 April 2011

*Mark Marsland/Getty Images*

*Below*: Sharing a joke with his sons at the Invictus Games at the Lee Valley Athletics Centre, London, in September 2014

*Yui Mok/PA Archive/PA Images*

*Middle left*: The Prince of Wales and Prince Harry attend the New Zealand Memorial Service in Turkey, April 2015, as part of commemorations marking the 100th anniversary of the Gallipoli campaign

*Paul Edwards/The Sun/PA Archive/PA Images*

*Middle right*: (From left–right) The Duchess of Cornwall, the Prince of Wales, Prince George, the Duke and Duchess of Cambridge, Queen Elizabeth II, Prince Harry and James, Viscount Severn on the balcony at Buckingham Palace following Trooping the Colour at Horse Guards Parade, London, June 2015

*Jonathan Brady/PA Archive/PA Images*

*Right*: Attending Royal Ascot, June 2014

*Ian Parker/Getty Images*

*Left*: Prince Charles and Camilla meet Pope Francis at the Vatican, April, 2017

*ABACA/ABACA/PA Images*

*Right*: At the Cenotaph, Whitehall, London, for Remembrance Sunday, 12 November 2017

*Jack Taylor/Getty Images*

*Left*: Arriving with the Queen for the formal opening of the Commonwealth Heads of Government Meeting in the ballroom at Buckingham Palace, April 2018

*Jonathan Brady/PA Wire/PA Images*

*Right*: With Indian Prime Minister Narendra Modi and dancers during a visit to the Science Museum during the Commonwealth Heads of Government Meeting, London April 2018

*Hannah McKay/PA Wire/PA Images*

*Top left*: The Prince of Wales and the Duchess of Cornwall emerge in colourful robes from the Sri Mahamariamman Temple – one of the four places of worship they visited in a day while on tour in Penang  *Robert Jobson/SJH Images*

*Top centre*: Taking a stroll in the Botanical Gardens in Singapore, during the successful 'Commonwealth' tour, November 2017  *Robert Jobson/SJH Images*

*Top right*: The Prince of Wales during an historic visit to Greece in May 2018, officially aimed at highlighting the two nations' longstanding maritime and military links  *Robert Jobson/SJH Images*

*Centre*: The Prince of Wales up close with orangutans at the Semenggoh Wildlife Rehabilitation Center, Kuching, Sarawak, Malaysia, November 2017  *Robert Jobson/SJH Images*

*Below left*: Charles after being made an honorary 'paramount chief' during a visit to the South Pacific nation of Vanuatu, April 2018.  *Robert Jobson/SJH Images*

*Below right*: The Prince of Wales is welcomed to Brunei by the Sultan of Brunei, November 2017  *Robert Jobson/SJH Images*

*Left*: The Prince accompanies Meghan Markle to the altar in St George's Chapel, Windsor Castle, for her marriage to his youngest son, Prince Harry, 19 May 2018

*Jonathan Brady/PA Wire/PA Images*

*Right*: With Doria Ragland, Meghan Markle's mother, following the wedding

*WPA Pool/Getty Images*

The Prince of Wales's 70th Birthday Patronage Celebration

*Left*: Prince Harry gives a speech during his father's seventieth birthday patronage celebration at Buckingham Palace, 22 May 2018

*Mark Cuthbert/Getty Images*

*Right*: HRH Camilla, Duchess of Cornwall with Meghan on her first engagement as Her Royal Highness the Duchess of Sussex

*Chris Jackson/Getty Images*

to curb illegal fishing by trying to 'bring to heel the recalcitrant countries who sanction, either directly or by turning a blind eye'. He suggested the use of the Royal Navy for enforcement activity, mentioning in particular illegal fishing of the Patagonian toothfish and continuing in a mournful vein, 'Until that trade is stopped, there is little hope for the poor old albatross, for which I shall continue to campaign.' He finishes by saying, 'Let us hope that, between all of us who mind about sustainable fishing, we can make a difference before it is too late.'

In another letter, to the Department of Health in 2005, Charles wrote about his concerns regarding the redevelopment of a hospital, stating that he was frustrated by the logjam that had prevented it. He said control of hospital estates had caused him growing anxiety. 'I fear that if the estates are transferred now without proper consideration, various chickens will come home to roost in your own department in coming years as the physical and mental well-being of future communities is affected.' he penned. He also asked to be consulted before any further decisions were made. 'I do pray we could discuss these matters more fully before irrevocable decisions are taken,' he added.

The prince had long been at loggerheads with aspects of our health service and in particular with the acceptance and use of alternative medicine. 'I would suggest that the whole imposing edifice of modern medicine, for all its breathtaking successes, is like the celebrated Tower of Pisa: slightly off balance,' he said at the British Medical Association's 150th anniversary in December 1982.

In another letter, to Tessa Jowell in 2005 – she was then

the culture, media and sport secretary – the prince asked her about the conservation of Antarctic huts built for the first polar expeditions. He wrote that he was at a 'loss' to understand why the restoration was considered to be an 'overseas' project, due to there being British territory in the Antarctic. 'Whatever the case, and however futile my plea to you for a bit of imaginative flexibility in the interpretation of these rules, I just wanted to emphasise the iconic importance of these huts,' he wrote. He also offered to help find wealthy individuals to help the conservation project if the government could not find the funding.

Writing to Prime Minister Tony Blair in February 2005, the prince then waded into the extremely contentious debate over whether to cull badgers to prevent the spread of tuberculosis in cattle. The prince told him, 'I, for one, cannot understand how the "badger lobby" seem to mind not at all about the slaughter of thousands of expensive cattle, and yet object to a managed cull of an over-population of badgers; to me, this is intellectually dishonest.'

In September 2004, the prince had written to Mr Blair saying it would be 'splendid if the government could find ways' to encourage consumers to demand British produce, as without their support British agriculture and the countryside would not survive. Despite acknowledging the fact that 'European rules preclude the government from running a campaign to promote, solely, British produce,' the prince writes, 'I only wish that more could be done to encourage people to buy British.'

The prince also wrote to Mr Blair warning him that the armed forces did not have adequate resources the year after Britain went to war in Iraq. He had particular concerns about problems with Britain's surveillance capability, crucial to the operations in Iraq. He told Mr Blair that he was worried about delays to replacements for the Lynx aircraft due to 'significant pressure on the defence budget'.

He also wrote of a major advance in monitoring technology, which he had seen in action in Northern Ireland, and warned, 'The aim of the Ministry of Defence and the Army Air Corps to deploy this equipment globally is, however, being frustrated by the poor performance of the existing Lynx aircraft in high temperatures.' He went on, 'Despite this, the procurement of a new aircraft to replace the Lynx is subject to further delays and uncertainty due to the significant pressure on the Defence Budget. I fear that this is just one more example of where our Armed Forces are being asked to do an extremely challenging job (particularly in Iraq) without the necessary resources.' Mr Blair wrote back saying the 'replacement of Lynx and Gazelle reconnaissance and surveillance capacity will be a priority'.

On reflection, had this drawn-out legal battle really been worth it for either party? After a fortune spent on lawyers' fees, frankly, the letters didn't expose anything significant, and certainly not some cancer at the heart of our democracy and constitutional monarchy. Had it been worth his while fighting it? That, of course, was a matter for the government. Indeed, the letters showed instead a man who cares profoundly about his country and who isn't simply prepared to sit idly and do nothing about issues where he sees solutions to failing systems. In public, through his speeches, television interviews and published articles, the prince has for decades chosen the more difficult path.

The prince has often challenged the current orthodoxy

and the conventional way of thinking. In many cases he has highlighted dangers ahead well before so-called experts have even acknowledged them. Clearly, while he is in a position to do so, whether prince or king, he will, those closest to him confirm, continue to try to raise the debate of areas he sees as important whenever he sees fit.

How he behaves and thinks in private is a question that officials – particularly among the Queen's senior officials at Buckingham Palace – would rather was not made a matter of public debate. The 'black spider memo' fiasco raised that spectre and it had deeply worried the Queen's senior advisers. Of course, the letters were examined for evidence of any pressure brought to bear by a hereditary monarch-in-waiting on elected ministers and for any evidence that government policy was changed following the prince's intervention. But the correspondence proved benign.

The future king hadn't overstepped the undefined mark. The prince is not naïve and anticipates that some politicians – even Privy Councillors, who have sworn an oath to be 'a true and faithful servant' to the Crown – are less than faithful. When he puts pen to paper he is aware his carefully worded missives would reach the public's ears. In reality, sources close to him admit that the inbuilt dissident in him would not mind that at all.

The prince has made his position on so-called 'meddling' clear. 'I think it would be criminally negligent of me to go around this country and not actually want to try and do something about what I find there. I think that's my duty to do so. If some people don't like it that's too bad, isn't it, frankly, because I think there are more important things to worry about, which is this country,' he said in an interview with Sir Trevor McDonald in 2006, in a documentary to mark thirty years of the Prince's Trust. He consummately believes in what he does and the way he does it. In his view, it is not prying or lobbying, scrawled in black ink in memos to ministers. His interventions are simply his 'demonstrating leadership', and that he is able to do so is acutely important to him.

In July 2018, Clarence House courtiers faced another 'tin hat' moment when they were called upon to defend their boss. There was nothing they could do but brace themselves and hope that too much flak didn't come their way. The prince and his team were certainly rattled by the Inquiry into his erstwhile 'friend', disgraced former bishop Peter Ball. The Prince of Wales was required to make a written submission to an Inquiry into the convicted paedophile stating that he did not seek to influence any police investigation. In the submission that was read to the Inquiry, he said he felt, 'deep personal regret' for trusting Ball when initial reports of abuse emerged, years before he was jailed in 2015.

In a 1997 letter, the prince said of a critic of Ball, 'I'll see this horrid man off if he tries anything.' And in a series of letters between Charles and the bishop, read to the Independent Inquiry into Child Sexual Abuse, Ball spoke of a 'malicious campaign' against him and 'harassment' by 'fraudulent' accusers. In another letter to Ball in 1995, the prince said, 'I wish I could do more. I feel so desperately strong about the monstrous wrongs that have been done to you.' And, in 1997, the prince wrote a letter in which he described an apparent accuser as a 'ghastly man...up to his dastardly tricks again'.

In 2015, Ball's world of lies collapsed around him and he was jailed for thirty-two months for offences against eighteen teenagers and men. In the written submission, read by the counsel to the Inquiry, Fiona Scolding, the prince said he had been 'misled' and, at the time, 'there was on my part a presumption of good faith' in relation to Ball. He added,

> Peter Ball told me he had been involved in some sort of 'indiscretion' which prompted his resignation as my local bishop. He emphasised that one individual that I now understand to be Mr Neil Todd had made a complaint to the police, that the police had investigated the matter, and the Crown Prosecution Service had decided to take no action. Events later demonstrated beyond any doubt, to my deep regret, that I, along with many others, have been misled.

Knowing what was known in 2018, there's no doubt the prince's letters to Bishop Ball in the 1990s, in particular his expression of sympathy for the 'monstrous wrongs' supposedly done to him, were acutely embarrassing and reveal a degree of naïveté on his part. But, to be fair, the prince wasn't alone at that time in doubting the allegations against the apparently beguiling and believable Bishop Ball. Major institutions such as the Church, NHS and BBC were also notably reluctant to ask uncomfortable questions and to make proper enquiries, either.

In the prince's case there was a sense, as his statement said, of 'deep personal regret' that he was one of the many deceived by the bishop. The fact that he opened his personal correspondence for scrutiny is a recognition, his officials insisted, of the importance the prince attached to the Inquiry. Clearly, he felt too that his 'presumption of good faith' in the Bishop Ball case was so badly betrayed. The prince said that the 'true context and details' of complaints against Ball 'did not come to my attention until the time of Mr Ball's trial and conviction in 2015', and, when they did, he immediately ceased contact with Ball once the judicial process had concluded and he was found guilty of such egregious offences against young people.

This case, of course, highlighted the danger the prince faces just through the nature of his position, which brings him into contact with prominent people who have subsequently been accused of serious wrongdoing. Rather than rushing to private judgement, he has always, and rightly, taken the view that the judicial process should take its course first. Inevitably, his private correspondence on a whole variety of matters can come back to haunt him.

That said, is it perspicuous that the prince continues to engage with people on a whole range of issues and in so doing continue to make unfeigned interventions that could be interpreted as political, even when king? Royal courtiers exist to protect the 'Boss' they serve and the institution of monarchy itself. The official line is that the moment the prince ascends the throne he will cease to exist as the man we have known on the public stage. He will, some officials suggest, simply wrap a giant ribbon around his life work as the Prince of Wales and consign it to history. Then he will continue, anointed as if reborn, to become a new person, our king. He will, they say, avoid issues that have been at his core all his adult life. That will not happen.

Not even the prince himself believes he will be overly constrained by the top job as monarch. He intends to make it work for him – for the good of his future subjects and his country, realms and wider commonwealth. To suggest he will not change his character and passions overnight is to fail to appreciate the man. He is more than capable of conducting himself properly as a constitutional monarch and still have passions about particular causes. 'He is bigger than that,' a senior inside source said. The prince has also decided that, unlike some monarchs, such as his grandfather George VI (who was Prince Albert, Duke of York, before ascending the throne), he will not change his name to become George VII, as has been speculated. He will be King Charles III, as he feels he is too old and too well known to be called anything other than Charles. Perhaps more importantly he will not change his style. As one close source put it, 'He will want a seat at the table, not just to be briefed or rubber-stamping the decisions after they are taken.'

When king, Charles will continue to lead as he always has: from the front. He will of course operate within the confines of our unwritten British constitution, but always 'thinking ahead'. For, just like the role of the heir, that of monarch is not set in stone. Although constitutional monarchy is a system of rules, controlling what a monarch can do personally and constitutionally, each king or queen regnant has largely been at liberty to adapt those guidelines as to how they see fit.

If they overstep the invisible line, it is for the sovereign Parliament to act and put a stop to it. Charles indubitably grasps the limitations placed on a constitutional monarch. In fact, there are few people better placed than he who appreciate the role, given his decades serving as the heir apparent. When his time comes to reign, he will patently be inspired by his mother's and grandfather's periods of so doing, but certainly not as a carbon copy. Essentially, however, it will be up to him to define those limitations and, in doing so, define the nature of his reign.

Predominantly, the public role of a king or queen of Britain (or the Commonwealth realms where many of the functions will largely be carried out by the governor general on behalf of the monarch) is to serve as constitutional head of state. That involves carrying out a number of ceremonies deemed essential to the existence and fabric of the government and can be performed only by the person who is the king or queen regnant. These formalities include the appointment of a prime minister to head up a government, the dissolution of Parliament prior to a general election as well as Royal Assent legislation. They appear to be redoubting powers but, in reality and explicitly, they do not allow for the personal views of the sovereign.

Other formalities include the business of the Privy Council, such as proclamations or legislative orders, passing into law appointments of new peerages in the House of Lords and Anglican bishops. The monarch also carries out a ceremonial role on state occasions such as delivering a speech at the state opening of Parliament at the start of each annual session. Again, even though it is called the king's or queen's speech, there is nothing personal about this, either, and simply has the sovereign reading out a speech written by Downing Street as a reminder that it may be his or her government, but in this case said monarch is little more than a figurehead.

The monarch is also expected to preside over state banquets and meetings with other visiting heads of state in a sort of benevolent diplomatic role. These functions are all carried out at the 'request' of the government, usually at Buckingham Palace, the official residence of the British monarch. Hence, during her reign the Queen has paid host to a number of despots and tyrants as well as great leaders and presidents and shown them all the same level of courtesy. The monarch also, in an extension of that diplomatic role, is expected to travel the globe on so-called state visits.

The Queen's age means these visits, such as the autumn 2017 Commonwealth tour starting in Singapore, opening the 2018 Commonwealth Games on the Gold Coast and the visit to Vanuatu, in April 2018, are now undertaken by Charles. During these visits, unlike other members of the Royal Family, the prince, as heir apparent, is not only representing the Queen but, effectively, assumes her role.

As well as being head of state, the sovereign holds two further roles of constitutional substance: Supreme Governor of the Church of England and Commander-in-Chief of the British Armed Forces. It would be wrong to assume that the prince is planning wholesale change to the monarchy when he ascends the throne. It would also be wrong to assume Charles is not obliged to reign in exactly the same way as his mother. She has updated the institution and made it sensitive to a changing public whilst maintaining its traditions. Charles knows that a modern monarchy must never be behind the times, but it must never be ahead of them, either. While heir apparent, he has always avoided running commentaries on how his reign will take shape. After more than half a century of public service, the prince believes few are better placed than he is to appreciate requisite and appropriate constraints on the role of a constitutional monarch. If fate calls upon him to serve, the prince will draw on his own experiences but also act within what he understands as the confines of the constitution.

The RAF Voyager on which I was travelling with the heir apparent and his team was flying towards RAF Brize Norton in Oxfordshire. I had typed up notes gleaned from the short chat I had about the prince's 'red spider memo' across my newspaper report. As I looked at the notes on my screen, one word kept jumping out at me: 'leadership'. Written at 30,000 feet in the air whilst the rest of the passengers tried to catch up with some sleep, it seemed to me that the prince's scribbled words over my commentary article had hit the nail on the head. His reaction could be seen as a barometer of how he intends to reign.

Leadership for the prince is pre-eminent. This is a man who intends to lead as monarch, not just follow. A constitutional monarch is, after all, defined as a sovereign who reigns but does not rule, but there is nothing to prevent them from leading. What makes Charles a good leader? Ostensibly, he has no fixed agenda, certainly not a partisan one, and is a good listener who takes enormous trouble to be on top of global affairs, different cultures and religion. 'He knows he has a unique ability as somebody who can convene important people who would not otherwise sit in a room together,' a close source said.

An example of his ability to convene powerful world figures with opposing agendas would be COP21, the UN conference of Climate Change held in Paris in 2015, not to mention his highly valuable tours of the Middle East and Gulf States. The Foreign Office has repeatedly asked him to visit the region to make use of his great understanding of the region and the respect in which he is held by the royal leaders there, perhaps more than any other member of the Royal Family.

With the prince's interventions on climate change, inner-city deprivation, architecture, alternative medicine and organic farming, he intentionally strayed into what could be deemed the party-political. His critics believe he has sailed too close to the wind. On occasions they have had good reason. His description of the proposed National Gallery extension during a speech to the Royal Institute of British Architects in 1984, calling it, 'a monstrous carbuncle on the face of a much-loved and elegant friend', drew widespread criticism from the industry and politicians, but, it seemed, received general support from the public.

The prince was condemned, too, when, on 11 December 1987, he forthrightly denounced plans for Paternoster Square beside St Paul's Cathedral saying, 'You have to give this much to the Luftwaffe. When it knocked down our buildings, it didn't replace them with anything more offensive than rubble.' And, in the case of the National Theatre building on the capital's South Bank in 1988, he referred to 'a clever way of building a nuclear power station in the middle of London without anyone objecting'.

He was even more scathing about plans for a skyscraper to replace the Victorian Mapping & Webb building in 1984. 'It would be a tragedy if the character and skyline of our capital city were to be further ruined and St Paul's dwarfed by yet another giant glass stump, better suited to downtown Chicago than the City of London.' It seems it is a battle the prince has lost, for, thirty-four years on, the modernists, led by his architectural nemesis Sir Richard Rogers, Baron Rogers of Riverside, appear to have won. For today Sir Christopher Wren's great work, St Paul's Cathedral, is indeed overshadowed by a host of giant glass edifices such as the Shard, the Heron Tower, the Cheesegrater (the Leadenhall Building), the Gherkin (30 St Mary Axe) and the Walkie-Talkie (20 Fenchurch Street). What the prince often finds difficult to fathom is how government-backed 'monstrous, elephantine building projects' that suck exchequers dry – such as the 'Scottish Parliament, the Parliamentary Offices in Parliament Square, and the Dome' – manage to achieve planning permission when they overrun costing and more money is needed.

The prince is not intentionally partisan in the way he approaches the causes he champions. He has always acted for the greater good. After the 2017 ten-day Commonwealth tour of Singapore, Brunei, Malaysia and India, Charles was off again on a solo mission to see at first hand the damage caused by the devastating Hurricane Maria in the Caribbean. Speaking to *The Sun*'s photojournalist, Arthur Edwards, he warned of a pending 'Armageddon' as he surveyed wreckage in Dominica. 'It is extraordinary people can't "read the tea leaves" and understand just what mankind is facing,' he told Mr Edwards. The recognition of climate change and global warming is a massive subject that the prince has made one of the core battles of his life. That is hardly likely to change when he is king.

On that visit in November 2017, he went to the remains of the home of local Sarah Charles. She and twelve members of her family had cowered there as Maria had struck just weeks earlier. Winds ripped off the tin roof and the house was flooded as a nearby river burst its banks. Visibly moved by the visit, the prince said, 'It looked like Armageddon had struck. But what I can never get over – and it fills me with immense admiration – is the way people are so courageous and so resilient.'

For Charles there is no choice for humanity to make, as we are already living on borrowed time. He went on, 'Some people seem to think it's somehow a threat to undermine capitalism if you mention climate change. It isn't. The whole point is to achieve a circular approach which enables us to work with nature. At the moment we are still fighting a battle against nature. You can't do that.'

He added, 'We have to remember there are so many people around the world in other parts who are suffering hugely from the accumulating effects of putting all this $CO_2$ into the atmosphere from all kinds of pollution – from coal-fired power stations to cars, and goodness knows what. All I have tried to do over the years is, along with others, draw attention to the fact that there is not a convenient series of holes in the atmosphere from which all this stuff can escape. So we are heating up everything and the more you warm it up the more you warm the oceans as well.'

It would never occur to the prince to make personal gain from any of his interventions. He is simply taking the initiative, passing on to those with influence to effect change. It shows, too, that when his chance comes Charles will reign in the best interests of the entire country his way.

Critics of the prince often quote passages from the work of Walter Bagehot as if that Victorian writer's work were gospel and cannot be questioned. It is as if, to them, nothing had changed with regard to the monarchy in the years since Bagehot penned his treatise. He wrote in his 1867 pamphlet *The English Constitution*, 'The Sovereign has, under a constitutional monarchy such as ours, three rights – the right to be consulted, the right to encourage, the right to warn.' This is often quoted and rarely challenged. He goes on to add, 'A king of great sense and sagacity would want no others.'

Bagehot's thesis rightly still gets traction. But, considering how the world and institutions, such as the monarchy, have changed since then, it should be put into context. Bagehot, after all, was a lucid political thinker of his time, a time when the working man or woman didn't even have a vote in the UK. His conclusions, perspicacious as they are on Queen Victoria, her family and her monarchy, are not necessarily relevant when examining our evolved monarchal system today. It was after a time of empire, deference and a rigid class system.

One must remember, too, that he also wrote of the British monarchy, 'Its mystery is its life. We must not let in daylight upon magic. We must not bring the Queen into the combat of politics, or she will cease to be reverenced by all combatants.' He penned this when he could not have possibly envisaged the internet, television and twenty-four-hour news media when modern royals, with the notable exception of Queen Elizabeth herself, are expected to give interviews, to explain themselves on camera and give reaction to events happening around them. Could Bagehot have imagined his queen with a Facebook or Twitter account? It would all have been alien to him.

As for 'daylight', it was Elizabeth who said sagaciously in the modern era, 'I have to be seen to be believed.' Encouraged by Princes Charles, William and Harry, the Queen has realised the influence of social media when it comes to getting one's message across. The monarch, unlike US president Trump, has posted on Twitter personally on only two occasions. For her aides, social media has become as important as the royal walkabout, the garden party and her Christmas broadcast in promoting the monarchy brand. Buckingham Palace, Charles at Clarence House and his sons at Kensington Palace use Twitter feeds for today's announcements and reports of audiences and ambassadorial hand-kissing, as well as Instagram timelines of followers, almost before bowing guests have departed the Queen's white drawing room. Images are swiftly pinged out into cyberspace – and without the sometimes unflattering filter applied by mainstream media.

For the royals, social-media platforms are a huge success. Harry's 'mic drop' antics with the Queen and the Obamas, promoting his Invictus Games, went viral on Twitter. Harry has also broadcast live on Facebook being tested for HIV, generating an enormous audience reach. Currently, the @RoyalFamily Twitter account has 3.7 million followers. The palace team also coordinates @KensingtonRoyal, which has 1.6 million followers, keeping abreast of the engagements of the Duke and Duchess of Cambridge and the Duke and Duchess of Sussex. The Prince of Wales is the social-media pioneer. His @ClarenceHouse Twitter account, which has more than 789,000 followers, and his Instagram page, which has 491,000 followers, were royal firsts and are both enjoying 20 per cent year-on-year growth.

For all three palaces, the aim is to increase engagement, particularly with a younger audience and overseas, too. There is no desire to hide away like Bagehot's queen/empress. This twenty-first-century monarchy seems to be doing the precise opposite of what Bagehot advised in Victorian times.

Today it is essential that royals have a voice on all media platforms, in newspaper interviews and in television interviews, too, to remain relevant and to show that, despite being part of a hereditary and unelected institution, they have evolved over the years into one that exists to serve. The Prince of Wales and his sons want to be seen and heard and feel they must embrace new technology and new communication platforms to stay relevant. Charles, after all, was also one of the first senior royals to try Google Hangouts: in 2014 he took part in a live webchat with young volunteers. William and Harry had already tried out the technology, speaking from Buckingham Palace to youngsters from five Commonwealth countries. This is a new Royal Family which, unlike widowed, reclusive Victoria, actively wants to engage with society and to have a loud voice.

Many constitution experts still bow too readily to Bagehot and his astute observations of his Victorian age and his Victorian monarchy. Republicans often quote passages of Bagehot's work as incontrovertible proof to make a point about the prince's so-called meddling. Times change and institutions, such as our monarchy (as well as the unwritten constitution of this country that embraces it) have evolved over time in order to stay relevant to the people who sustain it.

Half a century after Bagehot penned his famous thesis, monarchy was still by far the predominant form of government in Europe, with only three republican governments in place in France, Switzerland and Portugal (whose monarch was deposed in 1910). There were constitutional monarchies in Britain, Italy, Denmark, Norway and Sweden, Belgium, Luxembourg and the Netherlands. There was also the constitutional state of the Austro-Hungarian Empire, and the less 'constitutional' empires in Germany, divided into princely states with a Kaiser and Tsarist Russia. During and after World War I, most of these monarchies were deposed and, as result, today most European states remain republics.

Of the surviving European monarchies, with the exception of perhaps the Danish, the British monarchy is by far and away the oldest. Our Queen can trace her ancestry back to Egbert, King of Wessex, in the ninth century. Except for Oliver (and Richard) Cromwell's interregnum of 1649–60, the royal descendants of Egbert have reigned in England and then Britain for 1,200 years. The concept of constitutional monarchy, in fact, dates from the Magna Carta, drawn up by the barons and accepted by King John at Runnymede on 15 June 2015. But the significance of the Magna Carta lies less in its detailed provisions and more in the two implied underlying propositions. First, a king or queen regnant must rule according to the law and, crucially, must also be answerable to the way he or she rules; second, and equally as important, an individual's rights transcend the personal desires of the monarch. These fundamental principles have echoed through the ages.

Over time the power of the monarch has been eroded, the most physical and dramatic coming with the brutal execution of Charles I in 1649. His severed head not only signalled a brief period of Britain's being run by a form of republican government, but the interregnum ended the concept of the 'divine right of kings' – the doctrine that kings derive their authority from God, not their subjects. Since then, the power of the restored monarchy has been significantly reduced over time.

The Glorious Revolution of 1688 also significantly changed the relationship between monarch and parliament, demonstrating that parliament could alter the title to the throne in the case of what it saw as misgovernment, as in the case of James II. The Bill of Rights (1689) ensured all Catholics and those married to Catholics would be excluded from the throne, too. The Coronation Oath Act (1688) prescribed that the monarch had to swear to maintain the Protestant religion. The Act of Settlement of 1701 further defined the concept of constitutional monarchy, reinforcing the constitutional rule that Parliament had the right to determine not only the succession to the throne but also the conditions under which the Crown was to be held. The Reform Act of 1832 had the most radical impact on the evolution of our constitutional monarchy, sabotaging any remaining real power of the sovereign. It was a weakened position an immature Queen Victoria failed to understand fully when she ascended the throne in 1837 aged just eighteen.

Bagehot had many cogent arguments and undoubted talent, but seeing into the future was not one of them. When he wrote *The English Constitution* a depressed Queen Victoria was still dressed in black, mourning the death of her husband and consort Prince Albert, who had died at Windsor Castle in December 1861 aged just forty-two. It was a period that was to last until around 1876 and defined by her withdrawal from public life. It also marked the dawning of a rising republican movement. In the final period of her reign until her death in 1901, she re-engaged with her subjects and her government resumed the palpable bias against William Gladstone's Liberal Party.

Victoria had relied heavily on her first cousin and husband, Albert, perhaps more than any other monarch before or since. During the day, the royal couple would sit side by side at two desks working through the many red boxes of correspondence. After Albert's shock death, however, she would not allow her heir apparent, the future King Edward VII, access to the red boxes, much to his frustration (especially as Victoria did give his haemophiliac younger brother Prince Leopold, Duke of Albany, her eighth child, who died at just thirty in 1884, a key so *he* could read).

Queen Victoria's reign saw the evolution of constitutional monarchy into its modern form. It was her profound scepticism of the spread of liberalism and malevolence towards the expansion of democratic rule that, in many ways, saved the monarchy. Ironically, it was the growth of the power of a sovereign parliament with MPs elected by popular vote, and an executive formed from those elections, that strengthened the reputation and acclaim of the monarch and the system she represented. The kings and queen regnant who followed Victoria adopted the tenets of constitutional monarchy spelled out by Bagehot. Indeed, George V, George VI, Elizabeth II and Prince Charles himself have all been schooled in the English Constitution in depth. Since the end of Victoria's reign, there would have been no foundational revisions to the monarchal model or to the role of its head.

Perhaps the most significant outside intervention in changing our modern monarchy since Bagehot came from an unlikely source. It seems almost unimaginable that the perceptive writer and historian John Grigg – 2nd Baron Altrincham from 1955 to 1963 until he disclaimed that title under the Peerage Act on the day it received the Royal Assent, and who died at the age of seventy-seven in the Queen's Golden Jubilee year (2002) – was once regarded as a dangerous revisionist. Denounced as a crypto-republican, he was widely criticised after he penned an article in August 1957 arguing that the Queen's court was too upper class and British, and therefore harmful to the monarch and the institution it served. Instead, he advocated a more classless Commonwealth court and dubbed Elizabeth's court both 'complacent' and 'out of touch'. He went on to attack the Queen personally and criticised her style of speaking as a 'pain in the neck'.

Writing in the *National and English Review*, a publication that he also edited, he said, 'Like her mother, she appears to be unable to string even a few sentences together without a written text. . . The personality conveyed by the utterances which are put into her mouth is that of a priggish schoolgirl, captain of the hockey team, a prefect and a recent candidate for Confirmation.' Grigg utterly deplored the way a monarchy that should have been truly national and above class divisions was, in practice and reality, intimately and almost exclusively associated with the British upper classes. His article achieved exactly what they wanted, creating uproar in the popular press and other media. He was dropped by the BBC from *Any Questions*; the Duke of Argyll, rather extremely, said that he should be 'hanged, drawn and quartered' after he had gently reiterated his strictures in a television interview with Robin Day. He was even assaulted in the street when leaving Television House after giving an interview on ITV defending his article, when a member of the League of Empire Loyalists, Philip Kinghorn Burbidge, slapped him hard in the face, saying, 'Take that from the League of Empire Loyalists.' Burbidge was arrested and later fined twenty shillings, and outside court the defiant defendant said, 'Due to the scurrilous attack by Lord Altrincham I felt it was up to a decent Briton to show resentment.'

Grigg was hardly from revolutionary stock, which perhaps made his public criticism all the more serious. He was the son of Edward Grigg, a *Times* journalist associated with the imperialist circle of Joseph Chamberlain and also a member of Winston

Churchill's wartime government, who was created 1st Baron Altrincham in 1945. Eton, Grenadier Guards and New College, Oxford, meant John Grigg came from the very heart of the British establishment. What seems remarkable today, however, is the degree of outrage Grigg's reflections provoked considering how mild they were. In the 1950s you could hardly say a word against the royal family, let alone Her Majesty the Queen.

It wasn't the first time Grigg had shared his criticisms of the monarchy. He aired these ideas at the time of the coronation in 1953, yet at that time, as the country celebrated the crowning of the new Elizabethan era, nobody paid much attention. But, by 1957, the national mood had shifted, partly because the shine of the new queen had worn off, perhaps, but also because Britain had been through the trauma of the Suez Crisis, which ended in disaster and caused a great deal of soul searching in Britain. Suddenly, Grigg's ideas struck a chord. The irony about the 'Altrincham episode' was that, in reality, he was a supporter of constitutional monarchy, not somebody hell-bent on destroying it. His criticism was directed not so much at the Queen, but at the army of outdated courtiers whom he believed were failing the institution. He clearly spoke not as a revolutionist but as a free-thinking, enlightened Tory and as a strong believer in constitutional monarchy. He made it clear that he had no wish to be disloyal, merely to help what he saw as an outdated institution kicking and screaming into the twenty-first century.

The brouhaha had the desired effect. Her feathers ruffled, the Queen did what she does best: she listened quietly and said nothing; but, slowly and surely, changes were made. She accepted that the institution had to modernise to remain relevant so, ultimately, the monarchy adapted. Some of Grigg's suggestions, such as televising the monarch's Christmas message (introduced in 1957) and ending the class-ridden ritual of debutantes (upper-class young woman making her first appearance in fashionable society) being presented to the Queen, were also introduced by 1958.

Monarchy is, after all, only as good as the people doing the job. Today, commentators acknowledge that one of the Queen's great achievements has been to modernise the monarchy seamlessly and without destroying its traditions. As one of her former senior advisers said, 'She is not the type of person who would throw the baby out with the bathwater. But, when she needs to act, she has always acted decisively.' For some years she agreed to allow Charles access to all ministerial papers secreted in the Barrow Hepburn & Gale-produced scarlet cases, the so-called 'red boxes'. She has encouraged him to invite ministers and ambassadors to audiences with him, too.

Crucially, constitutionally, like the monarch as heir apparent, Prince Charles, too, has the right 'to be consulted, encourage and warn'. Like the Queen, he knows the parameters of his role only too well. Thus, when republican-minded critics complain that he is 'butting in' or 'overstepping the mark' they are missing the point. For the blunt truth is this dissident prince is simply doing his job.

Monarchy is the oldest form of government in Britain. Charles inherently knows, as does his mother, that its first duty is to 'inspire' – another of the Victorian polemicist Bagehot's observations. Doing nothing is hardly inspirational and, in his view, not an option. As 'Head of Nation' our sovereign already does this. She has become the beacon of stability and unity. This role may be less formal than that of head of state, but it is no less important for the social and cultural functions it satisfies. The sovereign provides a focus for national identity, unity and pride; for giving a sense of stability and continuity; for recognising success, achievement and excellence and for supporting service to others. Perhaps this is why Charles feels, before attaining the top job, throughout his life he has tried to justify his existence. His motto as Prince of Wales is the German '*Ich Dien*'. As we saw earlier, this means 'I Serve' – an aphorism that sums up Charles to the core. It is what he sees as his duty and what he has been doing all his adult life.

## Chapter Eleven

# DEFENDING
# FAITH

———~———

'When you begin to look at what. . .[they] are saying
you find that so much of the wisdom that is represented within
these religions coincides.'

The Prince of Wales in an interview with biographer
Jonathan Dimbleby, *circa* 1994

Successive English (and later British) monarchs since Henry VIII
have all been known by the title Defender of the Faith – *Fidei
Defensor* (feminine: *Fidei Defensatrix*). It was bestowed on the
tyrannical Henry by Pope Leo X on 11 October 1521 because he
was a good Roman Catholic. His first wife, Catherine of Aragon,
had been his sister-in-law, married to his older brother Prince
Arthur Tudor in 1501 before his premature death six months
later. She too was made Defender of the Faith in her own right
as Henry's Queen Consort. Ironically, the title was originally
conferred on Henry in recognition of his treatise *Assertio Septem
Sacramentorum* (*Defence of the Seven Sacraments*), which defended

the sacramental nature of marriage and the supremacy of the Pope. It was a work that was seen as important as it opposed the then radical ideas of Martin Luther and the Protestant Reformation that was sweeping across Europe at the time.

When Henry broke with Rome nine years later in 1530 and was established as head of his new Church of England, the title was revoked by Pope Leo's successor, Pope Paul III, and the king was later excommunicated. In 1544 the English Parliament conferred the same title, 'Defender of the Faith', on the king and all his successors, now not for defending Catholicism but for his role and position in the new Anglican faith, of which they remained Supreme Governors, with the exception of Henry's Roman Catholic daughter, Mary I.

It meant too that the monarch was formally of higher rank than the sitting Archbishop of Canterbury as primate. When Elizabeth II was crowned Queen Regnant at Westminster Abbey in 1953, she was styled Elizabeth II of the United Kingdom of Great Britain and Northern Ireland and Her other Realms and Territories Queen, Head of the Commonwealth, Defender of the Faith. *Fidei Defensor* is even represented on all British coins by the abbreviation, 'F D' or 'FID DEF'. It is therefore embedded in our history and the history of our royalty.

In 1952, when the Queen ascended the throne on the death of her father, she too, became Defender of the Faith and her coronation confirmed that. It was a very different, more religious and faithful society back then – an Anglican-led Christian society. Many of her subjects still believed that the Queen had actually been appointed by God.

The Prince of Wales will become head of a very different,

multidenominational nation, and where, by the time his son succeeds him, according to census analysis, Christianity could already no longer be the prevailing faith. Indeed, authoritative studies predict all Christians, including both Protestant and Roman Catholic, will be in the minority in the UK by the middle of this century amid surging growth in atheism and those who follow Islam. According to projections, the proportion of the British population identifying themselves as Christian will reduce by almost a third by 2050 to stand at just 45.4 per cent compared with almost two-thirds in 2010. The number of Muslims in Britain is predicted to more than double to 11.3 per cent, or one in nine of the total population, during that time.

Charles's more persistent detractors still cling on to half-truths and flimsy myths as proof that he is not made of the right stuff to reign. One such often-cited falsity centres on his 'faith', or, rather, his supposed lack it, and what it claims is his less-than-solid relationship with the established church, the Church of England. Unlike his mother, who is a devout High Church Anglican, Charles displays a willingness to embrace and work alongside other faiths, and that is frequently seen as a weakness rather than something to be encouraged.

Charles has even been accused of being a secret Muslim. Soundbites plucked from long, detailed speeches make headlines, claiming to show his conversion. He said in a speech titled 'Islam and the West' at the Oxford Centre for Islamic Studies on 27 October 1993, 'Islam can teach us today a way of understanding and living in the world which Christianity itself is poorer for having lost.' This was widely quoted as some kind of proof that he had abandoned Christianity.

It is fair to say that he has long espoused the positives about the religion where others have focused on the negatives. When he was widely criticised for this in the early 1990s at the time of the extremist militant Islamic factions, Charles, to his credit, was quick to point out, 'Extremism is no more the monopoly of Islam than it is the monopoly of other religions, including Christianity. He caused more controversy when he said on 20 June 1994 of Christianity, 'It has no right to challenge Islam or any other religion. It is merely a Western face of God.'

In that same keynote speech in 1993, he was even more supportive, calling on the West to recognise Islam as a part of its culture not a thing apart. 'Medieval Islam was a religion of remarkable tolerance for its time, allowing Jews and Christians the right to practise their inherited beliefs, and setting an example which was not, unfortunately, copied for many centuries in the West,' he said. 'The surprise, ladies and gentlemen, is the extent to which Islam has been a part of Europe for so long, first in Spain, then in the Balkans, and the extent to which it has contributed so much towards the civilisation which we all too often think of, wrongly, as entirely Western.'

In a 1997 *Middle East Quarterly* article entitled 'Prince Charles of Arabia', Ronni L. Gordon and David M. Stillman bizarrely examined evidence that Charles had actually secretly converted to Islam. They sifted through his public statements, some where the prince in their view defended Islamic law, praised the status of Muslim women and, apparently, saw in Islam a solution for Britain's ailments. Their conclusion was fudged but put on the record that, 'Should Charles persist in his admiration of Islam and defamation of his own culture', his accession to the throne would indeed usher in a 'different kind of monarchy'. That, of course, would go without saying. The key word in this conclusion is 'should'. The prince has long faced criticism over his acceptance of other faiths and willingness to embrace and understand other views and beliefs. It is something for which he should be praised rather than seen as having a failing.

Since 1993, he has been patron of the Oxford Centre for Islamic Studies, where he gave a speech in that year on 'Islam and the West' that was reprinted enthusiastically in newspapers across the Middle East and earned him widespread praise. But does an ability to see what is good in another religion make him a convert?

In truth, he is a very natural adapter, a broad-centred man, deeply aware of others. He sees the commonality between different faiths as a positive, not a negative. His religious life began conventionally enough. He was only thirty days old when Geoffrey Fisher, then the Archbishop of Canterbury, christened him in the Music Room at Buckingham Palace on 15 December 1948. His mother, then Princess Elizabeth, chose the first hymn to reflect the sacred significance of the event: 'Holy, Holy, Holy'.

Twenty years later, as an undergraduate student at Cambridge, however, he began writing to Mervyn Stockwood, then the Bishop of Southwark, who refused to dismiss 'psychic happenings' and believed that the miracles of Jesus demonstrated 'the Saviour's oneness with nature'.

Later, in his twenties, Charles grew close to Laurens van der Post, the South African-born writer and explorer, whom he would later ask to become one of Prince William's godparents. Van der Post introduced the prince to mysticism and encouraged him 'to see the old world of the spirit'. The prince was entranced by his adviser's history of bushmen in the Kalahari Desert, and travelled with him to spend a week in the Aberdare Mountains in Kenya. The friendship left a lasting impression on the prince's faith. He once spoke up for respecting the natural world for the glory of God.

The prince also admires the Orthodox Church, and has made regular spiritual retreats to stay in the monasteries of Mount Athos, the Greek republic run by two thousand monks. Officially, he goes there because he is interested in the architecture and spirituality of Athos. Of course, there is a family connection, too: his grandmother, Princess Alice (the Duke of Edinburgh's mother) was an Orthodox nun. He has also incorporated Byzantine icons in the Sanctuary, a simple chapel in the grounds at Highgrove. It is a very important place for him, where he goes to pray and to meditate.

His embrace of Orthodoxy has even led to wild speculation in some quarters. After one of his visits to Mount Athos, an Athonite monk was quoted in one newspaper declaring that there is no question that the British royal is Orthodox in his heart. Those close to the prince dismiss claims that he is a convert, insisting that he remains a practising Anglican. Indeed, those close to him say it is because he has read and thought so deeply about his own Christian heritage and is firmly rooted in it that he is able to engage with other religions.

During his visits around the country he makes sure he is balanced, visiting Sikh, Muslim, Hindu and Christian communities. He has studied the Koran in depth and has been a student of the Arabic language for years. He has also studied Judaism in depth and is close to Jonathan Sacks, the former Chief Rabbi. He believes that both faiths have 'a great deal in common' with Christianity. 'The future surely lies in rediscovering the universal truths that dwell at the heart of these religions,' he has said.

The prince's belief in interfaith dialogue has long been on his agenda. He believes wholeheartedly that talking openly and honestly can only help strengthen communities and understanding. He told his biographer Jonathan Dimbleby in 1994, 'When you begin to look at what. . .[they] are saying you find that so much of the wisdom that is represented within these religions coincides.'

Clearly, our next Supreme Governor of the Church of England plans to do the job a little differently. 'He is an individual who wants to chart new territory, and that will be very interesting indeed,' says Lord Carey, the former Archbishop of Canterbury. 'He is very outspoken.' Over the last four decades, this has become obvious. The prince has tested the boundaries of his public role by attending Catholic masses, and his private spiritual enquiry has been frequent fodder for satirists, forcing him to deny using ouija boards and 'dabbling in the occult'.

Such caricatures only serve to distort the prince and his position. 'All I have ever wanted to do is build bridges that span these chasms,' the prince explained. But his bid to build bridges has left some confused and his critics to point an accusatory finger, wrongly, suggesting a lack of commitment to being a Christian and to the Church of England. They could not be further from the truth.

Much of the doubt stems from Charles's admission of adultery during his marriage to Diana, Princess of Wales, and the bitter divorce that followed. His detractors even to this day seem hell-bent on ignoring the fact that he remained 'faithful and honourable' in the marriage until, in his view, it had 'irretrievably broken down, us both having tried'. There was wrongdoing on both sides.

It is also driven by his apparently telling biographer Dimbleby in the 1994 book *Prince of Wales* that he wanted to be seen as a 'Defender of Faith' rather than 'Defender of the Faith' when he ascends the throne. Dimbleby said that Charles was planning this symbolic change when he became king to reflect Britain's multicultural society. Understandably, it caused a furore at the time, particularly amongst senior Anglicans and politicians.

Changing years of established tradition over the title would, after all, mean Charles overcoming huge obstacles, including getting Parliament to agree to amend the 1953 Royal Titles Act, which came into law after changes were made for the Queen's coronation in the same year. While laudable, the coronation is an Anglican ceremony and any change would require legislation. One of Britain's foremost constitutional experts, Professor Vernon Bogdanor, Emeritus Professor of Politics and Government at Oxford University, speculated that after the coronation, which would take place at Westminster Abbey, it was plausible that a second service would be held for other denominations and faiths, such as the Muslims and Hindus. 'It would be a way of the new king showing their importance in the country,' said the professor, who is also Research Professor at the Institute for Contemporary British History at King's College London and Professor of Politics at the New College of the Humanities.

As sovereign, Charles will want to demonstrate that he can set an example for the entire country to follow and the coronation – which would follow his ascension within a few months rather than the usual year or even longer – would be a perfect vehicle to do that. But such a dramatic change to the service, with Charles revising nearly five hundred years of tradition when Dimbleby published, led to a predictable backlash from so-called 'outraged' MPs publicly reminding the future king that he would be playing a dangerous game, as Britain was a Christian country. 'It's our heritage and we should defend it,' came the message from parliamentarians. The directive to the tinkering prince was clear: 'Don't tinker with a state occasion without clearing it with us, the eyes, ears and voice of the people and your future subjects – first.'

Since then, Charles's position on the wording to be used at his coronation has categorically changed. It has been made clear to this author that Charles will 'absolutely 100 per cent' be named as 'Defender of the Faith' when he is crowned king. But he will also demonstrate in his reign that he believes wholeheartedly in the importance of his connecting with all faiths of the subjects he will reign over.

There is no doubt that Charles's faith is all encompassing. His appreciation of other religions comes from his wealth of study and reading over many years of interest. He makes all British citizens feel they are part of the grand historical narrative. As a result, he is the one Western statesman who is still held in a high standing in the Muslim world. This is why he has been asked to represent the Queen in the Middle East and Gulf States on numerous occasions. He is seen as an envoy who understands and respects both sides.

Views about his faith are typical of the issues that still swirl around the prince. The truth is, however, far from disturbing him, most of the time he actually enjoys controversy. It, after all, encourages debate. He has always seen himself as a freethinker working against an established consensus.

*Chapter Twelve*

# DISSIDENT AT
# HEART

—————∾—————

'He [Prince Charles] would readily embrace the political
aspects of any contentious issue he was interested in. . .
He carried it out in a very considered, thoughtful and
researched way. He often referred to himself as a dissident
working against the prevailing political consensus.'

MARK BOLLAND, DEPUTY PRIVATE SECRETARY TO THE
PRINCE OF WALES BETWEEN 1997 AND 2002

If Charles and not his mother had been monarch at the time
of the second Iraq War, when Tony Blair sent UK troops to
die for their country, his weekly Wednesday meeting with the
king would indubitably have been a verbal battle ground. Would
Blair have been so hawkish if his monarch and commander-in-
chief of the British armed forces, Charles, demanded he disclose
and discuss the so-called irrefutable intelligence that Saddam
Hussein had weapons of mass destruction? After all, it is a prime
minister's constitutional responsibility to tell the monarch what is

happening and the monarch's constitutional to probe and to ask questions about what they are told.

It is of course supposition, and we do not know what stance the Queen took with Blair. Like her, ultimately a King Charles would have had to remain politically neutral. That said, I cannot imagine that the prince, given his breadth of knowledge and contacts in the Gulf region and Arab world, would have remained silent. He was, after all, not alone in his grave reservations at the time. The United Nations secretary-general, Kofi Annan, said at the time he believed the US-led, UK-backed invasion of Iraq was an illegal act that contravened the UN Charter and the decision to take action in Iraq should have been made by the Security Council, not unilaterally. Blair's government responded by saying the attorney-general made the 'legal basis. . .clear at the time'.

Many close to the prince, however, believe in private that, while he might well, as monarch, feel he would have no choice but to acquiesce, he would undoubtedly have voiced 'his strongest possible objections' on the war. He most certainly would have 'advised and warned' against British military intervention. His advice to Blair would have been to heed the warnings of Arab leaders in the region, men with whom Charles had built up good working relations over the years.

Charles, after all, was diametrically opposed to the Blair–Bush Iraq War strategy, along with Labour's former foreign secretary, Robin Cook, who had tried to pursue an ethical foreign policy during his tenure, was demoted to Leader of the House in 2001 and quit the government in March two years later, saying nobly, 'I cannot support a war without international agreement or domestic support.' He went on to state that, because the public was unconvinced by the arguments for war, it was not the right step. Cook's words in the House of Commons echoed what Charles was saying in private to friends in high places, including leading politicians.

'There is no doubt Mr Blair would not have been given an easy ride from HRH over Iraq Two,' an ex-household source reiterated. 'I can say without any doubt that those weekly meetings would have been tough going for the PM. As king, he would have been given access to all the state papers and would have insisted on seeing the so-called proof that Saddam had weapons of mass destruction ready to use. Blair would not have had an easy ride.'

A British monarch's residual powers – the so-called royal prerogative – are mostly exercised through the government of the day. These include the power to enact legislation, to award honours (on the advice of the prime minister), to sign treaties and, crucially in this case, to declare war. But would the prince, given his deeply held conviction, simply have rubberstamped a decision to invade Iraq as the Queen did? I think it is at best doubtful.

Over the years, Charles has established close working and personal ties with royal Arab leaders. He is well respected in the Gulf States and Middle East, not least for his sympathetic speeches about Islam. Like Blair, he studied the Koran in depth and has even over years learned Arabic. When corresponding with Arab leaders he always signs his name in Arabic, another small nod to respecting the other culture. Indeed, he believes Islam can teach us all a way of understanding and living in the world, which, sadly, Christianity, he believes, is poorer for having lost.

Prince Charles believes that, by shackling Britain to the flawed

Bush administration, Tony Blair missed a golden opportunity to forge an alternative consensus, one that both secured the crucial support of Arab leaders and embraced their unique perspective and understanding of the often troubled region.

Among friends Charles was less diplomatic about the premier. Privately, he castigated both President George W. Bush and Prime Minister Blair's combative role in Operation Iraqi Freedom, the 2003 military invasion of Iraq. His views did not come with hindsight. Charles made his no-nonsense position clear to those in power at the time. He told political figures and those in his trusted circle that he regarded the Bush Administration as 'terrifying' and pilloried what he believes was Blair's lack of perspicacity. He believed Blair had behaved like Bush's 'poodle' and said so.

One of his circle put it, 'Whenever he followed in the wake of the Prime Minister on an overseas visit he would quote a phrase dryly, "Thou shalt go behind the rear of the Lord to declare his song." It would always get a laugh.'

Long before the BBC report in May 2003 the Prince of Wales cast serious doubt on the government's 2002 SIS intelligence 'dossier' (that it had been 'sexed-up' by Blair's spin doctor Alastair Campbell, and stated that Saddam's Iraq had weapons of mass destruction capable of being deployed within forty-five minutes). He believed the president 'lacked intelligence'. He said Bush would always remain a 'mystery' to him.

On Blair, the prince was even more condemnatory. With a heavy dollop of irony, he scornfully dubbed the premier 'our magnificent leader' whenever talking about him in private and derided him for ignoring the wealth of sound intelligence available to him at the time that contradicted the American view. The prince believed Blair's decision to send in our troops, thus endorsing the Americans' stance, had simply 'stirred up a hornets' nest' in the Gulf region. He repeatedly told friends that Blair should have listened to Arab leaders about how to act over Iraq. After all, Western style democracy in Iraq, the prince felt, was and always will be a 'pipe dream'.

But, at the time of this second invasion of Iraq, Charles was deeply concerned as the Arab rulers had repeatedly told him how uneasy they were about Blair becoming so closely aligned with Bush and how 'bewildered and saddened' they were by the UK's position in being 'tied to the USA's coattails' over Iraq.

Charles asked one high-level source damningly, 'Why did Mr Blair do it, despite what they must all have been telling him before the conflict about the dangers of stirring the hornets' nest up in this part of the world?'

'The prince,' one senior source and former member of the Royal Household said, 'had a very clear position on the West's so-called democratisation of Iraq and the region based on years of study and conversations with leaders there. HRH did try very hard to engage senior figures on this, but nobody in government wanted to listen to a word he said. Their minds were made up.'

When given the opportunity the prince would point out why the delicate differences in culture in the region were crucial to understand. It was a region dominated by tribal loyalties, and still is. So marching in carrying a banner for Western-style democracy was both foolhardy and futile. One of the prince's circle, who was fully aware of his views at the time, said, 'The prince was wise enough to foresee that. Why weren't the politicians of the day? It was as if they had. Perhaps it didn't suit their or the government's hawkish agenda at the time.' He never understood why politicians thought they had the monopoly on wisdom and, in his view, it was never more lacking than in the case of the second Gulf War.

The 2003 invasion of Iraq lasted from 20 March to 1 May. In the immediate aftermath of the war, Charles found the United States and United Kingdom government 'solutions' to be both naïve and inept. The prince privately questioned the legitimacy of so-called 'democratic elections' that followed when it was happening in a background of intimidation, violence and intertribal feuding. The exclusion of Baathists would particularly infuriate him. It was 'beyond' him, he would say, how a sufficiently stable government would be able to unify all the disparate and opposing elements in a country that had been through such traumas. 'How will it ever be formed, let alone succeed?'

One impeccable source said, 'Around this time the prince grew increasingly frustrated with the Iraq issue. It left him deeply depressed. Yes, there was a lot of talk about democracy, tolerance and people working together, but he felt this really lacked an appreciation for the people, their beliefs, and the innately tribal society we were dealing with meant these so-called solutions were incompetent.'

Another informed source told the author, 'I remember one evening when the Boss was particularly animated on this subject. He was animated and very critical of the Bush administration and the President in particular, saying that he felt our children's futures appear to be in the hands of what he described as an "awful" administration and it absolutely terrified him. He just didn't trust them one bit.

'The prince had spent many, many years cultivating high-level contacts in the region and enjoys close and mutually respectful friendships with the ruling families.' He 'believed it exceedingly difficult to introduce democracy to such a society and which has such tensions between Sunni, Shia, Kurds, Turcoman and Assyrians,' the source went on.

The prince, according to sources, maintained it was 'absolutely extraordinary' that neither the Americans nor those in authority in the UK ever seemed to listen to the Arab perspective or consider their knowledge of Iraq and its religious and tribal complexities when seeking postwar solutions there. Ignoring their perspective, the prince felt, was fatal and had led to what he described as 'the bewildering mess we are facing now at home and abroad'.

Charles believes such 'dismissive unwillingness' to pay any attention whatsoever to the advice of elders in the region was shown to be extremely costly and led to the influence of Al-Sayyid Ali al-Husseini al-Sistani (commonly known as the Grand Ayatollah Sistani in the West, born in 1930), the Spiritual Leader of Shia Muslims in Iraq and one of the most senior clerics in Shia Islam.

In May 2007, hundreds of Shia Muslims demonstrated publicly in Basra and Najaf over comments made by Ahmed Mansour during a television broadcast of Al Jazeera. Mansour voiced scepticism about Sistani, suggesting he was not aware of contemporary problems in Iraq, and claimed Sistani's edicts were, largely, written and disseminated by aides. Despite his great age, Sistani is one of the most influential figures in post-invasion Iraq. He issued a fatwa in June 2014. It called for 'citizens to defend the country, its people, the honour of its citizens, and its sacred places', and called on Iraqis to join the armed forces to fight the terror threat that at that time had taken over Mosul and Tikrit and was threatening Baghdad.

A direct result of US and UK policy in the post-Saddam era would eventually lead to the kind of situation everyone wanted to avoid: an extremist, religious form of government. The prince felt that intelligent voices in the region, such as Jordan's King Abdullah and before him his father King Hussein, were being muted, particularly by the Bush administration. The prince has a deep affection for 'the dear old Jordanians', who have always made him feel at home by their friendliness, courtesy and continuing regard for many things British, particularly at a time when so many of the British values and traditions viewed affectionately by the Jordanians are really no longer in existence in the UK as a result of 'deliberate cynicism and ridicule'.

One former member of the prince's household divulged that Charles was completely baffled by Bush and his stance in totally ignoring the advice of local leaders. 'The prince could not understand the sense in America's position,' the source said, 'which was a need to revisit the "crazy" de-Baathifican policy which had led to the exclusion of so many badly needed professional people throughout Iraqi society and turned so many people against the coalition.'

Charles, the source said, was particularly derogatory about Bush's Secretary of State, Condoleezza Rice – the first black woman to hold that post – and the extent of what he deemed US ignorance of the Middle East. The prince couldn't fathom why Ms Rice resisted all requests to visit the area. And some of her statements left him cold. 'The people of the Middle East share the desire for freedom. We have an opportunity – and an obligation – to help them turn this desire into reality.' But what does that actually mean and how on earth were they going to implement it? he would question.

In the prince's view, the only way proper democracy will ever be achieved in Iraq and the West and stand any chance of winning the war on terror is by dealing with the 'real toxin' infecting the whole world: the Israel–Palestine question. He maintains that the West must also focus on education and resisting what he believes is a 'terrible distortion' of Islam and how it is perceived. Only then – when the wider world embraces the real Islam, combined with a serious collaborative effort to find a workable solution to the Israel–Palestine question – will, in the prince's opinion, the rage that drives the war on terror start to wane. The lack of a realistic and satisfactory solution to the Israel–Palestine problem, in his view, is the fundamental reason for the hostility and all the 'pent-up poison' throughout the Islamic world.

'I have heard him [Charles] say time and again, "Remove the poison and you remove the cause of so much of the terrorism,"' the close source said. It is the prince's core belief on the issue, the source added.

A regular and welcome visitor to the Gulf States today, the prince enjoys close ties with the ruling houses, who include some of the world's last remaining absolute monarchies. On his visit to the UAE and Bahrain in November 2016, they afforded him great respect.

He is seen as a friend of some of the most powerful families on the planet. Among them are the Al Thanis of Qatar, the Husseins of Jordan and the Al Sauds of Saudi Arabia, all of whom have known the prince personally for many years and from whom he commands respect. Charles sees part of his role, whenever he visits the region, to make these rulers, so often ignored by the superpower USA, feel how valued they are to Britain and how important that long-standing relationship is.

Charles's Arab sympathies have led him to be accused of being anti-Jewish and anti-American. Perhaps that is one reason why it was his son William, not he, who was chosen by the Queen and Foreign Office to make the historic first official royal visit to Israel and the occupied Palestinian West Bank in June 2017 while his father stayed at home. William would have consulted his father before making the visit, but surely Charles, not William, should have been the one to go?

Positive headlines flowed from the moment William touched down in the region. He was predictably dubbed 'peacemaker' in the headlines and there is little doubt he should be lauded for his deft diplomacy. Inevitably, he found himself being drawn into the complex politics of the region and asked to act as a peace envoy when Israel's president asked him to take a message of hope to the Palestinian premier. British officials immediately stepped in and insisted that was not William's role, but hoped his landmark visit to the Jewish state and the occupied Palestinian West Bank would act as a catalyst, highlighting the need to kickstart a long-stalled peace process in the world's most intractable dispute. His Foreign Office-led move in embarking on the visit sparked a call for peace from Israel to Palestine's president Mahmoud Abbas and placed the second in line to the throne into the role of statesman.

The Prince of Wales's well-known public views on Islam and Arab friendships probably disqualified him from the role of peacemaker.

Instead, while William was predictably winning plaudits from the travelling British press, Charles was left to ponder back home, carrying out official duties such as bestowing a knighthood on Barry Gibb, the only surviving member of the Bee Gees.

Was this a missed opportunity for Charles to be appreciated as a world statesman and the peacemaker he undoubtedly is? Or was it an example of a dissident prince not having an opportunity because his views on the issue were too widely known? Was he seen by the Foreign Office as too much of an Arabist to achieve the best results?

The prince has, after all, never shied away from espousing his views. He is careful what he says in the speeches he writes with his reams of edits. Privately, Charles disagrees with the bans imposed in France and Belgium on Muslim women covering their faces with burqas and niqabs, seeing it as 'an infringement of human rights', which criminalises women rather than challenging the custom. He has made it clear to ministers, too, that he no longer wishes to be used to promote British arms in Gulf States. But anti-Jewish? That is certainly not his intention or his position. However, to this day he strongly believes a solution can be achieved only by listening to and acting upon the advice of powerful Muslim figures.

Indeed, Charles came under fire in November 2017 when his views, revealed publicly in a letter he penned to his friend and mentor Laurens van der Post in 1986, came to light, saying that he blamed the 'influx of foreign Jews' for causing unrest in the Middle East and he believed America should 'take on the Jewish lobby'.

The prince argued that the exodus of European Jews in the middle of the last century 'helped to cause the great problems' in the Middle East. 'I now appreciate that Arabs and Jews were all a Semitic people originally and it is the influx of foreign, European Jews [especially from Poland, they say] which has helped to cause the great problems.'

He went on, 'I know there are so many complex issues, but how can there ever be an end to terrorism unless the causes are eliminated? Surely some US president has to have the courage to stand up and take on the Jewish lobby in the US? I must be naïve, I suppose!' The letter was found in a public archive and was written on 24 November 1986, following an official visit the then thirty-eight-year-old Charles had made to Saudi Arabia, Bahrain and Qatar with his then wife, Princess Diana.

He wrote that the tour was 'fascinating' and that he had learned a lot about the Middle East and Arab outlook. He added in the letter, 'Tried to read bit of Koran on way out and it gave me some insight into the way they [Arabs] think and operate. Don't think they could understand us through reading Bible though!' Clarence House rather lamely said in a statement that the opinions expressed in the 1986 letter were 'not the Prince's own views' but instead reflected the opinions of those he met on his trip. It certainly did not read like that.

Charles's lack of trust of America is a recurring theme. He is not only critical of their lack of a coherent Middle East policy, but deeply concerned by the US's refusal to sign up to any international convention on climate change – a stance made even worse by the current incumbent in the White House, President Donald Trump. Charles is also 'horrified' by US agri-industrial activities – the appalling animal welfare and environmental consequences of the cattle-feed-lot system.

Charles believes the vast industrial-scale output of chemical-dependent and government-subsidised corn, which leads to economic surplus and is then turned into every conceivable form of fast food, is leading to an ever-growing health crisis in the USA. This is through obesity-related problems, not to mention that the rapidly increasing rates of diabetes make his 'hair stand on end', as does the huge lobbying power of the gigantic corporations and fast-food companies.

US administrations from George W. Bush to Donald Trump, Charles believes, have promulgated the industrialisation of nature throughout inherent unsustainable agricultural methods. 'The prince,' one of his circle told me, 'finds the US society – which in his view contains a "worryingly large element" of born-again evangelical, fundamentalist Christians for whom the Old Testament seems more important than the New, and who take it literally – deeply worrying.'

Today he is determined to use his personal relationships with the Arab leaders in the Gulf to the greater good. I was one of the few journalists who accompanied the prince and the duchess on their tour of the Gulf States in November 2016, including, controversially, to Bahrain, which has been widely criticised for human-rights abuses. The visit undoubtedly left many influential figures, both in the region and at home, feeling better about Britain and its place in the world.

One area he will not be drawn into – in such a lucrative potential marketplace – is marketing weaponry. This is despite his previous forays into this area. In Jonathan Dimbleby's 1994 documentary, Charles defended his appearance at the Dubai arms fair on the basis that he is boosting British trade, arguing without much conviction that the arms will likely be used as a deterrent, and if the UK doesn't sell them someone else will. Since then he has had a complete *volte-face*, and heaven help the royal aide who suggests slipping in such an engagement these days!

The photographs from the tour – of a smiling Charles sword-dancing in Oman or shopping in a Bahraini souk with the Duchess of Cornwall – told some of the story, but certainly not all. For, as the world tried to come to terms with the fallout after Donald Trump's victory in the US presidential election, Charles had once again been in the heart of the Muslim world, sent on behalf of the Foreign Office to strengthen and reinforce Britain's long-standing relationships with Oman, the United Arab Emirates and Bahrain.

I was taken aback not only by his workload but by the respect with which he is held in the region. His seven-day visit encompassed fifty engagements, four cities, five flights, numerous helicopter rides and serious talks with the most influential leaders and heads of state. It was seen as a requisite overseas visit by Charles, the Queen and the Foreign and Commonwealth Office and, from my ringside seat, its impact was palpable on so many levels.

It was exemplified by the fact that the visit could spark a Gulf-wide expansion for the British company Bluewater Bio – success that would last long after the royals have flown home and the flags and bunting have been binned. Charles is not some cheap dealmaker with slick patter and list of new proposals, promoting Great Britain PLC like a supersalesman. That is not what he does and never has been. He clearly commands respect on the international stage. He is aware and mindful of the economic needs of a post-Brexit Britain. This was his fourth visit to the region in four years, at the request of the British government, promoting the UK's partnership in the region in key areas such as religious tolerance, military cooperation, supporting women in leadership, creating youth opportunities, preserving cultural heritage and wildlife conservation.

In truth, it is the positive and unique longstanding relationship between our Royal Family – particularly Charles – and the royal families of this region that helps so many direct and indirect opportunities to flourish. During his visit, he opened a new welfare block at Britain's naval base in Manama, Bahrain, met sailors on board HMS *Middleton* and visited a plant, built on land gifted by the government, using wastewater-treatment technology deployed by Bluewater Bio. The award-winning British firm is a global specialist in technologies for cost-efficient, environmentally friendly water and wastewater treatment.

For, if you looked only at the images printed in newspapers and published online, the subtle diplomatic, business and cultural benefits could easily be lost. There is a much bigger picture at play here – the trip was a serious and complex undertaking, crucial for Britain's interests in the area.

Charles and Camilla's trip to Bahrain was the final leg of a tour in which they both embraced subjects close to their hearts – and some unusual photocalls. Their first stop, Oman, produced headline-grabbing photographs of Prince Charles wielding a three-foot sword in a ceremonial dance held to welcome the couple to the country. The prince also saw at first hand the impact of conservation work on the tiny island of Bu Tinah, where he raced along in a dune buggy and took a boat tour to see important marine and coastal ecosystems.

Charles, a long-time champion of the need for environmental and business sustainability, also made a powerful address to business leaders in Dubai in which he warned there was a 'very real risk' of a climate-change disaster. He told them, 'We are facing what I believe is perhaps the greatest challenge ever faced by our economy and society. I have been finding the struggle somewhat exhausting and frustrating over the past twenty-five to thirty years to overcome the deniers and sceptics. If we are honest, we know all too clearly that we can't go on as we are.'

Ultimately, Charles believes these international visits work because over time they break down barriers that he fervently maintains must be broken down, for, in his view, unless we embrace each other, humanity is on a path to self-destruction, with misinterpretation and misunderstanding over religion and borders at its heart. As he eloquently put it, 'The three great Abrahamic faiths [Judaism, Christianity and Islam] all come from the same root originally and it's crazy to be persisting in this continuing misunderstanding.'

## Chapter Thirteen

# IRISH EYES

———— ~ ————

'I hope and pray that during the rest of my life before I drop
dead I might have a chance to visit as many of the counties as
possible in this great country.'

HRH Charles, Prince of Wales, 11 May 2017,
Kilkenny Castle, Ireland

'I declined a taste of the most fiendish little drink,' Charles
quipped with a mischievous smile and glint in his piercing blue
eyes as he chatted openly to locals outside Kilkenny castle. He said
he had 'better be safe than sorry' when offered a tonic ominously
named Dragon's Fire, made from garlic. Like the Queen, he has
an aversion to garlic because they are always meeting new people
and the smell makes it a no-no. The prince was on top form. He
adores such visits to Ireland, the land, the culture, its people, its
poetry and ancient, rich Celtic history. The more recent history
of the island and the resolution of 'the Troubles' has long been a
passionate subject of his, for personal as well as diplomatic reasons.

Being able to cross from Northern Ireland into the Irish Republic is something the prince often dreamed of doing but in all honesty believed somebody of his royal rank would never be permitted to do in his lifetime. The speed of the peace process has meant that his cherished ambition has been realised.

Outside the castle on 11 May 2017, the royal couple spent time shaking hands with locals and toured a local farmers' market. Thousands of well-wishers had lined the streets nearby to greet the prince and his wife with enthusiastic cheers. He is a popular figure in this part of Ireland and he was visibly touched by the genuine warmth of the welcome. Once inside the walls, Charles tried his hand at hurling with former Kilkenny All-Star Henry Shefflin on hand to advise. Both he and Kilkenny hurling manager Brian Cody demonstrated the art of the sport before passing over the hurley to the prince, who expressed relief 'not to have disgraced myself entirely by missing the goal and hitting a member of the press corps between the eyes'.

At a function the previous evening, hosted by President Higgins in Áras an Uachtaráin, Charles said that it would be too much of a tragedy if all the hard work of reconciliation by the UK and Ireland were weakened in any way. He said he was fully aware of the challenges both countries faced.

'Our joint efforts have become a beacon for the rest of the world and I feel it is important to keep bothering you with my visits to demonstrate the United Kingdom's commitment to the peace.' He used a phrase in the Irish language, Gaeilge, in both his opening and closing remarks as a mark of respect.

Both Charles and the Queen are consumed by the Irish political situation and the peace process and are known to talk about it in minute detail, privately, for hours. The Queen is known to have an almost obsessive interest in the subject. 'She is a bit of an anorak about Ireland,' one former member of the household said. 'She has found many a government minister wanting when she has challenged them on a particular aspect of the peace process or Irish history.' Charles is an avid reader on the subject, too, and is proud of what his mother has achieved in the delicate arena of Ireland. Indeed, he believes that the Queen's historic visit to the Republic of Ireland in April 2011 was the crowning moment of her reign, her lasting achievement. Whenever he has been asked directly what he believes the Queen's greatest legacy will be, he does not say, as some might expect, her role as Head of the Commonwealth but, unequivocally, 'Ireland.'

For, in Charles's opinion, his mother's historic state visit to the Republic of Ireland between 17 and 20 May 2011 set the seal on the full normalisation of Anglo-Irish relations, and the warm response to her speech at a state banquet at Dublin Castle showed that she had pulled off one of the most successful state visits of her reign. Even Gerry Adams, the face and voice of the political wing of the IRA, Sinn Féin, lauded the Queen for her 'genuine' expression of sympathy for victims of Ireland's troubled past. Praising a British monarch is something Adams probably never thought he would ever do, but those four days in spring 2011 were of immense symbolic significance in showing that Britain and Ireland were, as she said in her speech, 'more than just neighbours'.

The most significant moment came on the first day of her visit, when she bowed her head in respect to those who died for Irish independence after laying a wreath at the Garden of

Remembrance in Dublin. After all, she had lost members of her family, too, not least her cousin Lord Louis Mountbatten and one of his twin grandsons, Nicholas (aged fourteen), and local boy Paul Maxwell (who was fifteen), who were killed when a bomb planted by the IRA exploded on their leisure boat in Mullaghmore, County Sligo, on 27 August 1979. Another passenger, Lady Brabourne, aged eighty-three, died the day after the attack. Only a handful of people know what was in the Queen's mind that day, Charles probably among them, and it was a gesture that will be remembered for many decades by nationalist Ireland.

Prince Charles was devoted to Lord Louis, one of the most influential figures in his early life, whom he has described as 'the grandfather I'd never had'. On 20 May 2015, he made a pilgrimage to the spot overlooking the bay where his great-uncle was assassinated. A small cross atop the cliffs marks it now and, as the prince's cavalcade drove up to the castle, it deliberately slowed down beside it, until it was almost stationary for the briefest of moments.

Earlier, a wistful Charles had stood and gazed out across the Atlantic from the small Sligo village on Ireland's west coast, where, thirty-six years earlier on a clear blue-sky day, the thunder of an explosion tore the perfect sky, shattered the calm and ripped the canvas from so many lives, including his. Surrounding him was a small knot of well-wishers and villagers for whom memories were also painful and vivid. 'It's been a long time,' Charles whispered to one, talking of his long wait to visit the spot. 'I never thought it would happen.'

On that fateful day in 1979, despite security advice and warnings from the Garda, Lord Louis went lobster potting and tuna fishing in a wooden boat, the *Shadow V.* But, unbeknown to him or his family, IRA member Thomas McMahon had slipped onto the unguarded boat that night and attached a radio-controlled fifty-pound (23kg) bomb. The bomb had been detonated by remote control at 11.39 a.m., when the boat was about two hundred yards from the harbour.

The IRA quickly admitted carrying out the bombing, saying it was designed to 'bring to the attention of the English people the continuing occupation of our country'. At the time of the explosion, McMahon, then thirty-one, was seventy miles away, in police custody; by chance he and a second man, gravedigger Francis McGirl, then aged twenty four, had been stopped at a checkpoint after he had laid the explosive. But McMahon had flakes of green paint from Lord Mountbatten's boat and traces of nitroglycerine on his clothes. He and McGirl were charged.

Gerry Adams of Sinn Féin said of Mountbatten's death at the time, 'The IRA gave clear reasons for the execution. I think it is unfortunate that anyone has to be killed, but the furore created by Mountbatten's death showed up the hypocritical attitude of the media establishment.'

Adams went on, 'As a member of the House of Lords, Mountbatten was an emotional figure in both British and Irish politics. What the IRA did to him is what Mountbatten had been doing all his life to other people; and with his war record I don't think he could have objected to dying in what was clearly a war situation. He knew the danger involved in coming to this country. In my opinion, the IRA achieved its objective: people started paying attention to what was happening in Ireland.' There was insufficient evidence to place McGirl at the fishing village of Mullaghmore; he was acquitted and he died in 1995. McMahon was released from jail in August 1998 as part of the Good Friday peace agreement.

At the Pier Head Hotel, where on that dreadful day the dead and injured had been brought on makeshift stretchers, local people gathered to greet Charles and his wife, the Duchess of Cornwall, who visited on 20 May 2015. Among those there was Peter McHugh, who helped pull the bodies from the sea and who described to Charles the events of that day. 'I didn't want to be too sombre. I just gave him the briefest outline of what happened,' he said. Timothy Knatchbull, Mountbatten's grandson, who was badly injured in the blast, guided Charles's gaze out to where the boat had set off on its fateful trip that morning. Knatchbull has since been vocal in applauding the reconciliation process, having found his own path to 'forgiveness and peace'.

The other child victim, schoolboy Paul Maxwell, had been on holiday from Enniskillen and was earning pocket money as a boat hand. His father, John, a teacher, had to steel himself to attend the royal visit, but did so, saying it was the right thing to do. For Paul's mother, Mary Hornsey, it was her first time in Mullaghmore since the day of her son's death, but she had accepted the invitation to meet the prince on a visit she said was 'extending the hand of forgiveness'.

Richard Wood-Martin, who with his wife Elizabeth was in a boat behind Mountbatten's, recalled how they pulled Timothy Knatchbull from the sea: 'There was a puff of smoke, a loud bang, a shower of bits of timber and the boat was gone. One person was blown to the left and it was Timothy. I managed to pull him into the boat. He was facedown in the water.'

Understandably, Charles was profoundly affected by the murder of his beloved mentor and great-uncle, Mountbatten. At the time he said that it 'made me want to die too'. To this day, as in many during the quieter, solitary moments, he talks to his departed loved ones and in that way keeps Mountbatten and many other dearly departed spirits alive in his heart. In many ways his death has contributed to Charles's fatalistic attitude towards his own mortality. On Australia Day of 1994 in Tumbalong Park, Sydney, when protester David Kang, then twenty-three, stormed a stage and fired two blank shots at Prince Charles, he was about to deliver a keynote speech. I was among the reporters who were there that day and watched the drama unfold. After Charles's PPO had checked that the attacker was on the ground he secured the prince, who remained cool, if a little bemused, throughout.

'Suddenly a man leapt out of the crowd to the right and started running flat out towards the dais, firing a pistol as he ran,' he recalled. Of course, the gun proved to be a starting pistol. Later, Charles even joked about the incident. Turning to an aide, he recounted an anecdote about how he was charged by a bull elephant while in Kenya. He said the African encounter was far more frightening.

A few years later, on 8 November 2001, I was inches away from another serious incident when the prince was attacked by a young person, later identified as sixteen-year-old schoolgirl Alina Lebedeva, who slapped him around the face with a flower during a walkabout in a protest over NATO'S involvement in bombing raids in Afghanistan. He later privately joked about returning home with facial scars from a 'crazed assault by a carnation-wielding, adolescent Latvian Bolshevik' that he admitted 'frightened me rigid' (she was a Latvian Communist of Russian ethnicity). The poor Latvians, Charles said, were mortified by this incident. The prince pleaded for her to be treated leniently and she was spared prison but sentenced to a year of educational measures by a court. He applauds the great strides former Communist countries have made towards freedom with some help from the UK, although he remains sceptical about how so many former Communists in all these countries suddenly succeed in becoming the wealthiest businesspeople and yet do not seem to be prepared to take any corporate responsibility for providing social assistance within the community. Not a fan of the system, he says it shows how 'crooked' the whole system was in the past.

His view on his own personal security is that he has to leave it to the professionals who surround him and just get on with his job. If advised not to do something, he will always take that advice, but he is not going to hide away. He once famously said to reporters during a reception trip in Spain, 'There is nothing you can do if your name is on the bullet.'

Mountbatten was paramount in his development from boy to man in almost every area. They wrote long and meaningful letters to one another, and the urbane Louis became his most trusted mentor, filling the void left by Charles's more complicated relationship with his father, Prince Philip, Mountbatten's nephew. There was nothing he couldn't share with Mountbatten, from affairs of the heart to advice on matters of state to his military career, that the old man didn't seem to have a handle on. Mountbatten had always been there for him, just like his beloved grandmother, the Queen Mother. When the IRA detonated that deadly bomb it robbed the future king of his wisest adviser. He was lost without him.

'At the time I could not imagine how we would come to terms with the anguish of such a deep loss,' Prince Charles told an audience in the nearby town of Sligo before the visit. 'Through this dreadful experience I now understand in a profound way the agonies borne by others on these islands of whatever faith or political persuasion.'

This following year, 2018, Charles and Camilla were on the Emerald Isle once again flying into Cork Airport on 14 June for a three-day visit. Following in the footsteps of Charles's great-great-great-grandmother, Queen Victoria, the couple undertook visits to Derrynane, Tralee and Killarney in County Kerry.

The freedom they both felt was clear. Camilla, ever aware of a picture opportunity for the loyal photographers who follow her, felt the sand beneath her feet when she joined her husband on a Kerry beach to highlight the problem of plastic pollution. She removed her heels when the couple walked onto Derrynane strand. There, they learned about the work of local schoolchildren collecting waste from the shore. Charles told his wife, 'You'll get sand in your shoes' when she later slipped them back on. She certainly didn't seem to let it bother her. Before getting into a helicopter, which had brought the royals to the southwest Irish coastline, she could be seen shaking the sand from her footwear. From there, the couple moved on to Derrynane House, the home of the nineteenth-century campaigner for Irish rights, Daniel O'Connell, taking a guided tour through the rooms where the man, known as 'the Liberator', lived and worked. O'Connell, who was born in the late eighteenth century, campaigned for Catholic emancipation, including the right to sit as MPs at Westminster.

Their last stop was a visit to Siamsa Tire, Ireland's National Folk Theatre, in Tralee, and a garden party at Killarney House. Queen Victoria stayed at the original Killarney House during her visit to Ireland in 1861. In neighbouring Cork, where they had dinner with Deputy Prime Minister Simon Coveney, Charles again paid tribute to Anglo-Irish relations that had made such a visit even possible.

'Our countries have travelled a troubled road together, but, with reconciliation and understanding as our guide, we have found a very important new path to share prosperity and security and together we are determined we must never lose our way again,' the prince told guests at the dinner at Crawford Art Gallery.

Louis Mountbatten will forever live in Prince Charles's heart and soul. And one could see the joy in his face at the christening of his grandson Prince Louis, so named in honour of Mountbatten, during the summer. Her Majesty's years and remarkably busy schedule meant that, by mutual consent, she did not attend Louis's christening by the Archbishop of Canterbury, Justin Welby, on 9 July in the Chapel Royal, St James's Palace, leaving Charles in the role of patriarch.

But the ninety-two-year-old monarch poignantly retained a place in an intimate family portrait taken in the Morning Room at Clarence House, watching over the next generation of her family. The oil-on-canvas portrait of the Queen, by

Michael Noakes between 1972 and 1973, appears to have been raised several inches up the wall from its previous position to ensure its visibility in the official picture by photographer Matt Holyoak. Below her, gathered together for the first time, were the faces of those who will carry the baton for decades, including one cradled in his mother's arms bearing the same name as his grandfather's most trusted confidant.

## Chapter Fourteen

# FUTURE HEAD
# OF THE
# COMMONWEALTH

———————∼———————

'I am deeply touched and honoured by the decision of
Commonwealth Heads of State and Government that
I should succeed the Queen, in due course, as Head of
the Commonwealth.'

HRH THE PRINCE OF WALES, 20 APRIL 2018

The Prince of Wales is an avid listener to BBC Radio 4's *Today* programme. When his son Harry guest-edited the flagship news show on 27 December 2017, Charles was given time to expound on climate change. Charles himself had been offered the chance to guest edit the show but, when his publicity-hungry younger son heard about it, he suddenly revived earlier interest in doing the gig. Harry had been offered to edit and appear in the show some months earlier but had done precious little about it. His father magnanimously withdrew to avoid any conflict. Perhaps as a compromise, Harry then invited his father to be one of his interviewees, along with former US president Barack Obama.

The prince took full advantage of the media platform given to his 'darling boy' (as he referred to Harry on air) with aplomb. He remained light-hearted throughout and joked that he was relieved people were finally waking up to his 'dotty' opinions on climate change. The pair joked, too, about the influence of Charles's opinions on his son, with the Prince of Wales saying it was 'amazing' that Harry had listened to him at all. The two royals agreed the biggest issue facing the world was climate change and the havoc it was wreaking.

'There's a whole lot of things I've tried to focus on over all these years,' said Charles, 'that I felt needed attention. Not everybody else did but maybe now, some years later, they're beginning to realise that what I was trying to say may not have been quite as dotty as they thought. But the issue really that has to go on being focused on big time is this one around the whole issue of climate change, which now, whether we like it or not, is the biggest threat multiplier we face.'

Harry told his father there was 'so much hope' among the younger generation about what could be done to combat the problem and many of the solutions already existed. 'The future lies in working in far greater harmony with nature and trying to make sure our own economy mimics nature's economy,' Charles said.

It had been a great success, an excellent platform for both the enthusiastic Harry and his father and great coup for my old *Evening Standard* editor and the new editor of *Today*, Sarah Sands. Recently, the BBC was not quite so accommodating or generous. A few weeks later, in February 2018, a so-called BBC exclusive 'revealed' what many, including me, had long known: that the Commonwealth had secretly begun to consider who might succeed the Queen as its next head. Charles was far from a shoo-in, it gleefully reported, and the BBC claimed its reporters had seen documents to prove it.

Worse still, *soi-disant* pundits on BBC's *Today* wrongly claimed that Prince Charles was not all that keen on the job anyway and that the Commonwealth didn't mean as much to him as it did to his mother. It was enough to make him choke on his wholemeal organic muesli and he was understandably furious.

In actual fact, Charles has been a vocal and active supporter of the Commonwealth for more than forty years – albeit in the shadow of his mother. But the Queen hasn't carried out long-haul flights for several years and now it is Charles, supported by his sons and siblings, who do much of the heavy lifting when it comes to overseas Commonwealth visits. As I discovered in my lengthy conversation with him on the royal flight back from Vanuatu to Australia, he is deeply passionate about the organisation that represents 2.3 billion people and fifty-three nations – a third of the world's population. 'I have long had an instinctive sense of the value of the Commonwealth,' he said, and has spoken of the 'pivotal role' the Commonwealth has to play in safeguarding our planet.

This was the kind of vision and leadership expected of a future head of the Commonwealth, stressing that its leaders must listen to the views of the next generation in London the following April at the CHOGM. Charles shows his support through official visits, military links, charitable activities and other special events. In April 2018 in Brisbane he opened the highly successful Commonwealth Games and then toured Australia before flying back for the Commonwealth summit in London and Windsor.

Since 1969, the prince has visited forty-four Commonwealth countries. Most recently, he has led the charge for member island states that face being wiped out by a rise in sea levels with his Blue Economy initiative. In growing the Blue Economy, he hopes to combat poverty and accelerate prosperity in these under-threat regions. But still some say he is not passionate. The problem for the monarchy is that the position of head is not enshrined in the constitution. It is symbolic, with no formal powers. The Queen has been working hard in private to ensure the Prince of Wales succeeds her as head of the Commonwealth. It is a responsibility she says she has cherished – but it is not one that her son and heir would inherit automatically.

The BBC was right to discuss the matter but it was also stirring the pot ahead of the CHOGM. It was true, prior to a formal decision on who would be the next head of the organisation, that the prince was by no means assured of securing the position. He was always going to rely on Commonwealth leaders giving him their formal blessing and wanting him to replace his mother. That said, there was little doubt, after years of distinguished service, that there were few better qualified for the albeit titular role.

On 20 April, Charles took another step closer to the chalice when Commonwealth leaders backed the Queen's 'sincere wish' to recognise that her heir, the Prince of Wales, would one day succeed her as the next Head of Commonwealth. Theresa May, the British prime minister, announced the decision from the fifty-three Commonwealth Heads of Government after private deliberations at Windsor Castle, where Commonwealth leaders said they had reached an agreement to honour Her Majesty's 'vision, duty and steadfast service' to the institution.

Speaking at a press conference after the retreat, Mrs May said that the Commonwealth itself exists in 'no small measure because of the vision, duty and steadfast service of Her Majesty in nurturing the growth of this remarkable family of nations. On behalf of all our citizens I want to express gratitude for everything Her Majesty has done and will continue to do,' she said.

'Today we have agreed that the next head of the Commonwealth will be His Royal Highness Prince Charles, the Prince of Wales. His Royal Highness has been a proud supporter of the Commonwealth for more than four decades and has spoken passionately about the organisation's unique diversity. It is fitting that he will one day continue the work of his mother, Her Majesty the Queen,' she said.

When it was finally and formally announced, the prince was typically self-effacing and declared, 'I am deeply touched and honoured by the decision of Commonwealth heads of state and government that I should succeed the Queen, in due course, as head of the Commonwealth. Meanwhile, I will continue to support Her Majesty in every possible way, in the service of our unique family of nations.'

*Sub rosa*, presidents and prime ministers from across the world convened to finalise plans for the future of the Commonwealth, enjoying the hospitality of the Queen's home at the end of a week that had seen senior members of the Royal Family out in force. President of Ghana, Nana Akufo-Addo, said the decision was reached by 'strong consensus', while Theresa May insisted it was unanimous. Grenada's prime minister, Keith Mitchell, said he had been convinced the decision was a good one thanks to his belief that the young men of the Commonwealth need a strong male role model.

It was made clear, however, that the decision was a one-off, and the leaders spelled it out that the ruling did not apply to Charles's own heirs, Prince William and Prince George, who would not be automatically in line to hold the office. It would remain, they said, a non-hereditary position.

That said, the Queen had left nothing to chance. The day before the ruling, as she spoke at the official opening of the CHOGM at Buckingham Palace, she made a heartfelt address spelling out for the first time her hopes for the future of the Commonwealth, and offering her unadulterated support to her son in the role.

'It is my sincere wish that the Commonwealth will continue to offer stability and continuity for future generations, and will decide that one day the Prince of Wales should carry on the important work started by my father in 1949,' she told the leaders gathered. There is little doubt that the Queen's public words galvanised the world leaders into pushing through the decision.

'We are certain that, when he will be called upon to do so, he will provide solid and passionate leadership for our Commonwealth,' Joseph Muscat, prime minister of Malta, said of the prince in the same ceremony. Later that day, Malcolm Turnbull, the Australian prime minister, confirmed that his country 'strongly supports the continuation of the king or queen of the United Kingdom as the head of the Commonwealth . . .Prince Charles in time will succeed his mother,' he stated unequivocally.

Speaking to media, Justin Trudeau, the Canadian prime minister, said, 'I very much agree with the wishes of Her Majesty that the Prince of Wales be the next head of the Commonwealth.' And Ralph Regenvanu, the foreign minister of the Pacific state of Vanuatu, disclosed, 'We see it almost naturally that it should be the British Royal Family because it is the Commonwealth after all.'

Others had expressed frustration that the issue had overshadowed more important discussions. Tevita Tu'i Uata, Tonga's trade minister, told ITV News that people in his country 'are drowning' due to rising sea levels, saying, 'Maybe sorting out who is going to lead the Commonwealth may be also an issue, but it's not as pressing an issue to [Tonga] as taking care of climate change.'

The Prince is expected to represent the Queen in the honorary role at future Commonwealth meetings, the next of which will take place in Rwanda in 2020, having previously attended the meeting four times: in Edinburgh in 1997, Uganda in 2007, Sri Lanka in 2013 and Malta in 2015 when he appeared *with* the Queen.

How does he propose to change things, if at all? The bottom line is that the Commonwealth is a fundamental feature of his life. His first Commonwealth visit was to Malta when I was just five. He has, over time, spoken to many of the giants of the club: Sir Robert Menzies, Kwame Nkrumah, Sir Keith Holyoake, Jomo Kenyatta, Pierre Trudeau, Kenneth Kaunda, Julius Nyerere and Lee Kuan Yew.

But for Charles it is not applauding past successes; for he believes that the modern Commonwealth has a vital role to play in building bridges between our countries, fairer societies within them and a more secure world around them. He hopes his role will enable member states not only to revitalise the bonds with each other but also to give the Commonwealth a 'renewed relevance to all citizens', finding practical solutions to their problems and giving life to their aspirations. That way, he believes, the Commonwealth will be a cornerstone for the lives of future generations.

## Chapter Fifteen

# THE GREAT CONVENER

---◦---

'I have been entirely motivated by a desperate desire
to put the "Great" back into Great Britain.'

<small>HRH the Prince of Wales in a private letter, January 1993</small>

In the impeccable garden of Clarence House, glass in hand,
stood Chancellor Angela Merkel of Germany and Prime
Minister Alexis Tsipras of Greece. They were locked in
conversation. The UK's under-fire prime minister, Theresa
May, was close at hand, too, with her newly appointed foreign
secretary, Jeremy Hunt. A gaggle of other embattled UK Cabinet
ministers were close by. It had, after all, been a tough few days
with the double resignations of Tory 'Big Beasts' Boris Johnson
and ex-Brexit Secretary David Davis. The Polish prime minister,
Mateusz Morawiecki, mingled in the throng with six other prime
ministers from the western Balkans with their ministers and
ambassadors shadowing their every move.

The Prince of Wales, the host, was steadily working his way

around his garden, cajoling, joking, jollying along the influential group as the evening sun dipped out of sight in the capital. The reception, held to mark the end of the western Balkans summit in London, was a success. When Charles stepped up to a small podium, however, he was not about to flatter those present with pleasantries and platitudes.

He delivered a short but powerful oration on the importance of reconciliation. Speaking from the heart, citing his own experience following the murder of his great-uncle, Lord Mountbatten, at the hands of the IRA, he said, 'Reconciliation is not simply a theoretical abstract concept: it is, of course, a matter of practical, difficult action, painful choices and hard, but essential, compromise.'

He went on, 'Blame, distrust and hatred are natural, instinctive responses to decades, even centuries, of conflict and injustice – but they do not help us to change course. That requires the really difficult business of forgiveness, understanding and, if I may say so, tremendous courage and enlightened leadership. I know this because, very nearly forty years ago, my great-uncle, Lord Mountbatten, was murdered in a terrible bomb attack.

'Ever since that fateful day, I have been determined to pursue the long, hard road to lasting reconciliation. We can, of course, never forget the wrongs of the past, which must always inform the choices we make about the future. But they cannot be allowed to limit our horizons or to constrain the opportunity to which future generations aspire,' he said. His words, so raw and personal, touched a nerve with the blue-chip audience.

Meaningful reconciliation, the prince argued, in the western Balkans was the only way of ensuring that the region's children did not endure the agonies of the generations before them. 'Much progress has been made in this regard over recent years,' he said, 'but much, much more needs to be done.'

Charles was speaking in the week that marked the twenty-third anniversary of the Srebrenica massacre of more than eight thousand Bosnian Muslims at the hands of Bosnian Serbs, the worst mass killing on European soil since World War II He had assembled a powerful audience on 10 July 2018 and he hadn't wasted it, for he had delivered a powerful and effective message, too, delivered by a statesman who still believes post-Brexit that Britain will remain a global power.

In the way he conducted the proceedings, he embodied what Britain can be in the early part of the twenty-first century and gave a hint at what kind of king he will be: a strong convener with the ability to bring together leaders with real influence.

Who else but the Prince of Wales could persuade Angela Merkel's office that she should spend another hour of her day in the UK at a reception such as this? Who else could lecture a group of heads of government about reconciliation but an experienced statesman and future monarch who had suffered personally from the violence of conflict?

The prince is not about to become our *de facto* foreign secretary, nor would he want to be. And, if 'global Britain' and 'soft-power' diplomacy were to mean anything going forward post-Brexit, then the government will have to provide answers to the big foreign-policy questions of the age themselves and not leave it to the prince to fill the void.

It was an example, if one were needed, of that at which the prince is exceptional. He is the great convener, the ultimate chairman of the board, if you like. His strength and charm is bringing people together and skilfully addressing the biggest questions without the feeling he is ranting or ramming home his message.

The Queen has told those closest to her, if she is still living at ninety-five, it is her intention to step aside so that Charles can become Prince Regent, although the prince's team insist 'they' are not aware of this. It is her call and she is prone to prevarication at the moment, so nobody is really sure whether to start actively preparing for the moment.

'At seventy years of age, at seventy-five years of age, at seventy-six, when the moment comes he is not going to change,' one aide who knows him well explained. And, as we saw earlier, he also won't change his name – which is convention – when his moment to be King Charles III comes. People know him as Charles and he will continue to be Charles.

In time, I believe, history will be kind on King Charles III. His reign will probably be short, maybe even the shortest ever in contrast to the longest wait to attain it, and, as a result, in historical terms, his time on the throne not a remarkable one. His contribution to the world during his entire lifetime, however, certainly *has* been remarkable. His legacy, whether as prince or king, will be as a regal philosopher, a courageous man prepared to take risks for what he sees as the greater good, and an unselfish and unflinching advocate for peace and global sustainability.

One must remember, however, that the taxpayer doesn't fund any of his lifestyle (with the exception of travel when he is on official business and the security bill to keep him safe); his landed estate, the Duchy of Cornwall – which he ultimately runs, and runs very well and profitably – does. The estate, which stretches over 135,000 acres and across 23 counties, mainly in the southwest of England, was last year estimated at £1 billion and Charles's net worth is said to be £306 million, according to a report by *Time* magazine. He is just a steward for this estate. The trust passes to the Duke of Cambridge when he becomes Duke of Cornwall (and Prince of Wales) and beneficiary of the Duchy on Charles's ascension.

With the multimillions his Duchy of Cornwall estate generates for his personal use every year (last year it was £21.7 million, up 5 per cent on the previous year, and the tax paid voluntarily increased to £4.85 million), he might well live a cosseted existence. Why shouldn't he? The money is, after all, his, just as the money generated by other landed estates such as the Duke of Westminster's extensive property portfolio is his. Unless there were to be some kind of Communist-style land grab, it is the way it is. Charles, therefore, could have happily lived the life of a playboy prince, a waster selfishly squandering his wealth on a debauched and lavish lifestyle. But he does not and, even though it is his 'private income', the prince has long chosen to be as open and transparent as possible.

From March 2017 through to March 2018, together Charles and Camilla undertook 620 official engagements in 45 counties across the UK and 15 foreign and Commonwealth countries around the world. The prince visited ten Commonwealth countries in this year alone, supported by the duchess on six of these visits. In his travels, sustainability and climate change – constant themes of his work for four decades – have been at the core of his message as he bids to raise awareness of the ways in which changes to our natural environment are having a negative impact on the world around us, particularly the case on low-lying islands, including across the Caribbean.

He attended, too, the Our Ocean Conference in Malta in October 2018, where his keynote address warned once again of the damage that is being caused by the dual threats of climate change and plastics pollution as humanity stretches nature to the limit. He had worked tirelessly to draw out the issue of religious tolerance and greater cultural cohesion, too, which he had addressed through his Easter message broadcast globally on Good Friday 2018, reaching a global audience of more than 10 million. In it he gave an emotional message of support for persecuted Christians around the world, describing his compassion for 'Christians who are suffering for their faith in many places around the world'. He started the speech by saying, 'I want to assure them that they are not forgotten and that they are in our prayers.'

The prince's detractors insist he is a drain on the public purse. The reality is in the relationship between private and public money, the taxpayer meets less than 10 per cent of the total costs for Charles and Camilla (excluding security costs) and those costs are usually for travel expenses when they are sent on official business and in a mode of transport the government, not he, selects.

The scope and diversity of the prince's work is wide-ranging, from state occasions through to work to support the military, not to mention communities of every faith and of every ethnic origin, helping to bind all people together as a single United Kingdom. According to an independent study in 2017, the prince contributed £1.4 billion of value to society in the last decade alone. His charities raised £170 million in a year, a figure they have repeatedly hit. On the environment, he practises what he preaches, too, with his household recording that 85 per cent of its energy now comes from renewable sources, including all of its electricity.

Despite all this almost obsessive devotion to duty, some still argue Charles is a pampered, over-opinionated hypocrite who has his elevated wealth and status only through the good fortune of his birth. If one chooses to ignore the facts about the man, it is easy enough to argue that point. After all Charles has a personal staff of over 120, a figure perhaps more suited to a Tudor monarch than a modern-day, pared-down prince. There are valets who prepare his clothes and polish his shoes, chefs to indulge his every organic culinary whim, and a small army of estate workers, gardening being one of his greatest passions, one that was sparked in childhood, playing with Princess Anne outdoors and spending a lot of time with his grandmother, the Queen Mother, at the Royal Lodge in Windsor.

Despite his considerable wealth and resources, Charles has devoted his entire life to public duty, supporting the Queen in her role as head of state as well as being a global philanthropist. His Prince's Trust, which has long been lauded, has created more than 125,000 entrepreneurs since its creation, too.

But, when the time comes to assess his legacy, it is his work as a pioneer and game-changer for which he will be best remembered. Even when he becomes king, I am confident he will do his best to find a way not to be suffocated by the limitations of the role and continue to strive to give a voice and platform to what he believes in.

He, more than anyone still living, is behind a global sustainability revolution to make world leaders – indeed all of us – think more deeply about how we are treating nature and our planet, and to realise for the sake of future generations our lifestyles must change. He, more than anyone, has led the charge in changing how people think, and to realise, as he would say, 'Right action cannot happen without right thinking.'

In his seventy years, the prince has striven to make a real difference and to enlighten others. He has championed organic farming and spoken up for sustainable urbanism, emphasising the need for local character to be preserved. He has encouraged a more balanced approach to business and healthcare and a more benign holistic approach to science and technology. In doing so, he has placed himself in the firing line and faced widespread criticism for daring to challenge the current orthodoxy and the conventional way of thinking.

But what he has actually been revealing is that all of these areas are totally interrelated and we must all see the whole picture – what he often calls 'the big picture' – to appreciate the problems that we, as the human race, face.

Writing this book has been both a challenge and a journey. Its research has taken me around the world in the prince's slipstream, which has forced me to examine and explore closely his complex beliefs and personal idiosyncrasies.

It is clear that in Charles we are blessed to have a future king of high intelligence and drive. He may not be an intellectual in an academic sense, but he is a deep-thinking, spiritual man, not cynical but intuitive and instinctive. He is sentimental, too, and perhaps overemotional at times; but he is somebody who cares very deeply about the world and environment we live in, today and for the future. He may be born into huge wealth and privilege, but he has always tried his best to justify that good fortune by working to improve the lot of others.

He has a great love of the arts, too, of books, of Shakespeare, of J. K. Rowling's *Harry Potter*, of the Goons, of the poetry of Dylan Thomas, of the music of Bach, Hubert Parry and Leonard Cohen, of art, particularly the work of Johan Joseph Zoffany, and of the classical architecture of Rome and Wren, and, more recently, of Quinlan Terry. Charles, Prince of Wales, is fundamentally a decent man of integrity and honour who has always tried to put duty before himself.

Two days after my extended conversation with the prince on board the Australian Government BBJ jet during the Australian tour, on 10 April 2018, at a reception at Government House in Darwin, the final engagement of the visit, the two of us had another, much shorter exchange. Vicki O'Halloran, Administrator of Australia's Northern Territory, escorted him through an insufferably humid room that uses ineffective, colonial-style giant ceiling fans for ventilation, and I was formally introduced to the prince, as is custom even though we both knew perfectly well who each other was. Without prompting, he again mentioned HMY *Britannia*. It was clearly something that touched a nerve in our previous conversation. I then informed him how well he personally and the monarchy as an institution had fared in a poll in *The Australian* newspaper that day. It reported that I had said that the support for the monarchy Down Under was at an eighteen-year high. Perhaps, I should have known better.

The prince just smiled purposely, then shrugged his shoulders.

'Polls mean nothing to me,' he said, before looking me straight in the eye and adding, 'You see, I'm in it for the long term.'

# POSTSCRIPT –
'I HAVEN'T
GOT TIME'

---~---

'When Dumfries House first came to my attention in 2007, my vision for this Palladian mansion and its contents was to restore them to their former glory. In doing so, I hoped that present and future generations would be able to visit and enjoy the different facets of life and times of a bygone era and to appreciate British craftsmanship at its best.'

LETTER FROM HRH THE PRINCE CHARLES, DUKE OF ROTHESAY

Prince Charles, known as the Duke of Rothesay when in Scotland, is proud of his Scottish ancestry. Claude George Bowes-Lyon, fourteenth Earl of Strathmore and Kinghorne, and father of the Queen Mother, was his great-grandfather. He died in 1944, aged eighty-nine, in Glamis Castle, Scotland, four years before Charles was born.

Charles's Scottish titles, and the responsibility that comes with them, really matter to him. When on duty in Scotland he is often pictured wearing a traditional kilt with a matching tie and smart jacket, and will happily and publicly enjoy a dram of a local single-malt whisky, even when the cameras are present. He seems, those close to him say, to love every minute when he is north of the border, on and off duty.

The Prince's full style when in Scotland is His Royal Highness Prince Charles Philip Arthur George, Duke of Rothesay, Earl of Carrick, Baron of Renfrew, Lord of the Isles and Prince and Great Steward of Scotland. Just as the Dukedom of Rothesay is held by the incumbent heir to the throne, so too is the Earldom of Carrick, a title applied to the ruler of Carrick; a district which is now in southern Ayrshire. It has been strongly associated with the Scottish crown since Robert the Bruce, who had inherited the earldom from his maternal kin, became King of Scots in 1306, reigning until his death in 1329. Since the fifteenth century the title has automatically been held by the heir apparent to the throne, hence Charles is the current earl. Why does this matter? Because it shows the prince's personal passion for a United Kingdom and the monarchy's ties with the Scottish nation. It is also key to who and what the prince is.

In September 2018, shortly before publication of this book, I was invited, along with other representatives of the British media, to the Dumfries House estate, situated near the old mining town and village of Cumnock and New Cumnock. It is a stunning part of the world, but the closure of mines and factories has had a devastating impact on the local community. Many, many jobs have been lost, leading to the area being called the worst place to live in the country. To say that, however, is to ignore the breathtaking landscape around New Cumnock, a village that is rightly proud of its association with Scotland's national bard Robert Burns. There is even a statue of him in the main street, which is not surprising because his famous lyrical poem 'Sweet Afton' immortalised the Afton Water, which rises in the hills of New Cumnock and joins the River Nith at the heart of the village. There is a trail dedicated to Burns, too, and plaques, mainly donated by New Cumnock Burns Club, on several buildings in and around the village.

The Dumfries House story is certainly worth hearing, not least because it neatly encapsulates who and what the prince – Earl of Carrick – is all about. In 2007, the Palladian house, nestled in the Ayrshire countryside, was about to be sold off and with it much of the old furniture and antiques inside. The prince was saddened by this and saw an opportunity to save it and also support the community he serves. He acted quickly and decided to use his various charities to buy it, putting down £20 million of the £45 million needed, to start the process and save the house for the nation. Built in the 1750s, the house was designed by John and Robert Adam for the fifth Earl of Dumfries, and was sold to the nation – effectively, to the group headed by Prince Charles – in 2007.

Saving an old house is commendable, but what Charles has achieved in a decade has also helped save a community depressed by years of neglect after the closure of the coal mines. The pit closures in Ayrshire had a devastating effect: a loss of jobs, a failure of the local economy, and the slow, painful demise of the entire community.

Some question the importance of saving one stately home through his charitable foundation. Can it really make a difference? But the fact is that it has. Opening the grounds to people free of charge, employing local people to carry out the work to renovate the house and transform the grounds, building cottages for rent and hiring out the estate for weddings have certainly helped. The prince has gone further, however. Kitchens have been built to train the local people, many of whom had never even considered cooking as a career. The long-term unemployed have been trained in front-of-house hospitality; schoolchildren are regular visitors to the estate for lessons on how food is grown or produced. He has gone further, building a sports hall for locals to hire, creating accommodation for Scouts and Guides and for companies wanting a place for team-building. The profits from Dumfries House have paid for the renovation of the local town hall and for the rebuilding of New Cumnock's outdoor swimming pool, only the third in Scotland, as well as stimulating the construction of new affordable housing. The impact on the grateful community has been positive and dramatic.

What impressed me after my visit there was how successful Prince Charles's idea has been. He is rightly proud that his idea has given New Cumnock in particular, often voted one of the worst places to live in the UK, a lift. The renovation of the town hall, which doubles up as a cinema, as well as of the swimming pool, have made a huge difference to the village. Dumfries House is now the second biggest employer in the area: the 200 employees include the staff on the estate, the lifeguards at the new swimming pool, and the man working in the reception of perhaps the best village community hall I have ever seen. Before the money came from Dumfries House to renovate the hall, the local council was planning to knock it down. Even the prince's wife, Camilla, was sceptical when she first visited the spooky old building. (It is even understood that an exorcism was held there before the renovation began.) Now it is returned to its former glory. It was only Charles's vision and courage to take on a huge loan that have breathed new life into the house, the estate and the local community.

Charles and Camilla chatted freely when at the house with me and the select group of UK media representatives in a friendly, off-the-record get-together ahead of the prince's seventieth birthday. They were in good spirits and excellent hosts. Later we all attended a black-tie dinner attended by supporters of his project. I sat next to Michael Fawcett, who has done so much to make the Dumfries House project a success. Michael, so often derided in the media, told me over dinner that the one thing out of all the stories written about him that still irks him is the claim that when he was Charles's valet many years ago, he squeezed toothpaste on the prince's toothbrush. 'It is just not true,' he said. I believed him. He also said when I asked him what stands out for him about the prince, 'His sense of humour.' I couldn't help but agree.

After dinner I spoke to the prince again and asked him what he would like for his birthday from the British media. 'Well, not a garden gnome' he joked. (This was because the UK royal photographers had commissioned a gnome with a long telephoto lens for his sixtieth birthday.) He thought about it for a second or two, and said he would like two park benches for Dumfries House made by students in the workshops on the estate – the inscriptions he would leave to us. Sadly, my colleagues from the national press did not want to contribute, but fortunately I managed to secure the funding for the benches.

My few days at Dumfries House were an illuminating experience. It was chance to join the dots and finally appreciate what the prince is all about; how his vision is becoming a living, working reality. Here was an old estate with a fine house set to be demolished by the local council. It was saved by his vision, tenacity and courage to invest. The result, eleven years on, is a project in which the positive effects permeate into many places in desperate need of help.

Of course, Cumnock, New Cumnock and the surrounding area still need more jobs, more shops, more investment and businesses to employ more people, including the local apprentices trained by Charles's charity, the Prince's Trust. Of course there are also many places where the housing is poor. But without Charles's intervention in saving Dumfries House I dread to think what the area would be like today.

One of the first people I met when I turned up a day early for the media get-together at The Lodge of Dumfries House was Rodney Cook, of the Hearst Foundation, the philanthropic organisation founded to reflect the concerns of the American newspaper baron William Randolph Hearst. Rodney, from Atlanta, Georgia, told me he was there to see the prince about a panelled room from Gwydir Castle in North Wales. William Randolph Hearst had acquired all the room's panelling about a century ago and shipped it to America, and Rodney was there to discuss with the prince how it could be returned to the original castle to restore it to its former glory.

Rodney is the son of civil rights leader Rodney Mims Cook, a close friend of Dr Martin Luther King. Together the two men worked with the leadership of the black community to help keep

Atlanta peaceful during the volatile 1960s and 1970s, when there was so much death and destruction.

It just so happened that, on his deathbed at the age of eighty-nine, Rodney's father had charged his son to rebuild Atlanta's Mims Park, a peace park in the city centre established by his family in the nineteenth century. Later, a school had been built on the original park, which by around 1917 had grown greatly, almost taking over the area. The local community, like that in Cumnock and New Cumnock after the closure of the mines, languished over time.

In 2009, Atlanta's Democrat mayor, Shirley Franklin, asked Rodney to meet with the Prince of Wales at Poundbury, Charles's experimental new town on the outskirts of Dorchester in Dorset. After the meeting he became the first American trustee of the Prince of Wales's Foundation for Architecture.

During their exchanges the prince recalled the original Mims Park, and then asked Mayor Franklin to allow his protégé Rodney to rebuild the park, noting that the peace narrative and distinctive beauty of the design would rehabilitate thousands of acres well beyond the organic centre of the park.

Now, years later, the $60,000,000 development is under way and will be half completed by December 2018, the other half and the buildings by the following year.

On 27 August 2018 Dr King's daughter Bernice wrote to Rodney: 'I would like to sincerely thank you for honoring my parents in developing Cook Park. My mother and father had an indelible impact not only on our great country, but also on the world and I am delighted to see that your park is honoring their legacy in such a powerful way'

To a considerable extent, all of this happened because of the Prince of Wales. His influence is considerable; he inspires others to do their best to reach the pinnacle by connecting people, tapping into those he knows can do certain things, and letting them run with it.

Rodney told me at Dumfries House, 'His Royal Highness completely changed my life, and now my city of 6,500,000 people will see his influence for the better for centuries. I can never thank him enough.'

# SELECT
# BIBLIOGRPHY

Bagehot, Walter, *The English Constitution*, 1867

Bedell Smith, Sally, *Prince Charles: The Passions and Paradoxes of an Improbable Life*, 2017

Benson, Ross, *Charles: The Untold Story*, 1993

Berry, Wendy, *The Housekeeper's Diary*, 1995

Bogdanor, Prof. Vernon, *The Monarchy and the Constitution*, 1995

Bower, Tom, *Rebel Prince: The Power, Passion and Defiance of Prince Charles*, 2018

Charles, HRH, Prince of Wales, *Harmony: A New Way of Looking at Our World*, 2010

Dimbleby, Jonathan, *Prince of Wales: A Biography*, 1994

Hamilton, Alan, *The Real Charles*, 1988

Holden, Anthony, *Charles, Prince of Wales*, 1979

Jephson, Patrick, *Shadows of a Princess*, 2000

Jobson, Robert, *The New Royal Family*, 2013

Junor, Penny, *Charles: Victim or Villain?*, 1998

———, *Prince William: Born to be King: An intimate portrait*, 2013

———, *The Duchess: The Untold Story*, 2018

Loades, David, *Princes of Wales: Royal Heirs in Waiting*, 2008

Mayer, Catherine, 2015, *Charles: The Heart of a King*, 2015

Wharfe, Ken, and Jobson, Robert, *Diana: Closely Guarded Secret*, 2002; new edn 2016

———, *Guarding Diana: Protecting the Princess Around the World*, 2017

# INDEX

# INDEX